STUDENT ACHIEVEMENT THROUGH STAFF DEVELOPMENT

Fundamentals of School Renewal

Second Edition

Bruce Joyce
Beverly Showers

Foreword by Michael G. Fullan
Afterword by James M. Wolf

Longman *Publishers USA*

Student Achievement through Staff Development: Fundamentals of School Renewal, Second Edition

Longman, 10 Bank Street, White Plains, N.Y. 10606

Associated companies:
Longman Group Ltd., London
Longman Cheshire Pty., Melbourne
Longman Paul Pty., Auckland
Copp Clark Longman Ltd., Toronto

Acquisitions editor: Virginia L. Blanford
Production editor: Linda Moser/Saxon House Productions
Cover design: Anne Pompeo, Pompeo Design
Production supervisor: Richard Bretan

Library of Congress Cataloging-in-Publication Data
Joyce, Bruce R.
    Student achievement through staff development : fundamentals of
school renewal / by Bruce Joyce & Beverly Showers.—2nd ed.
        p.   cm.
    Includes bibliographical references and index.
    ISBN 0-8013-0782-1
    1. Teachers—In-service training—United States.   2. Continuing
education—United States.   3. Career development—United States.
4. Academic achievement—United States.   I. Showers, Beverly.
II. Title.
LB1731.J69 1995
371.1'46—dc20   94-6678
                                                        CIP

5 6 7 8 9 10 -CRW -99

We dedicate this book to the colleagues from whom we have learned so much and whose courage we so admire:

- Teachers who have surpassed our skill with the models of teaching we have introduced to them
- School administrators who have suffered the uproar endemic of the times as they have created the programs that allowed us to reach beyond our capacity
- The scholars of innovation, who tolerate the incredible ambiguity of the attempt to build a new world in education and other organizations
- The steady scholars of teaching who, with few resources and coping with a world not entirely friendly to research on education, have created teaching practices that make a difference to children
- The children who have patiently helped our teachers in their struggle to learn how to teach them how to learn

Paraphrasing Ernest Hemingway's reminder: "We are all apprentices in a craft where none of us will be a master."

Contents

Foreword

Bruce Joyce and Beverly Showers have written more than a second edition of their highly acclaimed book on *Student Achievement through Staff Development*. They have written a new book that advances the field enormously. At the first level, and unlike the majority of staff developers today, they pursue with clear thinking and careful assessment the relationship between continuous staff development and student achievement. With an array of powerful propositions linked to numerous case situations in which they have directly worked, Joyce and Showers reveal what quality staff development looks like, why it works, and with what results.

The major contribution of this new edition, however, is its integrating and synergizing advancements—conceptually, empirically, strategically. With all the talk of systemic reform, and without overusing the term and its elusive abstract connotations, Joyce and Showers knit together a system of proven reform which powerfully and organically link the individual, the school site, the district, and governing agencies.

The authors long ago discovered that staff development must be continuous and focused on the improvement of practice which results in measurable advances in the learning of students. Now, they demonstrate that this cannot occur unless staff development is part and parcel of fundamental reform in the culture of the school, and indeed in the ethos of the profession of education. They lay out the elements of this reform clearly, but go further by strategically designing what the system must look like and do.

Joyce and Showers are able to do this clearly and convincingly because along with their colleagues in Richmond County, Georgia; Ames, Iowa; and in several other jurisdictions, they have already implemented prototypical systems which got results, and which point the way to further, even more systematic designs for the future.

These new designs represent a quantum leap forward because they confront directly the problem of how to go to full scale. Now that we know something about how to achieve substantial success in some schools, and even some districts (and Joyce and Showers are pioneers on this front), how could we realistically accomplish reform in *all* schools? Joyce and Showers do not underestimate the complexities and difficulties in this journey, but the pathways and their interconnections can be mapped out according to their research and the lessons contained therein. What is needed, they claim, is a giant but simple self-learning system of inquirers in which every educator is inevitably implicated. This community of learners uses building blocks of coaching teams (two teachers), study groups (three coaching teams), school improvement councils (the principal and study group leaders), and cluster networks that represent schools at the level of district coordination.

What is elegant about the design is that it anticipates and incorporates the dilemmas and tensions that are endemically characteristic of complex social systems. There is a place for individual differences as well as for collective action; school autonomy is respected while allowing for district priorities and coordination; evaluation and public accountability is a requirement, but so is inquiry and discovery. The technology of effective staff development for student achievement is specifically spelled out, providing much more detail than in the previous edition. There are many more insights into the nature of training, the evolution of peer coaching, the role of content, the evaluation of staff development, and the types of outcomes to be accomplished.

Joyce and Showers' crowning achievement is integrating this new knowledge into wider governance and support systems that are designed to achieve comprehensive vertical and horizontal synergy.

Michael G. Fullan
Dean of Education
University of Toronto

Preface to the Second Edition

We wrote our first articles together, "Improving Inservice Training: The Messages of Research" (1980) and "The Coaching of Teaching" (1982), when the field of staff development was still learning to conduct "needs assessments," and the problem of just organizing smorgasbords of seminars and workshops for volunteers was taxing to most staff development offices. The content of those articles—basing the design of staff development programs on the results of research on training; using tested Models of Teaching and curriculum as the substance with student learning as the goal; and organizing teachers to provide their own "follow-up" through peer coaching—appeared ambitious to many planners. Experience has shown that many teachers and administrators liked strong substance, skill-oriented training, the colleagueship of shared effort, and the satisfaction of implementation. That genre has found a niche in staff development.

Now, the staff development field has developed ambitions that would have seemed impossibly challenging in 1979, and the messages of research and experience have much to promise those expanded aspirations. The combination of an increasing orientation toward school improvement and systemic change with a recognition of past mistakes has fueled the larger ambition. Many highly publicized and expensive initiatives to change curricula, tend individual differences, and neutralize the effects of poverty have had modest results or even failed because of what is now recognized as an absence or near absence of staff development. The staff development field is being asked to tool up to respond and ensure that future initiatives will not fail. Site-based "restructuring," "systemic" reform, and "quality management" possess sufficient history now to enable us to recognize a disturbing prospect: Failure is in store for them if they are not accompanied by extensive staff development of a strength and responsiveness that would be barely recognizable in the arrays of short courses provided 15 years ago. The commitment to a learning system for educators has to be made simultaneously with the creation of any approach to school renewal, whether that approach puts teachers at the center of the process or intends to bring the results of research and development to the workplace.

Although the program organizers of the 1970s could take satisfaction in serving bands of volunteer teachers and administrators, school improvement has turned out to be a matter of total faculty involvement. The development of the colleagueship that can sustain real reform requires learning by people in every facet of the system, and staff development must sustain that learning. In addition, all the reported successful school improvement efforts—successful in that there has been better learning by students—have made changes in curriculum, instruction, or technology, changes supported by intensive staff development.

As if those challenges were not enough, current scholars of change maintain that significant levels of innovation demand changes in the very culture of educators. The creation of a culture of educator-learners is necessary if significant improvement is to be sustained and future innovations are to be permitted without monstrous effort. We need to learn from the scholars who study innovation. Although changing the culture of education was far from our thoughts when we first became active in the field and began to study it, we now recognize that serious involvement with staff development efforts leads us, properly, into the business of cultural change.

In fact, the development of a pervasive staff development system is, in itself, a major cultural change; and that change will spawn others by changing the relation of professional to professional and between all professionals and the knowledge base and the process of inquiry.

We hope we are at the threshold of the creation of staff development systems that not only will possess effective component programs, but will, through their pervasive sustenance of people, regenerate the organization and the quality of life as well as the competence of every individual in it. We hope this small book will make a modest contribution to the energy to boost us over that threshold.

Preparing to write, we reflected on the first edition and whether our emphases of 1986 are similar to the ones of today, taking into account eight more years of research and experience by the staff development field and by ourselves as individuals. In 1986, we advocated the development of a system that would serve educators as individuals, as school faculties, and as part of an education agency. Initiatives come from individual teachers and administrators; from faculties, which are the basic collegial unit of the school system; and from the faculties of education agencies acting in concert.

Today, we still advocate the creation of a system that will serve these same parties. However, the parameters of cultural change are clearer now as is the consequent need for the staff development system to become the infrastructure of spiritual reformation. We believe now, as we did then, that the content of staff development should promise effects on student personal, social, and academic learning. We believe that any other considerations are secondary with respect to the selection of content. Educators serve students.

Nevertheless, the creation of a learning system for educators will change the workplace dramatically and will greatly alter the power relationships within the educational bureaucracy; it will equalize roles and provide everyone within the system with the means, heretofore lacking, to "get things done" and have a voice in what those things will be.

We opposed then, and do now, dichotomizing "top-down" and "bottom-up" initiatives. The "top" should be democratically governed and create cohesive and concerted efforts to improve the education of all students and ensure equality of educational opportunity. The school is the unit where education takes place, and faculty synergy is essential for quality and effectiveness in the unit. Individual initiative is glorious.

We have changed in that we emphasize more centrally the position of the school. Both district and school initiatives depend on concerted study and action at the faculty level. Individuals are greatly enhanced if the quality of the school is good, and they are impeded if it is not healthy. Much of our personal experience and our research over the last few years has been in schoolwide school renewal, and we are increasingly committed to its place in facilitating individual efforts and concerted district initiatives.

We are clearer that the key to student growth is educator growth. They happen together; each enhances the other. Altogether, a "win, win" proposition.

Good design in training continues to fascinate us. Refinements have made it possible for us to assert, even more emphatically, that "teachers are wonderful learners" (Joyce and Showers, 1988), and refinements in training design bring most Models of Teaching and curriculum within reach of most teachers and, thus, students. Designing the workplace so that teachers can work together to implement changes (through peer coaching) is still the key to transferring the content of training into the repertoire of the classroom and school, whether the content is over teaching and curriculum or over processes for collegial action. We have been saddened by the cooption of the term "peer coaching" by the field of supervision. We believe that staff development should replace "supervision," which is an obsolete concept in our opinion.

We emphasize the conduct of staff development as inquiry (continuous data collection, analysis, and interpretation) even more than we did a few years ago. The staff development system needs to be operated as a large-scale action research project and improved continually as the community of people operating it—everyone in the school system—studies effects.

We have also come to appreciate how much staff development is needed in the area of data collection and analysis, and how essential learning to collect and manage data is to improvement efforts at all levels of the organization. In the field of staff development itself, failing to collect data about implementation and student learning leaves planners without the ability to judge the effects of the components of the system or the system as a whole. Failure to manage data about student learning leaves teachers, schools, and systems unable to assess clearly how productive they are. Undoubtedly, many wonderful acts of teaching and school improvement are not available to us because of a simple lack of knowing how to collect information economically and how to use it meaningfully. Staff developers need staff development on data collection and management.

Time to study and support innovation was important ten years ago; it takes on more meaning today, when we recognize that time for collegial study, planning, staff development, and assessment needs to be built into the job of educators. Embedded time for study is one of the structural features of the new culture we hope to become.

Will is still important. Concern about potential obstacles undermines will. We need to love children and ourselves to a greater degree than our concern over the barriers we have to overcome. We need to create a respectful, positive, worldwide community of educators whose devotion to children is manifest in our reverence of learning. Those goals are the raison d'etre of the staff development system and we all need to commit to them. We have to allow ourselves to believe that the levels of student learning in personal, social, and academic domains can always rise and that our job is to enable that to happen. We have to give up the notion that school improvement will be a matter for those who happen to be interested—and take on the idea that it is a vital matter involving us all.

part I

Goals, Means, Ends

In the first three chapters we examine the roles ideally played by comprehensive staff development systems; the types of support they can provide to individuals, schools, and districts engaged in change and improvement efforts; and the roles and relationships needed in democratically governed groups if staff development systems are not only to function but to thrive.

Chapter 1 addresses both the source and the audience for staff development systems—individuals, schools, districts, and governing agencies. Assumptions are developed about the roles of a comprehensive staff development system when the goal is service to each of the three audiences. A brief review of literature in staff development builds a rationale for our belief that creating pervasive staff development systems is eminently practical. The first chapter ends with a set of beliefs/theses about staff development to which readers are invited to respond. Throughout the book we revisit these theses to clarify for ourselves and others the relation between belief and practice.

In chapter 2, we advance the notion of staff development systems as service organizations within educational settings and discuss the types of support they might reasonably provide. If the improvement objectives of individuals, schools, and districts are to be achieved, the service organization must facilitate the growth of knowledge and skills about teaching and learning, the processes of school improvement and change, and the implementation of district initiatives that reflect the aspirations of the community for all its children.

Chapter 3 addresses the development of democratically governed staff development systems.

chapter 1

The Essential Role of Staff Development Systems

Proposition: Much of the stress felt by educators is traceable to the lack of a solid staff development system. A well-designed system will empower educators as individuals, as school faculties, and as district faculties. Thus, it will empower those whom they serve.

Whether people think their schools are in relatively good shape, but can always be improved a little, or whether they think radical changes are required, *everyone* agrees in principle that the capability to make things better is a good thing. Partly because of the widespread concern that changes of a considerable magnitude are needed, school renewal receives much attention these days; the meetings of boards of education, concerned citizens' groups, school district officials, and teachers and principals are filled with proposals for making education better.

Generally speaking, proposals for school renewal come from four frames of reference; they differ considerably in terms of who is pictured as the source of the renewal process.

1. The individual practitioner as the source
2. The school site as the source
3. The district office as the source
4. The roles of governing agencies (local boards of education, the legislative and executive branches of state and federal government, and state boards of education) as the source

Each of the four concepts has merit.

THE INDIVIDUAL PRACTITIONER AS THE
SOURCE OF SCHOOL RENEWAL

Teachers and principals deliver education. Preparation for their roles has often been weak; they have had to teach themselves most of what they know, borrowing ideas from their colleagues as they can. Time to study is not built into their paid duties, and in most settings they get very little help from sources external to the school, though they are the most knowledgeable people about the problems they face. Providing them with the resources and opportunities to strengthen their skills and help them carry out their work in a reflective, inquiring mode makes very good sense.

THE SCHOOL SITE AS THE SOURCE
OF SCHOOL RENEWAL

While classrooms are the scene of instruction, the school needs to have a coherent renewal program; there are many aspects of schooling and school renewal that cannot be effected by individuals working alone. The school climate and the curriculum can be incoherent unless there is a faculty in the real sense of the word, assessing the health of the school and making decisions for ways of making it better. Thus we have the movement toward "site-based" approaches to school renewal. Increasingly, school districts are dividing the discretionary monies for school improvement among the schools and states are providing grants directly to schools. Some "charter" schools are beginning to operate as if there were no district organization.

Many districts are, regardless of philosophy, literally "forced" to take the site-based route as the central offices are stripped of personnel previously in support roles. Whatever the motivation, learning to handle the renewal at the level of each particular school is a matter of great importance.

THE DISTRICT INITIATIVE AS THE
SOURCE OF SCHOOL RENEWAL

While classrooms and schools are the stage where the play of education is enacted, curricular coherence, technological improvement, and matters of equity for all students impel districts to make initiatives in those areas. Even with greatly reduced central office personnel, curriculum guides continue to be written, computers are purchased, assessment systems developed, and ways of evaluating personnel and supervising them are adopted.

The district is the political unit for education; it has the responsibility to view the schools and teachers with some objectivity and generate ways of improving education. The technical rationale for district initiative depends to a large extent on the argument that the unit can "see" things that may not be apparent to the school-based personnel and can marshal the resources for a quality of curriculum that may be beyond the development capability of the smaller units.

THE GOVERNING AGENCIES AS THE
SOURCE OF SCHOOL RENEWAL

With the responsibility for communicating the will of the public to the schools, the governing agencies (local boards, state boards, and state and federal government agencies) also can have the advantage of perspective. No school could have written *A Nation at Risk*. Accurate or not, the work necessitated persons with a national and international perspective on the overall system to write it. It helped bring people together to think about the health of the educational system in a way that no local report could have. At the local level, boards can see and feel the needs and pressures from our ethnically diverse population. They can also compare education to other units in the society, and raise questions about education for the workplace and the maintenance of the arts and the values that are important to citizenship. They want to see a system that is accountable to the public and generate initiatives for "strategic planning," "quality management," "restructuring," and "management by objectives," most of which are borrowed from practices in the private sector.

Initiatives from all four sources *can* have a very positive effect on the education of children. There is merit in the potential of all of them. However, at present all four suffer from weaknesses that greatly reduce their effectiveness. Oddly, all four, despite apparent differences, have the same problems which, fortunately, can be corrected.

THE ACHILLES' HEEL OF ALL FOUR SOURCES

Initiatives generated for or from any of the four sources, operating as a sole source, have a very poor probability of success for two interlocking reasons:

> None will succeed in their goals unless they are supported by, and their initiatives nested in, an extensive and potent staff development system, one far more powerful and pervasive than the one that exists in the education agencies of today.

> To build an adequate staff development system will require effort by and coordination of all four sources. (In other respects, building such a system is not technically difficult.)

How the lack of a pervasive staff development system impedes each one is not difficult to perceive.

Individual Practitioners

For years individual teachers and principals have been carrying the system. The old saws: "How many schools do we have? Count the classrooms" and "How many districts do we have? Count the schools" have large measures of truth in them. The recent attention to the "reflective practitioner" and the "teacher as researcher," as well as studies of the states of growth of teachers and how teachers expand their teaching repertoires, all indicate the substantial capability of practitioners to reflect on their work and engage in innovative practice.

However, the situation of the classroom that constitutes the workplace of teachers and principals is terribly isolating in most school districts, and the process of innovations is such that people need each other if they are to sustain change. Also, in most settings there is a sore lack of the kind of staff development that helps practitioners reflect on fresh ideas and acquire Models of Teaching new to them. Without companionship, help in reflecting on practice, and instruction on fresh teaching strategies, most people can make very few changes in their behavior, however well-intentioned they are.

A staff development system can change these conditions easily.

Faculties

Some schools, with great cohesiveness and good leadership from lead teachers and principals, have made great strides. Unfortunately, the operative word is *some.* Site-based school improvement has to hurdle many obstacles. Many of these are the same hurdles that individuals have to jump. Usually, the workplace is not only short in time for individuals to study, it is not structured to facilitate collective study. Consequently, few schools have developed the collegial processes and norms that permit collective decision making to proceed smoothly. Thus, many schools have great trouble making collective decisions or engaging in schoolwide action research. And, like individuals, faculties need support and training in order to learn how to study their settings, become knowledgeable about alternative solutions to problems, and learn new curricula and teaching strategies. From studies of site-based school renewal (Calhoun, 1994; David, 1989, 1990; David & Peterson, 1984; Little, 1982, 1990; and Seashore-Louis & Miles, 1990), we estimate that only from 5 to 10 percent of schools can overcome these obstacles unassisted, even when given large grants to facilitate "restructuring" or "systemic change," or any of the other strategies now in vogue. Yet, much is known about the kinds of leadership that can make a difference (Hallinger & Murphy, 1985; Leithwood, 1990, 1992; Murphy & Hallinger, 1987; and Murphy & Louis, 1994). Again, we can easily envision changing the workplace and building a staff development system that will provide the necessary support and make site-based school improvement the odds-on winner it should be.

The District

Here, again, we have some stunning examples of districtwide initiatives that have made substantial differences in student learning (see chapter 4). However, few districts currently have the means to carry out successfully initiatives of sufficient magnitude. The successful programs all have some easily identifiable characteristics: All have had specific student-learning goals in mind, have employed procedures tailored to their goals and backed by rationales grounded in research, have measured learning outcomes on a formative and summative basis, and have employed substantial amounts of staff development in recognition that the initiative involved teacher and student learning of new procedures. Data about the progress of implementation was collected regularly and made available to project personnel.

The dependence on staff development is obvious from the list.

The Governing Agencies

Because the governing agencies act through the districts, schools, and individuals, all that has been said above applies to initiatives made by official policy-making bodies. In other words, they are helpless without a comprehensive system of staff development. However, many agencies have tried to get along without it and, in so doing, have created a lot of difficulties for themselves and others (and spent a lot of money) with little effect. An example at the federal level is Chapter I, a federally funded compensatory education program designed to help children of poverty (Anderson & Pellicer, 1990). The program, from a nationwide standpoint, has been notably ineffective in compensating for the effects of poverty; the inner cities and poor rural areas continue to suffer academically. The probable cause is that, without adequate staff development, the program used the same educational procedures that had not worked before, albeit with a lower student-teacher ratio, a variable that will not by itself do the job. At the same levels, programs providing funds for restructuring to schools have had very little effect for reasons described above. In California, a massive initiative that provided as much as $100,000 per year to each of 3,600 schools had such little effect that the evaluators recommended that the secondary school phase of the program be discontinued entirely (Berman & Gjelten, 1983). At the district level, magnet schools are turning out to be a social disaster, despite their popularity, for much the same reasons (Moore & Davenport, 1989). The newly popular "Total Quality Management" and "Systemic Reform" approaches are relatively untried in educational settings and, unless backed by very strong staff development, will have no greater effect than their predecessors of a few years ago, like "Strategic Planning" and "Restructuring." Finally, some governing agencies (and district managers) have recently tried to compel personnel to improve by changing assessment systems; they still need to recognize that people can only use the tools they have. Without training, changes from accountability-based assessment systems are likely to be small.

Nearly all scholars of school improvement are now convinced that a strong and responsive staff development system—essentially an investment in people—

combined with the provision of time within the workday for study and collaborative planning is essential to school improvement efforts. Such a system will support and legitimize individuals, schools, and district initiatives.

FROM HERE TO THERE

As this is written, the field of staff development is evolving gradually from a patchwork of courses and workshops into a system ensuring that education professionals regularly enhance their academic knowledge, professional performance, and image as professionals. States, school districts, intermediate agencies, and teachers' organizations are searching for ways to increase the investment in and styles of staff development. They are trying to develop a system that will embed professional growth opportunities into the work life of teachers and all other personnel, including administrative and supervisory personnel. Research on the knowledge and skills of teachers is increasing rapidly and the study of programs and designs continues to mature.

The focus of this book is on the planning of a comprehensive system and the governance, design, and implementation of the dimensions of that system and specific programs within it. Much of the book consists of recommendations that are based on the study of a wide range of staff development programs, research on teachers and teaching, information about the workplace, research on how teachers learn and ideas about how to design effective programs. The authors have accumulated and organized the research on staff development and teaching, conducted studies on training, studied several dozen staff development programs, collaborated on research involving more than 5,000 teachers and administrators (including case studies of about 400), and conducted staff development programs for several thousand teachers and administrators. They have helped approximately 100 agencies plan programs, including several states, many districts, a number of teacher organizations, and a half-dozen foreign countries. One of the net results of this experience is a sense of not only what is known but what is not known, and the reader will find that we believe that there is solid evidence on many issues but that many others need thoughtful attention and careful research as we progress into the future.

The time is ripe for creating rich staff development systems. To do so, we need to build working assumptions on our data and experience as it exists now, proceeding with a firm step but in a spirit of inquiry that exposes our assumptions to continuous examination. Embedded formative evaluation needs to characterize our system, probing both our strongly based assumptions as well as those that of necessity are based on our best judgments but not on evidence.

ASSUMPTIONS

First is the belief that we should develop comprehensive resource-development systems for education personnel. We will argue that the institutions that employ educators have the responsibility to ensure that all personnel regularly study teaching, school improvement, and academic substance. Further, educators have the obligation to insist that employment contains the provision for a pervasive system. The operational word is *all*. The time when administrators generate workshops for teachers but do not participate in them should be buried without ceremony. As we discuss the workplace, we will emphasize that the original task-assignments of teachers and administrators neglected to include time to prepare for teaching, for the study of teaching, for cooperative efforts in school improvement, or for academic study. These issues were simply not part of the job description. The implicit assumption was that preservice teacher education provided all the knowledge and skill that one would need throughout the career. Salary incentives and recertification requirements were used to induce teachers to return to school for courses, workshops, and institutes, but the responsibility for further study was largely that of the individual. Essentially, if the incentives failed to work the practitioner was unsupported. The response to the opportunities provided by universities and other agencies has varied widely. Some persons responded early in their careers, attending a number of courses to achieve a permanent certificate or reach a certain point on the salary scale and then did not engage in further voluntary activity for more than 20 years.

We believe that the study of academic substance, teaching, and school improvement should be an inescapable part of the job and that the organization should arrange and pay for the system. Incentives are not a good substitute for the embedding of staff development support within the context of the workplace.

Education is the only complex occupation where institutions have been ambivalent about providing continuing education for their employees. We believe that ambivalence should end and that agencies should take responsibility for the academic and clinical health of their personnel.

Second is the assumption that student learning can be greatly increased through human resource programs. While an important reason for staff development is to benefit the personnel themselves, organizations invest in human resource programs to reach their objectives. In the case of education there are two interrelated broad goals. The first is to enable the students to learn the information, skills, concepts, and values that comprise the curriculum. The second is to increase the students' ability to learn in their future.

Research on teaching and learning has resulted in a considerable array of curricular and instructional alternatives that have great promise for increasing student learning (chapters 4 and 5). These include a large number of models of teaching that have a strong research base under them (Joyce, Weil, & Showers, 1992) and a much clearer picture of the things that more effective teachers do to plan and carry out instructional programs for their students (Wang, Haertel, & Walberg, 1993).

The potential is great. Many researched teaching strategies have enough power to help the average student (the student normally at the 50th percentile) achieve what the top 10 percent of students achieve and can help the students who usually achieve in the upper quartile to make comparable gains in rate of learning.

The fundamental task of teaching is to help the students "look good" as learners—that is, to help them behave with confidence and skill. The tools now exist where any faculty can help its students look as good as or even better than the students in our highest-achieving schools.

Third, recent research on staff development has demonstrated that virtually all teachers can learn the most powerful and complex teaching strategies provided that staff development is designed properly. We are in a position where curricula and models of teaching that are now rarely employed by teachers can be learned and used by them (Joyce, Weil, & Showers, 1992; also, see chapter 7). Research on curriculum implementation and staff development has demonstrated that difficulties in implementation and the low frequency of use of the more powerful teaching strategies has been a product of weak preservice and in-service programs, not in the learning ability of teachers.

Fourth, the norms of the workplace of teaching change if powerful staff development is to be implemented; reciprocally, when it is implemented, the energy of the workplace increases considerably. Teachers and administrators have worked in relatively isolated environments (Lortie, 1975), and faculties have had relatively little experience in cooperative planning of school improvement or staff development programs. Effective staff development requires cooperative relationships that break down the isolation and increase the collective strength of the community of educators who staff the school.

Fifth, embedded staff development will have a great effect on the ethos of the profession of education—the beliefs and behavior of the professional community. Currently teachers have to rely on their personal knowledge of teaching for most of their decisions. The products of formal research and study of teaching are unknown to many of them and few have had the opportunity either to study formal knowledge or to learn how to make it work in the classroom. A strong system of preservice and in-service education will contribute to that hallmark of the great professions—a common knowledge base and the skills to use it.

Sixth, the staff development system needs to be operated as a large-scale action research project and improved continually as the community of people operating it—that means everyone in the school system—studies its impact on teachers and administrators. Teachers and administrators need to study the experiences they have, their use of the content in their work, and the effects on students. Organizers need to collaborate in those studies and respond to the effects of their efforts. The instructors in any workshop, course, or consultative activity need to study the effects of what they do. And these studies need to reach far beyond opinion about whether activities are attractive and perceptions about whether they are having a positive effect. Participants in every workshop need to count the uses and types of use they make of the workshop content and study the responses of the students and whether the students are developing greater capability to learn. Essentially, the staff development system is a very wide door to school renewal and needs to be treated as such.

The final assumption is that professional knowledge consists of three overlapping components: the study of academic content, that which undergirds the content that is to be learned by the students; the study of curricular and instructional strategies, the process of organizing content and helping students study it; and the process of school improvement, the cooperative work by faculties to make the school better. The school has its impact in three ways: One is what is taught, the second is in how it is taught, and the third in the kind of place it is—the social dimension of the learning environment (Downey, 1969). Teachers and administrators need to be engaged in the continuous study of all three, continually increasing knowledge of academic content, models of teaching, teaching skills, and models for school environments and how to create them (Levine & Lezotte, 1990; Goodlad, 1984; Sizer, 1991). We strongly believe that all personnel need to study how to build not only school-improvement programs but how to develop self-renewing organizations as well. Unless all personnel are sophisticated managers of change, they will be dominated by those who know, or believe they know, how to innovate. Creating staff development systems and creating self-renewing organizations are now one and the same. All need to participate in governance, and, if there is to be a level playing field for all participants, knowledge will have to be equal across role groups. We need to move from a condition where some manage and the rest teach to one where all manage and all teach. But, and this is a significant "but," not in the way either managing or teaching has been done before.

THE DEVELOPING BASE OF RESEARCH

In the first edition of *Student Achievement through Staff Development,* we drew heavily, as we do now, on research on teaching and curriculum as the content of staff development programs; in particular, we ferreted out the teaching skills, strategies, and curricular approaches that are known to have a positive effect on student learning in the personal, social, and academic domains. There was no lack of them (see chapter 5) and, thus, no lack of options for high payoff content for staff development. In addition, we mined research on training and curriculum implementation (see chapter 7) for designs for staff development that have a high likelihood of transferring into the classroom and other instructional settings. We also drew on studies of teachers, especially with respect to those aspects of psychological makeup that generate orientation toward growth, an aspect of personality that appears particularly relevant to staff development. We drew on sociological studies of the workplace, especially those that depict the norms of collegial groups and the effect of those norms on responses to initiatives promising change and innovation. We drew less on research on school improvement strategies, although they were continually in the background of our stance that the raison d'etre of staff development is student learning.

In this edition, we are able to profit from developments in a number of lines of research, some of which extend knowledge and some of which have opened up new avenues for exploration. Six domains of research have been especially useful: explorations of school renewal strategies, training, staff development involving entire faculties of schools and districts, large-scale programs where the link between staff development and student achievement was directly explored, teachers as researchers and reflective practitioners, and teaching skills and models of teaching. To these we have added our clinical experience in school districts.

Research on School Renewal Strategies

The intense worldwide attention to school renewal has resulted in greater definition of strategies that faculties can use to generate actions ranging from relatively complete redesigns of the curriculum to small-scale initiatives for relatively modest goals. Evaluations of school-improvement projects make up much of the research, which is naturalistic (describes what happens naturally rather than reporting an experiment) and intensely pragmatic. Most of the evaluators want to find out if a given project *works* rather than testing out the theories on which it is based. Spawning comparison groups is, in most cases, virtually impossible, so questions like "Is strategy A working better than strategy B?" are rarely addressed. Fortunately, many of the important questions in staff development can be informed by the naturalistic, evaluation-oriented studies.

For example, quite a number of studies have tracked schools that applied for and were given resources (sometimes as much as $200,000 or more per school but generally much less) to develop and implement school improvement plans. David and Peterson (1984) and Berman and Gjelten (1983) reported two such studies and found that most of the schools had been unable to produce collective initiatives or, if they had, to organize the training needed to implement them, let alone study the effects on students. Advice to "restructure" or engage in "systemic reform," become "an essential school," or institute "total quality management" have not, for the most part, yielded evaluations that are promising. Essentially, the "site-based" approach to the management of school improvement is having a hard time. Whether other approaches to school reform would have fared better in those settings is open to question. However, most important, as we examine these studies, we are able to generate some ideas about what so often goes wrong and how to make site-based initiatives work. What often goes wrong is that faculties are not, for the most part, very well organized to study themselves and make decisions for collective action, nor does the structure of the school provide much time for collegial study and decision making. Schools are organized into classrooms peopled by largely autonomous teachers who are unaccustomed to collective action-taking and can find it aggravating and inefficient. As Myrna Cooper (1988) put it so well, "Idiosyncrasy makes their culture distinctive." Left to themselves, somewhere between eight and nine out of ten faculties will have a terrible time trying to change themselves from an operating school to a school that not only operates but devotes a great deal of energy to self-study. However, that frustrating struggle does not have to be. Were the school nested in the envelope of a full-service staff development system to help with process, resources for study, and training when needed, and were time built into the workweek for substantial amounts of collective study, we might see an entirely different picture. Studies of schools engaged in schoolwide action research have found that, with expert consultative support, faculties can slog through the mire of school improvement with surprising alacrity and satisfaction. From our perspective, there is no more compelling data-based ground to support arguments for a comprehensive staff development system than the research on school renewal. Whether in urban areas (Seashore-Louis & Miles, 1990) or rural and suburban ones (Huberman & Miles, 1984), faculties need help to redefine their workplace and get going on the business of improving education.

Research on school improvement has yielded much additional information about the social system of school faculties, types of leadership, and the problems attendant to changing the culture of educators, all of which we will draw upon as relevant throughout the book.

Research on Training

In the first edition, we summarized research on training, especially research on training in staff development, and drew heavily on it to provide principles for designing effective staff development programs for individuals, faculties, and to support district initiatives where transfer into the workplace and consequent effects on student learning are the objectives. By the mid-1980s, we could assert that the art and science of training design had reached the point where designs could virtually assure that nearly all educators could master just about any teaching skill or model of teaching yet developed; follow-up activities by the educators themselves (peer coaching) could assure that nearly all of them would find satisfaction through implementation of the additions to their repertoire and the responses of the students. Over the last ten years, a number of studies have affirmed those assertions and consolidated some of the elements of the training design. The major advances have been in a greater understanding about how to "design" the workplace to facilitate peer coaching and training and in a greater understanding of the grouping of participants for training and the functions of leadership in the workplace. In successful projects, administrators and lead teachers are not organizers only; they participate fully in training, the study of implementation, and the effects on students.

Research on "Whole-Faculty" Participation

Large-scale projects involving entire faculties of schools and, in some cases, school districts, have demonstrated that "whole-school" and "whole-district" programs often achieve higher rates of transfer than do programs that involve small groups of volunteer teachers from schools (see chapters 6, 7, and 8). When groups of volunteer teachers are organized into study groups and engage in peer coaching, the proportion who transfer the content of training to classroom practice is very large (75 percent to 90 percent), but when the entire faculty is involved, the transfer rate approaches 100 percent (Joyce, Murphy, Showers, & Murphy, 1989). Without the study-group/peer-coaching organization, the rate for even very enthusiastic volunteers can be as low as 10 percent (see Figure 1.1). The reason appears to be that, when the entire workplace is involved, the colleagueship generated provides powerful social support as people practice teaching strategies that are new to their repertoire or implement the difficult areas of a curriculum change. The small groups from a variety of schools, although they may be cohesive, simply cannot receive the pervasive support or collective sense of purpose that ensues when the whole gang is involved.

This finding is very good news indeed when the purpose of a staff development entity is school improvement with ambitious goals for student learning. Such efforts necessarily involve everyone in the school and, frequently, many parents and community members, as well. Small groups of volunteers simply do not make a school faculty.

A concomitant finding has good news for participatory governance at the school level. When school faculties decide that they will make decisions about staff development options on the basis of 80 percent agreements that bind all the members, the entire faculties participate with very little discord stemming from those members whose option did not get priority "this time around." In our own clinical work, we take a "more the merrier" approach, preferring to work with whole faculties of schools and even districts.

We will deal with a number of other recent findings in the chapters to come, but our assumption that teachers are wonderful learners remains unchallenged; their ability to work collectively to master new and difficult models of teaching and curriculum is more than adequate to generate high levels of implementation

FIGURE 1.1 Level of implementation by pattern of participation and training design

Pattern of Participation	Level of Implementation
No peer structure for follow-up—participation by volunteers as individuals	5–10% implementation
Participation by peer-coaching teams from a variety of schools	75% implementation or better
Participation by whole-school faculties organized into peer-coaching teams for follow-up	90% implementation or better can reach 100%

of anything thus far generated for the storehouse of educational alternatives. The condition is well-designed training and a well-designed workplace, and those are not difficult to achieve. Good people (which we have) combined with well-designed staff development programs (which we can create) will result in meaningful change that, if the content is good (we have plenty), will help students learn more in all respects.

Research on Models of Teaching, Teaching Skills, and Curriculum

Ten years ago there was plenty of research to draw from to fill the content of staff development programs with teaching strategies, skills, and curriculum options that had proven value in enhancing student learning capability. Today there are more (see chapter 5), and there have been refinements in some of the older ones (Joyce, Weil, & Showers, 1992). Advances in the use of the statistic of "effect size" (Glass, 1982) enable us to estimate the magnitude of effects of various treatments, whereas tests only of the probability that a difference between treatments is real did not permit estimates of the importance of the size of the differences. (The concept of effect size is explained more fully in the introduction to Part II, page 47.) Thus we are able to establish goals more meaningfully. For example, when we say that the inductive approach to the teaching of the reading/writing connection in language arts has an effect size of 0.67 (Hillocks, 1987) compared to textbook-oriented instruction and interpret that to say that the median student in the inquiry-oriented treatment moves to about the 73rd percentile of the median student in the textbook-oriented treatment, the goal of using the inductive approach becomes clearer and more meaningful. Meta-analyses of research on models of teaching (Joyce, Showers, & Rolheiser-Bennett, 1987) and teaching skills (Wang, Haertel, & Walberg, 1993) combine with studies of particular approaches to curriculum (Bredderman, 1983; El Nemr, 1979) to display the knowledge base so that choices among options can be made with anticipated levels of gain in student learning as the clear goal. Imagine an individual teacher, a faculty, or a district contemplating variations in cooperative learning. They can choose from ones that will have an effect size of 0.10 or 0.20 to ones that have an effect size approaching 2.0 (where the median student reaches the 95th percentile of the comparison treatments) (Sharan & Shachar, 1988). The catch is, of course, that the stronger treatments in this example require a greater investment in staff development if implementation is to take place. We, of course, do not regard that as a "catch." All reported projects that have achieved student effects included substantial amounts of staff development.

The storehouse of options now contains quite a few items which, in combination, promise really remarkable gains in student learning. We will deal with a number of these in detail in chapter 5. The message is that there is real strength "out there" and there is no good reason not to use it.

Research on the Reflective Practitioner

Ever since the publication of Schon's (1982) very popular book created interest in shaping environments to facilitate reflection on practice and the conscious development of skill through personal inquiry, staff development designers have been challenged to create such environments. Several hundred case studies have been published that support what practitioners can do when they turn a reflective eye on their practices; recommendations range from "training" to engage in individual action research, to developing networks of support groups, to providing consultation that bears a strong resemblance to personal counselling but concentrates in the personal/professional dimension of life. David Hunt's *Teachers' Personal Theorizing* (1981; Hunt & Gow, 1984) is a marvelous guide to how individuals can elevate their reflective thoughts into conscious theorems for the guide of practice. Kenneth Leithwood's (1990) work provides a similar frame of reference for work with administrators. Materials to help teachers carry out research in the curriculum areas are beginning to appear. For example, Myers' (1985) *The Teacher-Researcher: How to Study Writing in the Classroom* is a marvelous guide that provides many tools, offers important questions to ask, and connects the teacher to the research on the teaching of writing. Even supervision is being shaped to promote reflection, despite its history as a practice more often associated with regulation and evaluation. The approaches to supervision of Glickman (1990), Goldhammer (1969), Cogan (1973), and Sergiovanni (1985) have many elements in common with the reflective teaching movement. Hunter's (1980) work provides a structured framework that can certainly be used to promote reflection, although most advocates of support for reflective teaching are much more on the Rogerian side of the coin of interaction.

At this time the "Teacher-Researcher" movement offers much to the individually oriented component of a staff development system, regardless of the philosophical orientation taken. In our view, there is no reason why teachers cannot facilitate one another's reflection. There is little formal knowledge about the amounts and kinds of help they may need, but there is no reason why that cannot be figured out in the course of time or why communication components cannot be built into the system so that teachers and administrators can share the results of their individual study.

Some of the literature advocating the development of programs to assist teachers to become researchers also suggest that knowledge about teaching and learning developed by "professional" researchers, especially in universities, is irrelevant to classroom practice; some go so far as to say that helping teachers learn the results of that research on teaching is denigrating. In other words, they argue that there is no knowledge-base relevant to schooling or socially supportive of teaching as a profession (see, for example, several of the essays in Hollingsworth & Sockett, 1994). We obviously do not agree with all these authors or understand why they make some of the assertions they do, but we strongly advocate components that help teachers become better knowledge producers, whether for their own personal/professional use or to share with others.

Research on the Link between Staff Development and Student Achievement

The development of really fine staff development systems does not take place unless policymakers believe there is a link between the investment in staff development and the learning of children. Staff development as such does not lead automatically to increased student learning—it can contain content that will not change student learning. An example is assessment. Assessing learning is an important professional tool, and educators should become very good at it, but improving assessment simply changes how things are measured rather than changing what is learned. As near as we can tell, only content dealing with curriculum, instruction, or technology is likely to improve student learning. However, content of the highest quality will not change student learning unless it is implemented. For example, we recently worked in a district where large numbers of faculty members had studied a very potent form of cooperative learning with expert trainers in a series of workshops, but almost none implemented the strategy. The workshops had become exercises in futility. None had thought to organize study groups, develop peer-coaching relationships, or study implementation. The trainers returned month after month to a situation in which they were well received (nearly everybody enjoyed the workshops) but the purpose had been lost. There could have been, but was not, a link between those staff development activities and student learning. To have a link, there has to be potent content and good design, not only of the workshops, but of the workplace in which that content is to be implemented. In that district, we had to reorganize the training so that implementation could occur and, then, effects on student learning could be investigated.

The testing of various models of teaching demonstrate a direct link between staff development and student achievement in that the testing requires that teachers learn how to implement the models (and other teaching skills). Thus, the many studies demonstrating the effects of inductive, concept-learning, social, and behavioral models provide a knowledge base relevant to staff development. Most of those tests, however, are conducted with volunteer teachers who are relatively close colleagues of the engineers of those teaching strategies.

Convincing demonstrations of a potent link between student learning and staff development need to be large-scale and include teachers who are at some distance from the designers of the educational treatments. It is even better if the demonstrations can include students who are regarded as very difficult to teach, either because their "backgrounds" place them at risk in the educational system or because they are believed to be already achieving as well as possible. Note that these criteria are meant to make it difficult for the relationship between staff development and student learning to be demonstrated by being large-scale and involving *all* the personnel. Several such programs are dealt with at length in chapter 4.

THESES ABOUT STAFF DEVELOPMENT
AND SCHOOL IMPROVEMENT

As the literature on staff development has matured, there is a greater clarification both of the findings of research and also the assumptions that program planners make as they design programs. We hope that stating the assumptions, examining how they affect decision making, and locating evidence relative to them will help planners understand better why they and others choose particular options and will increase the likelihood that the chosen courses of action will achieve the planned goals. In the next few pages, we present a number of the "theses" that appear in the literature and also are used by program planners, and we will return to them throughout the book as we attempt to clarify the stances that drive various conceptions of staff development. The reader is invited to take a position on each of them. Throughout the book they will appear and be discussed in terms of their popularity, implications, and relevant research. At the end of the book we will present our syntheses of the research on each of them and indicate our own preferences.

On Personal Motivation, Selection
of Options, and Probable Effects

Thesis One: If individual teachers select their own staff development options, "buy-in" will ensure satisfaction and implementation.

_____ Strongly agree

_____ Agree

_____ Neutral

_____ Disagree

_____ Strongly disagree

Thesis Two: Personal motivational factors and knowledgeability vary considerably, and individually designed staff development programs will have equally variable effects and satisfaction.

_____ Strongly agree

_____ Agree

_____ Neutral

_____ Disagree

_____ Strongly disagree

On Collegial Locus of Control

Thesis Three: Staff development should be based at the school site, with the faculty making the decisions about directions and how to get there.

_____ Strongly agree

_____ Agree

_____ Neutral

_____ Disagree

_____ Strongly disagree

Thesis Four: Many schools are "stuck" and site-based restructuring efforts create frustration and disappointment unless the faculties transform themselves into problem-solving groups.

_____ Strongly agree

_____ Agree

_____ Neutral

_____ Disagree

_____ Strongly disagree

On Credibility and "Buy In"

Thesis Five: Start with a group of enthusiasts, and, when the others see what they are doing, they will buy in.

_____ Strongly agree

_____ Agree

_____ Neutral

_____ Disagree

_____ Strongly disagree

Corollary Thesis Six: Action research is best conducted by individuals and small groups.

_____ Strongly agree

_____ Agree

_____ Neutral

_____ Disagree

_____ Strongly disagree

Thesis Seven: Schoolwide action research knits the faculty and gets results for children.

_____ Strongly agree

_____ Agree

_____ Neutral

_____ Disagree

_____ Strongly disagree

On Central Planning

Thesis Eight: Carefully articulated initiatives in curriculum and instruction generate colleagueship and bring about changes in curriculum and instruction that are satisfying to teachers and effective for students.

_____ Strongly agree

_____ Agree

_____ Neutral

_____ Disagree

_____ Strongly disagree

Thesis Nine: Centralized initiatives are doomed to failure because of resistance and lack of "buy-in."

_____ Strongly agree

_____ Agree

_____ Neutral

_____ Disagree

_____ Strongly disagree

On the Culture of the School

Thesis Ten: Begin with the development of collegiality, then initiatives will emerge.

_____ Strongly agree

_____ Agree

_____ Neutral

_____ Disagree

_____ Strongly disagree

Thesis Eleven: Begin with initiatives and generate collegiality through action.

_____ Strongly agree

_____ Agree

_____ Neutral

_____ Disagree

_____ Strongly disagree

On Time and the Culture of the School

Thesis Twelve: The implementation of an initiative in curriculum, instruction, or technology takes three years or more.

_____ Strongly agree

_____ Agree

_____ Neutral

_____ Disagree

_____ Strongly disagree

Thesis Thirteen: Well-designed initiatives can be implemented during the first year.

_____ Strongly agree

_____ Agree

_____ Neutral

_____ Disagree

_____ Strongly disagree

Thesis Fourteen: Well-designed initiatives can change the culture of the school immediately in certain ways and, by steady increments, create self-renewing schools and school districts.

_____ Strongly agree

_____ Agree

_____ Neutral

_____ Disagree

_____ Strongly disagree

Thesis Fifteen: Changing the culture of the school takes from five to ten years.

_____ Strongly agree

_____ Agree

_____ Neutral

_____ Disagree

_____ Strongly disagree

On Age and Experience

Thesis Sixteen: Age decreases motivation and the stresses of teaching lead to "burnout."

_____ Strongly agree

_____ Agree

_____ Neutral

_____ Disagree

_____ Strongly disagree

Thesis Seventeen: Maturity increases strength as learners and problem solvers.

_____ Strongly agree

_____ Agree

_____ Neutral

_____ Disagree

_____ Strongly disagree

On Technical Assistance and Research

Thesis Eighteen: To get "moving" most schools need technical support, especially to bring the research base to bear on problem solving.

_____ Strongly agree

_____ Agree

_____ Neutral

_____ Disagree

_____ Strongly disagree

Thesis Nineteen: Knowledge is personal and situation-specific. External sources provide little of value to local problem solving.

_____ Strongly agree

_____ Agree

_____ Neutral

_____ Disagree

_____ Strongly disagree

SUMMARY

A pervasive staff development system serves the needs of individuals, schools, and districts, both by nourishing the professional growth of adults in the system and by directly addressing student learning. Research on school improvement processes, training design, curriculum, and instruction provides ample content for the design of comprehensive staff development systems.

The design and implementation of staff development systems, however, is likely to be influenced as much by the beliefs held by people in the system regarding school improvement and change as by research on successful programs. We acknowledge the link between beliefs and practice in the field of staff development and invite readers to examine their own beliefs as together we search for ways to design and conduct effective systems.

The chapter that follows is organized around the design of a staff development system that pervades the school and is the responsibility of the organization. The system will be built on research on how teachers and administrators learn and how to design effective programs within an embedded system of staff development. The powerful teaching strategies and curricula that have been developed over the last two decades need to be available to all personnel. The major goal is to increase student learning; however, there will be great changes in the workplace by increasing the study of teaching and learning and the strengthening of faculties as they work together for their students.

chapter 2

A Service Organization

Proposition: Staff development is a service organization within the educational system.

In this chapter we sketch a version of a comprehensive staff development system. Governance and design are the major topics. We are concerned with developing a governance system that brings everybody together to make decisions and carry out programs. We are also concerned that the content and processes serve individuals, faculties, and district initiatives richly and effectively, and that student learning be kept central as the system is developed.

To ensure that educators grow continuously is the goal. The idea seems innocuous enough. Given the awesome responsibilities of educating the young and the current rapid changes in both knowledge and social conditions, investing in people seems like an obvious and natural thing to do. Yet, the creation of a comprehensive educational service system feels like a "big" innovation to most people. Although staff development is technically and organizationally straightforward (the "educational warehouse" contains all the tools and materials needed to manufacture a good system and more good ideas turn up every day), putting it in place requires changes unusual enough that very few school systems have developed anything approaching the operation we envision. Notice the term *unusual* rather than *difficult*.

Creating pervasive staff development systems does not require exotic or arcane skills so much as the willingness to change routines. The increase in staff development time will, in itself, constitute a major change. Change, however, is not inherently stressful and the development of a staff development system will actually reduce many of the current stresses that people feel within the system.

25

As this is written, the average teacher in the United States engages in the formal study of teaching and schooling, including new content and curricula, for only about three or four days per year and has advisory conferences with teachers or supervisors only two or three times each year, less frequently in many cases. (Of course, there are some teachers who engage in a great deal of formal study, but this text is directed toward the average situation.) A small amount of support can be worse than none at all, for tasks such as trying to implement a significantly revised curriculum with just a couple of days of orientation can be painful in the extreme.

The system we envision would provide 15 or 20 days of study each year for everybody, embed provisions for cooperative planning into the workplace, and enable teachers to visit each other regularly to borrow ideas.

For many policymakers, the biggest change is attitudinal and involves views on two subjects: One has to do with perspective and the other with conditions.

The first view deals with responsibility and is a change from the perception that professional growth is solely the responsibility of the individual practitioner—something to be done on one's own time—to an acceptance of the obligation of the organization to provide for growth. The old view derives from a stance toward the life of the professional, and worker, that was popular in the nineteenth century, when advanced study by professionals was almost entirely self-study; and managers tried to divide work in factories and commercial entities into narrowly defined jobs that required little training for any one worker. This view minimized the need to make learning a central part of the organization. Fortunately, it has changed with respect to most occupational groups; however, with respect to education, many board members and not a few superintendents are not yet convinced.

The related second subject has to do with the conditions necessary for people to learn new skills and content to the point where they can use both effectively. A familiar position emphasizes educational improvement through coercion, essentially a view that people can be pressured to change by evaluation and accountability-oriented procedures. Thus, not a few initiatives by states and districts emphasize the use of assessment and "accountability" to attempt to make changes in education. The recent discussions around creating a national assessment program with national standards is similar. The essence of the rationale is that measurement, with public results, will force teachers and principals to change. In turn, that argument depends on an assumption that people, once made accountable for changes in education, can teach themselves how to make those changes. The assumption that people can, without support that includes training, teach themselves the magnitude of teaching skills and curricular changes that will make a difference to student learning is just not valid. Teachers are good people and work hard. They are doing the best they can. Aside from the questionable sensibility and morality of attempting to build a control system that does not include teachers and principals, the attempt to improve education by "accountability through testing" is doomed to failure on technical grounds. On the other hand, a pervasive staff development system that includes everyone in its goals and procedures will have tremendous positive effects, be a whole lot more pleasant, and reside much more comfortably within our democratic tradition. Organizational sensibility, social morality, and efficiency come together in the provision of ways that educators can grow.

Policymakers are not the only ones who need some persuading when it comes to building a going system. Many teachers and principals are not charmed by their first encounter with the idea, either. A fair number have come to enjoy the autonomy of the job and regard staff development as an intrusion on their self-supervised work. We would persuade them of the benefits. Also, the history of staff development as "something done to others" is probably one of the chief impediments to be overcome. Teachers and principals are rather tired of weak offerings and workshops that are conducted less as an inquiry into teaching and learning than as a carrying down of tablets of dicta. Good quality is the antidote, and inclusion in planning is one of the most direct routes to high-caliber programs.

PURPOSES

We suggest that there are three general purposes to be served and around which strands of the system can be organized.

Enhancement of Individual Clinical Skills and Academic Knowledge

One purpose is to ensure that all practitioners—teachers and administrators alike—are continuously polishing and expanding their current repertoires of knowledge and skill throughout their careers. Knowledge and skill are important, and neither are enhanced automatically. Adding new content and teaching strategies to the existing repertoire to the point where they can be used effectively in the instructional setting has turned out to be difficult and requires very hard work. (See chapters 7 and 8 for the research on which this assertion is based.)

The Study of School Improvement

Although the most familiar image of teachers and administrators is one of individuals at work, the improvement of the environment of the school requires collective work. The social climate of the school and the attitudes and patterns of behavior it promotes greatly influence the process of education. For example, rigorous standards for students are promoted not so much by what individuals do as by what the faculty does as a whole. A teacher who works alone to impose standards not promoted by the faculty as a whole is in for a very frustrating and largely ineffectual experience. A major function of staff development is to unite the staffs of schools in the study of ways to improve the school and to implement procedures likely to make it better. Outstanding schools have faculties who work hard at school improvement. Schools whose programs are neglected become less effective quite rapidly.

Districtwide Initiatives to Improve the Educational Program

The classroom and the school exist in the context of the larger agency that has responsibility for curriculum development, implementation of that curriculum, and the allocation of resources for facilities and technologies. Curriculum improvement and the introduction of new technologies require extensive study and training if they are to be implemented successfully. The staff development system needs to ensure that existing curricula and technologies are updated regularly and that districtwide innovations are of high quality and are conducted in a first-class manner

RATIONALE

As Fullan (1982; Fullan & Stiegelbauer, 1991) has pointed out so carefully, an innovation is not sustained unless there is a shared understanding of its purposes, rationale, and processes. Staff development is still an innovation—certainly the creation of a fully modern system is—and we need to reflect on our beliefs and ensure that our ideas are congruent enough to keep us working together.

Supporting the Continuous Study of Teaching and Learning

There is a considerable reservoir of effective curricular patterns and teaching skills and strategies (see chapters 4 and 5). The currently weak system of staff development does not bring these to the attention of very many teachers and administrators and often does not include training that can ensure that selected strategies are mastered and used (see chapters 6 and 7). Yet, programs can be designed in ways that enable virtually any practitioner to develop high levels of skill with them. We have confidence that, during the next few years, there will be an even greater increase in knowledge about effective teaching than we have had from the last 20 years. We have increasingly better tools for research, more rapid and complete communication among scholars, and the growing international community generates more perspectives that enrich inquiry. In addition, experience develops skill, particularly if the conditions are created to help people reflect on their experience and experiment with their teaching.

Thus, the rationale for the first goal is that there is much to learn and the means of doing so are at hand.

Supporting Faculty Study of School Improvement

The reality is that the school climate is developed through collective action. There is considerable knowledge about the dimensions of the climate that enhance learning; the isolation of practitioners in what Lortie (1975) has called the "cellular" nature of the school has prevented faculties from acting collectively to study what works and how to achieve it. The nature of the school has caused most teachers and administrators to concentrate on the instructional and leadership skills that they can employ alone rather than the skills that are employed in close cooperation with other people (Goodlad, 1984). Coherent curricula and social systems, however, are made by communities of people. The tools are available to help faculties plan collective action (Calhoun, 1994; Fullan & Park, 1981; Fullan, Miles, & Taylor, 1980; Schmuck, Runkel, Arends, & Arends, 1977).

Supporting District Initiatives in Curriculum and Technology

The implementation of curricular and technological changes is virtually impossible without very strong staff development (Fullan, 1982; Goodlad & Klein, 1970; Joyce, Hersh, & McKibbin, 1983). Curricular change involves innovations in content and instructional processes and materials. The current staff development system is too weak to support curriculum change beyond a simple change in textbooks in all but a handful of school districts (Fullan & Pomfret, 1977). Technological change is in the same situation. Even common media, like film, videotape, and broadcast television, are almost unused in schools, despite their enormous educational value. The computer comes late and lumbering to our schools. Initiatives like mainstreaming of handicapped students have labored dreadfully, denying the children its full benefits (SRI International, 1981).

Again, research has progressed to the point where the knowledge exists to engineer staff development programs on behalf of curricular and technological initiative at the district level. Individuals, faculties, and district policy makers can be empowered equally through effective staff development.

DIMENSIONS OF A COMPREHENSIVE SYSTEM

The system that we visualize is not particularly complex, although in large education units the logistics can challenge the best managerial skills. In any setting, creating the system requires a many-sided effort. The core is the development of many small communities of teachers and administrators carefully linked within and across schools and supported by human and material resources.

Study Groups and Coaching Teams: Building Communities of Learners

Each teacher and administrator has membership in a team whose members support one another in study. For example, each person can have membership in a peer-coaching study team of two to three people. Each team is linked to one or two others, forming a study group of no more than six members. The principal and the leaders of the study groups in a school form the staff development/school improvement council of that school. A representative from each school within a district cluster (usually a high school and its feeder schools) serves on the District Cluster Network Committee, which coordinates staff development efforts between schools and the district; it also works directly with the director of staff development (see Figure 2.1).

This governance structure is illustrated by the staff at the Onyx Elementary School whose faculty numbers 36. One teacher, Adriene, has a coaching partner, Katherine. They belong to Study Group A, which has six members. Aldrin is, with five others, a member of the Onyx School staff development council. She and the principal are members of the Cluster Network Committee which consists of representatives from one high school, two middle schools, and six elementary schools in the Opal district. Through a council of teachers and administrators, that cluster, with the three others in the district, is linked to the District Office for Educational Programs and Staff Development. The director of that office is an associate superintendent and reports directly to the superintendent.

The coaching teams and study groups are the building blocks of the system. Team members support one another as they study academic content and teaching skills and strategies. The study groups within each school are responsible for implementing school improvement efforts and districtwide initiatives.

FIGURE 2.1   A district staff development goverance structure

District Office for Educational Programs
and Staff Development
(Director is associate superintendent)

Cluster Network Committees
(Each of the clusters has representatives
from a high school and its feeder schools)

Staff Development/School Improvement Council
(School principal and study group leaders)

Study Group
(Three coaching teams)

Coaching Team
(Two faculty members)

Governance: Three Types of Operation

The comprehensive staff development system is designed to generate three kinds of effort. One is that each practitioner will be regularly engaged in the study of some aspect of academic content or clinical skill. We refer to this as the *individual* component, because the product is to be manifested in the individual's clinical competence as an instructor. The second effort is the faculty refining or renovating some aspect of the school program. We refer to this as the *collective* component, because it requires the cooperative enterprise of the school faculty. Third is that a district wide initiative in curriculum or technology will be in some stage of implementation. We refer to this as the *systemic* or *district* component, because it requires coordinated effort among the members of all branches of the district organization.

In Adriene's case, her study group is exploring how to organize their students into cooperative learning groups (Slavin, 1983; Johnson & Johnson, 1975). They have attended a workshop and are helping one another put into practice what they have learned. The Onyx School's improvement initiative for the year is focused on attempts to develop a more affirmative climate for the students and to increase the amount of cooperative study in which they engage. They have based their effort on research showing that an affirmative school climate and increased study, especially cooperative study, are related to student learning (Joyce, Weil, & Showers, 1992). Third, the district initiative for a two-year period focuses on increased use of the computer for instruction in writing. The Onyx School has combined this with its own effort to increase independent and cooperative study.

How are the three components (individual, collective, and district) governed? Two levels of decisions are to be made: One is about participation and the other is about the provision of support personnel and materials. In the case of the individual component, all teachers and administrators are expected to be engaged in the study of at least one aspect of academic content or teaching skill or strategy. Each individual can select the type of study to be engaged in during any year, within the limitations of feasibility. The district staff development committee is responsible for collecting suggestions from the schools, study groups, coaching teams, and individuals, and generating the program of offerings that will be supported during any given year. The program will be balanced so that individuals receive support for their first choices fairly regularly.

Similarly, the school committees make choices for the collective component and the district committee tries to support the choices that are made for the school foci.

The focus for the systemic or district component is selected by the district committee after a study of the alternatives. The focus needs to be narrowed as much as possible. In the past many districts have diffused their staff development programs by selecting more initiatives than could be supported adequately. We have witnessed the chaos that ensues when the curriculum unit generates two or three initiatives, the special education, Chapter I, and "Gifted and Talented" departments generate theirs, and the evaluation unit asks each of the schools to create its own new assessment program—all at once and uncoordinated with one another. Then each of these simultaneously provides "training" to one or two members of the faculty of each school who, it turn, are supposed to pass the content along to their colleagues. As many readers know, this is not a parody. The teachers and administrators on the district committee need to discipline the process so that such a diffused mess does not occur.

SUPPORTING THE SYSTEM

Each of the components depends on training and study opportunities for support. The components do not so much require different kinds of training and consultatory help as they do different patterns for accomplishing their ends.

The Individual Component

The individual component requires patterns of courses, workshops, and consultant services to enable individuals and coaching teams to study some aspect of teaching and to enhance their skills. Adrienne and Katherine have chosen to work as a team and selected cooperative learning from a set of alternatives that included offerings from the following categories:

Academic Courses.   For elementary teachers these included courses in mechanics, literature (contemporary poetry), children's literature, the geography of Africa, and a variety of other subjects.

Workshops on Teaching.   There are several levels of study (introductions and advanced study) on a variety of subjects. Cooperative learning includes three levels of topics. In addition to cooperative learning strategies, the offerings include several models of teaching (concept learning, inductive teaching, synectics, memory models, etc.), several offerings on lesson design (Hunter & Russell, 1981), and a series on classroom management for beginning teachers.
    There are workshops on teaching each of the core elementary school subjects. This year there is an extensive series on the teaching of writing.

Workshops on the Study of the Student.   Each year there are workshops on two different ways of looking at the learning styles of students and the design of instruction to maximize student strengths and to help students develop in areas of weakness. This year there is a course on self-concept and one on developmental psychology.

Workshops on Technology.   There is an extensive series on the use of the computer, a set of short workshops on television and video recording, and photography.

The courses and workshops are offered in a number of ways. Some are distance-based courses offered from the state university which use readings, broadcast television, and television recordings as instructional modes. A larger number are workshops taught by district personnel. A few are taught by university personnel and other consultants who come to the district on a regular basis.

The Collective Component

The offerings to support the collective component are similar to the ones offered under the individual component except that they have been requested by particular school faculties and are offered for the faculty as a whole. Also, there are workshops on the study of schools thought to be effective and on the process of school improvement. Workshops for the school-based facilitation teams are a critical element in the offerings for the collective component.

The personnel who offer the workshops are available to the school for on-site consultation on the topics they teach. Whenever qualified district personnel are available, they teach the courses.

The Systemic or District Component

The systemic component, being districtwide, is a more complex operation. A cadre of administrators and teachers representing each school study the initiative for a year and conduct many of the in-school offerings connected with the innovation. University personnel and consultants are enlisted, if needed, to help provide the training for this core group and work with the component's members as they provide workshops and other support for their peers. The study groups and peer-coaching teams provide assistance to their members as the difficult process of implementing the initiative takes place.

Support in the Opal District. Bilingual education has come to Onyx and the other schools in the district as large numbers of Spanish-speaking students for whom English is a second language have moved into the district. A very important initiative is under way to enable about 50 of the teachers to study Spanish intensively and learn how to implement the CIRC program (Calderon, Hertz-Lazarowitz, & Tinajero, 1991), so that these students can be taught with students who speak only English, each learning both languages in a multilingual community.

Every person in the district has responsibility for cooperating with the systemic and collective foci and for developing a program for personal growth, possibly in conjunction with a peer-coaching partner or a study group.

THE SUPPORT CADRE

An essential component of an effective system is personnel who can offer instruction and support to others in the areas that are under study. These persons need to develop a very high level of competence in an area to the point where they can deal with its theory, demonstrate it, organize practice with it, and help coaching teams and study groups sustain its use in the instructional setting. There needs to be a relatively small group of specialists in curriculum and instruction who study the alternatives, study staff development and school improvement, and organize the offerings that support each of the three substantive components. In addition, as areas are selected for study, instructional teams made up of teachers and administrators with an interest in the area need to be organized in teams who will offer the instruction and support on specific topics. For example, if inductive teaching is selected, the instructional team would study its theory, practice it with students, and prepare demonstrations for use in workshops and courses.

Because it takes time to develop competence to the point where one can offer instruction to others, the instructional team should be selected a year before any offerings are to be made in the area, so that they have ample time for preparation. From whom do they receive guidance? If there are already qualified district personnel, then they should be utilized. If not, consultants may have to be utilized or the team may have to travel to a setting where they can study the innovation, such as a university, an institute, or extended series of workshops, or a district that has made much use of the content.

The important feature is that the system includes a commitment to the development of in-house competence wherever feasible, relying on external consultants primarily to build the capability of the within-district personnel.

Returning to Adrienne, she and her partner are members of an instructional team that specializes in the use of the teaching strategy synectics for the teaching of writing. During the year they will offer a series of workshops as part of the collective component to the faculty of an elementary school that has chosen writing as its school improvement thrust for the year.

Even where offerings are distance-based or staffed primarily by external personnel, an instructional team needs to be organized to provide leadership for the individuals, coaching teams, study groups, and faculties who are participating. In fact, during the first year or two that a topic is supported, the instructional team might work with the external personnel as co-trainers while they develop their competence to generate offerings without outside support.

SUMMARY

The proposed system is straightforward. Its organizational building blocks include coaching teams combined into study groups within faculties that are networked within clusters of schools. Its three components serve individuals, faculties, and the system as a whole. The governance structure provides for teacher, administrator, and policymaker participation at all levels of decision making. Support offerings are selected on a basis of careful study of the alternatives and perceived needs of personnel. Offerings are probably fewer than in many operating systems but are in-depth. Within-district personnel are heavily utilized as training teams to the point where as many as one out of ten teachers and administrators is serving as an instructor at any given time.

Leadership at all levels is vital to the development of the system. The broad governance structure ensures that ideas and energy from the teaching and administrative corps are driving forces. The energy and dedication of the district, cluster, and school committees are essential elements; and the personnel designated to lead and coordinate those committees need to be real students of the field as well as capable organizers. Essentially, everybody needs to go to school for the processes of staff development and school renewal and make the best decisions they can about what will or can work. They need to conduct the entire program as an inquiry rather than as the implementation of certainties. Things are tried, studied, and revised rather than being regarded as certitudes. The community brings everyone into the process and brings the study of the crafts of education, including the crafts of staff development, into a central place in the organization. The traditional role-distinctions between supervisee and supervisor disappear. With everyone studying and helping one another, the traditional supervisory dimension in relationships becomes obsolete.

chapter **3**

The Synergistic School

Proposition: That membership in a faculty is membership in a self-study
community that learns to work together to make decisions.

The keystone, if there is one in this loosely coupled system (Baldridge & Deal, 1975),
is the social organization of the school. As we struggle to change the entire system
so that educators can become communities of scholars of their craft, no aspect of
the educational enterprise will need to change more dramatically.

The social organization of the school is critical to the success of staff
development initiatives not only those that are generated by or addressed to the
school but also those that are addressed to individuals and the district. The
reasons are not difficult to fathom; however, in practice many otherwise promising staff development efforts have faltered and even failed completely because
insufficient attention has been paid to the development of a social organization
that is congenial to change and growth (Fullan & Stiegelbauer, 1991; Little, 1982).
As we will see, training to reach an adequate level of competence in new skills
and knowledge requires intensive study, many demon-strations, and opportunities
for practice in the training setting. To elevate the new learning to the point where
it can operate effectively in the instructional setting, teachers and administrators
have to engage in extensive practice. Both the training and the practice have to
reside comfortably in the school setting and are intensely collaborative activities—
people depend on one another in a serious way during the early stages of practice
with unfamiliar skills and knowledge.

Because most staff development systems in the past have been relatively
weak, the establishment of effective programs—ones that enable teachers to

strengthen existing knowledge and skills significantly and to add fresh knowledge and instructional models to their repertoire—has to be regarded as innovative in itself (Fullan, 1990; Fullan & Stiegelbauer, 1991; Huberman, 1992; Joyce, Hersh, & McKibbin, 1983; and Miles & Huberman, 1984). As Fullan has carefully pointed out, shared understandings sustain innovations. If success is to occur in a system designed to sustain study and change, all personnel have to study both the content of innovations and the innovative process as well, developing the common knowledge that will guide their collective behavior. The activities depicted in the scenario in the previous chapter are examples. When Adrienne selects a workshop and attends it, she needs the support of her study team and coaching partners in order to practice the skills she has learned until they become a smooth and powerful part of her repertoire. When the school selects its focus for the year, the faculty works together both to select the goals and to engage in the process for making the changes. When the district selects the area that will receive its attention, the school has to be organized so that the innovation can be understood and the faculty cooperates in ensuring that they receive appropriate training and profit from it. All of these participants need a shared understanding of the nature of the system, the purposes of the three components, the nature of training and how to profit from it, and the determination to work for the common cause so that all of the initiatives pay off. Thus, to create a full-blown staff development system is to engage in cultural change as well.

The necessity for collective decision making and collaborative activity requires changes in the traditional relationships among teachers and between teachers and administrators. As Lortie (1975) has so eloquently described, not only has teaching been conducted in relative isolation, but the isolation has given rise to the particular normative culture that characterizes schools. Time provided for preparation of instruction is meager, as is time for the meetings that are necessary to discuss the state of the school and its program. Teachers rush from one activity to another with little time to catch their breath. As a high school science teacher put it to us the other day, "We're like a bunch of truck drivers careening down our own expressways, locked in our little boxes with no adults to talk to. We know the other guys are out there somewhere, but it's almost surprising when we gather in a faculty meeting to find that there are 200 others and you haven't had a decent conversation with any of them since the last meeting."

In the course of adapting to the isolation, school faculty have worked out patterns of behavior that fit the isolated conditions and the low degree of collaborative action. Essentially, teachers have had to learn to work alone, relying on themselves, unentangled for the most part by group decisions or the necessity to coordinate activities with others. The development of the conditions that will sustain effective training requires substantial changes in the patterns that have developed over the years. The study of teaching and curriculum becomes public, decisions become collective and, thus, more complicated, and connections between teachers and administrators become closer and more reciprocal. Some of these changes cause temporary discomfort that is alleviated only by continued contact with others until the benefits of collaboration overwhelm the spurious sense of security conferred by the conditions of isolation.

THINGS TO GIVE UP AND TO TAKE ON

The process contains social and intellectual parallels to deciding to lose weight and get in shape. We are trying to both give something up and take something on. In the early stages, the exercise appears to fight our bodies and the diet feels onerous. We find that giving up weight causes no psychological or physical pain. It's going hungry that hurts. The vision of a trim, exercised body feels great. The process of building strength and flexibility is what hurts. Yet, if we stick to it, we will succeed, largely because it's not really that hard. The first little pains made us think the later stages would be seriously miserable, but it turns out that our overactive imaginations were much of the problem.

Giving up isolation is probably the area that causes the greatest concern in the process of developing a collaborative school. We find we *liked* autonomy. Thrashing out collective decisions is much more complicated at first. Studying teaching together is more aggravating than deciding how to teach one's own classes with one's best judgment unfettered.

In the personal sense, however, a collaborative life is much more satisfying. Synergy is the reason. Our collective energy is greater than the sum of our individual energies. In the professional sense, what we can accomplish is immeasurably greater. Probably the clearest example is in the development of the social climate of the school, where the impact we have as a group in creating an environment of caring and excellence is far richer than anything we can accomplish alone and makes our individual efforts much more powerful.

Adopting new behaviors is not nearly as difficult or aggravating as giving up or modifying familiar behaviors, and we need to make the process palatable. Effort must be expended to deal with the anxiety that is contemplated during any change process. Yet, we reiterate, the new behaviors are not difficult to learn per se, and many people have navigated the changes that occur when the propositions for schoolwide change discussed below are applied and the social organization of the school changes. In other words, we have passed the point where creating collaborative, high-energy environments in schools can be regarded as a formidable enterprise. Rather, solid, methodical effort is needed with confidence that personnel can adapt to the needed changes without undue stress.

PROPOSITIONS

The research we can draw on to understand how the social organization can facilitate staff development is now substantial (Fullan, 1990). Rather than reviewing it formally we have distilled it into a series of propositions on which we believe healthy school organizations can be built and sustained. The focus is the collective energy of the school and how to ensure that all school faculties have a high degree of synergy and cohesiveness.

Generating Active Leadership

The call for active instructional leadership (Goodlad, 1984) has been so consistent that it has virtually become a cliché, but what an important truism of practice it is (Crandall et al., 1982; Fullan & Miles, 1992; Leithwood, 1990; Leithwood & Montgomery, 1982; Murphy, 1992)! Probably the most astounding aspect of the current discussions about the important role of the formal leadership at the site level (the principal and assistant principals or deans) is the notion that there could be anyone in those roles who does not perceive leadership as the critical element in their work.

Leadership needs to be very active in bringing about cohesion in the faculty, involving community members, developing study groups, and connecting the school to systemic initiatives. Specific tasks include:

1. Organizing the faculty into study groups and coaching teams. Meeting with those teams and facilitating their activities.
2. Organizing a staff development/school improvement council to coordinate activities, select priorities, and ensure facilitation of clinical and systemic components (see Wolf, 1994, for a thoroughgoing discussion and resources).
3. Arranging time for the collaborative study of teaching and the implementation of curricular and instructional innovations.
4. Becoming knowledgeable about school improvement and staff development (see chapters 4 to 7) and ensuring that the staff is knowledgeable.
5. Participating in training and implementing collective and systemic initiatives; knowledgeability is the key here, for an in-depth understanding of innovations in curriculum and instruction is necessary to plan facilitation.
6. Continuously assessing the educational climate of the school—feeding information and perspective to the faculty for use in decision making about possible areas for study and improvement.

The specific details are less important than the commitment to the role as curricular and instructional leader (Murphy, 1992; Murphy & Hallinger, 1987; Hallinger & Murphy, 1985). Imagine the following description of one principal in action:

> Lauren is principal of a 20-classroom school in a rural area. In addition to the 20 teachers who are assigned to classrooms, there is a full-time librarian and special education resource teacher. Lauren has organized the faculty into four study groups. Each group is responsible for exploring a particular teaching strategy and preparing itself not only to use that strategy but to demonstrate it for the other groups. Lauren, together with one member of each study group and five parents elected by the parent community,

constitute the school committee (see Joyce, Hersh, & McKibbin, 1983, for a detailed description of the "Responsible Parties" in the school improvement process). The committee is responsible for organizing parents and community members to examine the educational health of the school and suggesting ways of improving curriculum, instruction, and social climate. Instructional strategies are the focus for the current two-year period. Each Wednesday the students leave at 2:00 P.M. The faculty gathers for an informal meeting in a social setting with refreshments. Ordinarily, study groups report on their progress and watch a videotape of one of the teachers using one of the new instructional strategies.

In addition, Lauren, the librarian, and the resource teacher each teach one period each day, taking over classes from the other teachers, freeing them so that the coaching partnerships can function effectively. Lauren also visits the classroom of one teacher each day, trying to identify areas of need that can become the focus of the weekly meetings. It is on those visits that she makes the tapes that provide some of the substance of the weekly meetings. Also, she is preparing herself to think through what she believes should be the next focus for school improvement—more effective use of the computer as an instructional tool.

Only a handful of the teachers are expert computer-users. She is discussing options with a consultant from the State Department. Lauren knows that resources are available to increase the numbers of computers in the school, and she is determined to work out a feasible plan and ensure a good implementation. However, she is also concerned that the science curriculum is very weak and wonders if strengthening the science curriculum is a greater priority than the computer or if the two objectives can be combined. She already plans to build on the study of instructional models to strengthen the science program, but she wisely doesn't want to overload the faculty by asking them to deal with too many initiatives at once. She also knows that the entire group has to think out what will be done and how it will be done. She wants to be the best possible consultant to her staff.

One of the keys to Lauren's achievements as an instructional leader is that she has no doubt at all that it is her chief responsibility. She believes that she has the duty to organize the faculty and involve community members in the development of the healthiest social climate, curriculum, and instructional setting that she can. Although Lauren is integrative and gentle, she is quietly forceful—everyone is involved in the decision-making process, but steady improvement is central in every meeting.

Generating Faculty Cohesion with Clear Understanding of the Obligations for Collective Action

The relatively solitary norms of teaching need to be replaced with a sense of the obligation for collective action. One of the major obstacles to school improvement efforts is that teachers and administrators have perceived the instructional role primarily in terms of what one individual does with classes of students and there has been a much less clear picture of the role as a collaborative faculty member. *Specifically, the governance of staff development and school improvement efforts depends on an understanding that the faculty and administration can make decisions that are binding to the members of the group.*

Continuing the example above, Lauren and the school committee suggested that instructional strategies become the emphasis for a couple of years, and the faculty voted on that proposal and several others. About three-quarters of the members placed instructional strategies first. The remainder of the faculty understood that they were obligated by the majority decision with respect to the collective component of staff development. (They were, of course, free to pursue other interests as part of the individual-governed component.)

One of the essential aspects of Lauren's leadership is helping the faculty understand the difference in the dynamics of decision making between the several components. For example, no one is obligated to become a member of an instructional cadre offering training to others. However, once a school-improvement focus has been selected or the district has decided on an initiative as a faculty, then all the members of the group are obligated to participate. As Glickman (1993) explains so well, the essential task is to build a faculty democracy that both functions to govern the school and also, equally important, serves as the social envelope within which students are brought into this democratic society.

It is not uncommon for districts and schools to sidestep the issue by attempting "lateral diffusion" strategies, whereby, even when a majority decision is made, it is understood that they will begin with volunteer participation and rely on the success of the initial effort to spread the innovation. That strategy simply does not work in the social system of faculties as presently constituted (Joyce, McKibbin, & Bush, 1983). Also, a schoolwide effort in curriculum, technology, or school climate requires collaboration if it is to work. To confine it to a group of volunteers is to deny the role of collective activity in implementation.

Needing the District Office Personnel to Develop a Close and Facilitative Relationship with the Faculties of the Schools

The central office personnel and school leadership have to be closely connected to build shared understandings about the importance of staff development and to ensure that it is focused properly. A district council of teachers and administrators needs to select the areas that will receive systemic attention during any given period and these areas must be few and solidly backed. District office personnel need to be well-coordinated so that the school is not deluged by initiatives made by departments that end up competing for the time of teachers. In one district that we studied (Joyce, Bush, & McKibbin, 1982), a single school actually received more than 40 initiatives from the district office in one year.

How can this happen, one might ask? The answer is that the zeal of the central office personnel was not accompanied by the tempering effects of coordination. Reading specialists were initiating a drive to improve the reading curriculum and offering workshops to primary teachers. Supervisors were initiating training in the ITIP mode as well as offering workshops to principals and administrators (Hunter, 1980, 1981). Special education supervisors were offering workshops on the integration of students with learning disabilities in the classroom. A new program in education for the "gifted and talented" was initiated. A new shipment of microcomputers arrived and was distributed along with a round of workshops on how to use them. We could go on and on.

The effect of this barrage of initiatives from the central office is to trivialize all of the initiatives. With only a few persons receiving relatively weak training in any one of them, the entire range of efforts simply evaporates in a short period of time.

Such a diffused message simply confuses the schools that are disposed to cooperate and fuels the cynicism of those that are less disposed. The alternative is clear; the district staff development council needs to screen initiatives and select only one or two for a major effort. These systemic initiatives need to be communicated through the school representatives on the council to the school faculties, and preparations must be made to cooperate with the initiative. School councils need to take the system initiative into account as they establish the collective initiatives, pyramiding energy wherever possible. The study groups and coaching teams, of course, will be essential to both.

The district personnel also need to help administrators get the training and support they need to fulfill their roles effectively; they must provide training in content options for school-based initiatives and in the skills needed to organize councils, study groups, coaching teams, and training.

A spirit of cooperation is essential. Principals and teacher members of the district council need to approach the decision-making tasks to build cooperative relationships. They simply *must* understand that the clinical and collective components provide ample room for individual and school initiatives and *not* view the systemic component as an objectionable mandate simply because it requires decision making and implementation for the entire district organization.

Active leadership from the superintendent is another priority. Richard Wallace, the superintendent in Pittsburgh, demonstrated the importance of his role, even in a large system, during the organization of the Schenley program. Named for a school that became a staff development center (see chapter 4), the program was organized so that in the three-year period beginning in the fall of 1983, *all* of the secondary teachers in the Pittsburgh school district spent two consecutive months, during one of the school years, in residence at Schenley. The school was restaffed with outstanding teachers drawn from all over the district, and the visiting teachers worked with the resident staff and with a staff development team that conducted workshops on the analysis of teaching. A cadre of supernumerary teachers released the faculty members so that they could attend the Schenley program. The members of that cadre rotated from school to school, relieving teachers and providing program continuity (Wallace et al., 1984). Such a program could not be thought out, maintained, or implemented without a superintendent who is a highly visible and active instructional leader for the entire district. Administrators, teachers, teachers' organizations, the school board, and the community at large have to develop and maintain a shared understanding powerful enough to sustain the substantial innovations in relationships that are necessary to carry out a strong staff development program.

Returning to Lauren, her relationship with her district office helps sustain her activities. Although she is in a rural setting where it is difficult to have the regular contact that is easy to arrange in a more densely populated area, her superintendent and the rest of the central office staff have no doubt that her primary role is as instructional leader of her school. They do not deluge her with initiatives but maintain a council where she and a faculty representative meet periodically with their opposite numbers to define the systemic initiatives and divide resources. For example, the district has provided consultant services to her staff to maintain the program on instructional strategies. Reciprocally, she prepares her staff to cooperate with those systemic initiatives that are selected. She and the central office staff are well aware that curricular change has been extremely difficult in many districts (Muncey & McQuillan, 1993; Shirley & Anderson, 1994) and that substantial training and hard work in each school are necessary to implement any initiative of worth (Hall, 1986; Hall & Loucks, 1977). The message we obtain from the last ten years of research on site-based decision making is that nearly all schools need active facilitation from persons who are not part of its internal social system. In Rosenholtz's (1989) terms, they become "stuck." We suspect that the central offices of our districts are equally "stuck" unless they have reciprocal relations with the schools and have to respond to their realities and learn to facilitate them. In a real sense, everybody has to help everybody get unstuck.

Needing Vertical and Horizontal Solidarity

The research on organizational development (Crandall et al., 1982; Fullan & Park, 1981; Schmuck, Runkel, Arends, & Arends, 1977) indicates clearly how important social cohesion is to the innovative process, and we stress again that many features and most of the worthy content of staff development are innovations in themselves.

Successful innovations have both strong building-leadership by administrators and teachers and have strong sponsorship and facilitation from the district office. Not only must we build synergistic faculties with the shared understandings that permit a shared vision but district synergy is necessary also.

In Texas, where the state legislature has "mandated" that all schools use a site-based decision-making model for school improvement, the Marshall district has developed a seminar for all its principals. Principals meet monthly with a facilitator to share progress toward identifying needs, arranging for training, organizing faculties into peer-coaching study teams, monitoring implementation of planned changes, and designing formative evaluation programs. The seminar is the district's acknowledgment of its responsibility to support site development, and it also helps the district keep abreast of what the schools are doing and enables resources to be combined where appropriate. We worry at times that some districts virtually abandon their schools when there is a move toward site-based management. The evidence is clear that district support will be a major factor in the success of site-based school improvement.

SUMMARY

All of the propositions discussed above have as one of their major purposes bringing people together for collective decision making and action. Shared understanding about both content and process are necessary for collective action to occur. The development of study groups is symbolic of the need for cooperative action to implement the substance of staff development. The coaching partnerships are symbolic of the notion that teachers can learn from other teachers and share the process of learning new content and teaching methods. The existence of the councils is a statement that trust can be built to develop a place in which learning by teachers can be given an important place in the life of the school.

We hear much these days about the difficulties in the workplace (McLaughlin et al., 1986; McLaughlin, 1990) and the dilemmas of leadership in a time when members of the teaching staff feel burned-out and unsupported. The antidote is an active workplace that propels educators into collaborative, growth-producing activity. A strong, upbeat staff development program is a major part of the prescription.

part II

The Pursuit of Student Achievement: The Proximal Principle

Proposition: The student as learner is the key. The closer an innovation is to the interactive process that helps the learner manage learning better, the greater the effects will be. The choice, then, is innovations that directly touch the child. Reciprocally, the farther the innovation is from the environment where teachers and learners interact, the slower and lesser will be the effects, if there are any.

In this section of the book we begin the hunt for content that will have a good probability of paying off for students and for staff development processes that generate implementation. The essence of staff development is inquiry: individuals studying teaching and learning; faculties exploring together to make the learning environment better; and districts learning to build the larger communities of educators to create and implement changes in curriculum, instruction, and technology. Optimally, in each case, the content of any given staff development event or any long-term program of study is learned and used, and the effects, or some of them, are studied.

As content is selected or created, we want it to be *good*, meaning that it can help students increase their capability to learn. Thus, planners need to find good programs from which educators can choose; faculties must search for content that is worthwhile; and districts and even states must seek content that will make a difference.

The history of both staff development and school renewal gives us information about content that has made a difference and contemporary ideas that are our present storehouse of professional alternatives. As we search the history, we have to sort out the content of initiatives from the staff development processes that have often accompanied them. For example, the Academic Reform Movement of the 1950s and 1960s generated some fine curricula that brought new ideas to children, helping them gain greater conceptual control of both the academic disciplines and problem solving (see, Bredderman, 1983 and El Nemr, 1979). In other words, the content was promising and the structures of those curricula have messages for us today. Unfortunately, the staff development system was too weak at that time to permit implementation of even those high-quality curricula in more than a small percentage of schools. The result was great disappointment. The good news is that we can learn much from the problem. We do not have to make the same mistakes, as Cuban (1990) puts it, "over and over again."

Recent proposals for both content and process are being more closely studied than ever, so that our knowledge is increasing more rapidly than in the past. Our "turn around" time between the start of a new initiative and evidence of its results is shorter than ever before. For example, during the last few years the state of Vermont (Flanagan, 1994) has developed a "portfolio assessment" initiative that is intended to generate a more meaningful dialogue among educators about student learning and bring those teachers together to develop ways of improving, among other areas, quality in student writing. During the initiative period, much staff development has been provided by analyzing the quality of writing in the portfolios that have been collected. The state formative evaluation program has discovered, however, that the level of reliability of scoring is low enough that the scores should not be used to measure student learning. The state now needs to determine whether to: provide more (and possibly better) staff development; improve the scoring system and follow with staff development; or settle for the degree of dialogue that is permitted by the current level. Whatever they do, there are lessons for the rest of us.

In chapter 4, we will study the lessons from large-scale initiatives designed to improve schooling. In chapter 5, we will deal with research on specific curricula, teaching strategies, teaching skills, and unusually effective schools as we search for content for staff development and, while doing so, tease out any lessons we can for generating the staff development system we envision.

THE CONCEPT OF EFFECT SIZE

We use the concept of "effect size" (Glass, 1982) to describe the magnitude of gains from any given change in educational practice and thus to predict what we can hope to accomplish by using that practice.

To introduce the idea, let us consider a study conducted by Dr. Bharati Baveja (1988) with the authors in the Motilal Nehru School of Sports about 30 miles northwest of New Delhi, India. Dr. Baveja designed her study to test the effectiveness of an inductive approach to a Botany Unit compared with an intensive tutorial treatment. All of the students were given a test at the beginning of the unit to assess their knowledge before instruction began and were divided into two groups equated on the basis of achievement. The control group studied the material with the aid of tutoring and lectures on the material—the standard treatment in Indian schools for courses of this type. The experimental group worked in pairs and was led through inductive and concept attainment exercises emphasizing classification of plants.

Figure P.1 shows the distribution of scores for the experimental and control groups on the posttest which, like the pretest, contained items dealing with the information pertaining to the unit.

The difference between the experimental and control groups was a little above one standard deviation. The difference, computed in terms of standard deviations, is the effect size of the inductive treatment. Essentially, what that means is that the experimental group average (50th percentile) score was where the 80th percentile score was for the control group. The difference increased when a delayed-recall test was given ten months later, indicating that the information acquired with the experimental, concept-oriented strategies was retained somewhat better than information gained via the control treatment.

Calculations like these enable us to compare the magnitude of the potential effects of the innovations (teaching skills and strategies, curricula, and technologies) that we might use in an effort to affect student learning. We can also determine whether the treatment has different effects for all kinds of students or just for some. In the study just described, the experimental treatment was apparently effective for the whole population. The lowest score in the experimental group distribution was about where the 30th percentile score was for the

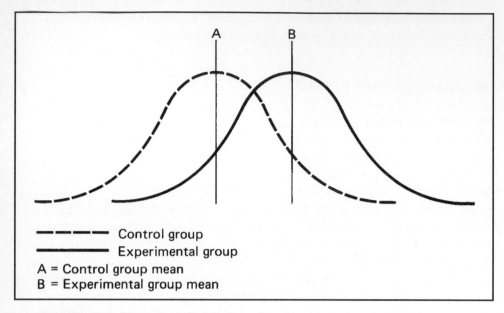

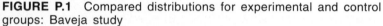

FIGURE P.1 Compared distributions for experimental and control groups: Baveja study

control group and about 30 percent of the students exceeded the highest score obtained in the control.

Although substantial in its own right, learning and retention of information was modest when we consider the effect on the students' ability to identify plants and their characteristics, which was measured on a separate test. The scores by students from the experimental group were *eight* times higher than the scores for the control group. The inference is that the inductive treatment enabled students to apply the information and concepts from the unit much more effectively than the students from the tutorial treatment.

Although high effect sizes make a treatment attractive, size alone is not the only consideration when choosing among alternatives. Modest effect sizes that affect many persons can have a large payoff for the population. A comparison with medicine is worthwhile. Suppose a dread disease is affecting a population and we possess a vaccine that will reduce the chances of contracting the disease by only 10 percent. If a million people might become infected without the vaccine but 900,000 if it is used, the modest effect of the vaccine might save 100,000 lives. In education, some estimates suggest that during the first year of school about one million children each year (about 30 percent) make little progress toward learning to read. We also know that lack of success in reading instruction is in fact a dread educational disease; for each year that initial instruction is unsuccessful, the probability that the student will respond to instruction later is greatly lowered. Would a modestly effective treatment, say one that reduced the lack of success in the first year for 50,000 children (5 percent) be worthwhile? We think so. Also, several such treatments might accumulate. Of course, we prefer a high-effect treatment, but one is not always available. Even when it is, it might not reach some students and we might need to resort to a less powerful choice for them.

Also, there are different types of effects that need to be considered. Attitudes, values, concepts, intellectual development, skills, and information are just a few. Keeping to the example of early reading, two treatments might be approximately equal in terms of learning to read in the short run, but one might affect attitudes positively and leave the students feeling confident and ready to try again. Similarly, two social studies programs might achieve similar amounts of information and concepts, but one might excel in attitudes toward citizenship.

Throughout the remainder of the book we will refer to the sizes of effects obtained in studies of educational practices in three categories:

Modestly Effective. These are practices that increase learning of particular kinds by up to one-half of a standard deviation. Compared to standard treatments, these increase the learning of the average students to between the 60th and 70th percentile of a control group in an experimental study.

Substantially Effective. These practices can increase student learning from one-half to one standard deviation. The average student, when these treatments are used, falls between the 70th and 80th percentile when compared to a control group receiving standard instruction.

Very Effective. These practices can increase learning more than one standard deviation. In the most dramatic instances, when the effect size reaches five or six standard deviations, the lowest-scoring student in the experimental treatment exceeds the highest-scoring student in the control treatment! This is a rare event, of course, but when it does occur, it gives us great hope about the potential of educational practice.

Again, as we describe some practices and the effects that can be expected from them, we should not concentrate on magnitude of effects alone. Self-instructional programs that are no more effective than standard instruction can be very useful because they enable students to teach themselves and can be blended with agent-delivered instruction. Broadcast television, because of its potential to reach so many children, can make a big difference even though it is modestly effective in comparison with standard instruction. "Sesame Street" and "The Electric Company" (Ball & Bogatz, 1970) are examples. They are not dramatically more effective than first-grade instruction in reading, but they produce positive attitudes and augment instruction handsomely, enabling a certain percentage of students to virtually teach themselves.

Learning the size of effects of a year's instruction can be very informative, as we learned from the National Assessment of Writing Progress (Applebee et al., 1990), which discovered that the effect size of instruction in writing nationally is such that the average eighth-grade student is about at the 62nd percentile of the fourth-grade distribution! Schools may want to learn how much better they can do than that!

Some procedures may not have been studied directly, possibly because they are products of recent development, but we can make inferences about them by referring to studies of similar treatments. For example, the new curriculum developments modeled after the recent Mathematics Standards (NCTM, 1989) will not be evaluated until after several years of implementation; we can infer, however, that where those curricula are well implemented, they will have positive effects on student learning because programs like SMSG Mathematics, studied more than 30 years ago, had such positive effects. The current movement toward "Integrated Curriculum Units" also will not be tested for several years, but we can infer from studies done between 30 and 60 years ago that, in terms of raising student learning, they are unlikely to have much effect, although they are justifiable on other terms.

Some procedures can interact productively with others (or unproductively). One-to-one tutoring has a very large effect size (Bloom, 1984) and might interact productively with some teaching strategies. Or, as is evidently the case within the "Success for All" (Slavin et al., 1990; 1991) and "Reading Recovery" (Pinnell, 1989) programs, it is incorporated within a curriculum-management system that enables short periods of tutoring to pay off handsomely. On the other hand, "tracking" hurts the effectiveness of any procedure (Oakes, 1985).

Measures of learning can be of many kinds. School grades are of great importance, as are measures of conduct such as counts of referrals and suspensions. In fact, staff development programs want to give close attention to those measures as well as simple measures such as how many books students read. Content analyses of student work are very important, as in the study of quality of writing, and will be more important as the movement toward "portfolios" and "products" continues. (Of special relevance to this book, they require careful design and very large amounts of staff development.) Curriculum-relevant tests (those that measure the content of a unit or course) are important. Finally, the traditional standardized tests can be submitted to an analysis that produces estimates of effect size.

So, as we proceed through chapters 4 and 5, we will pay close attention to the magnitude of effects that we find and, thus, can expect if there is a very good implementation.

chapter 4

Successful School Improvement Efforts

Proposition: To increase student learning, approach it directly, and bring the energy of everyone in the school or district to bear on the effort.

We begin with the analysis of some fairly large-scale school and districtwide initiatives that generated effects on student achievement and an examination of their common elements. They are not, by any means, the *only* successful programs, but they are so thoroughly described in the literature that we can try to learn what they did that might have made them successful. Four characteristics are obvious from the outset.

1. *Content.* First, these programs all focused on content in curriculum, instruction, and technology. As near as we can tell, only content dealing with curriculum, instruction, technology, or the overall social climate of the schools is likely to improve student learning.
2. *Implementation.* Content of the highest quality will not change student learning unless it is implemented. All these programs developed adequate training, and they organized the teachers and administrators to implement the content of the programs.
3. *Inclusion.* The programs described here involved all the teachers and administrators in particular schools or, in some cases, all the personnel in the school districts where they took place. We are unable to find examples of school improvement where the entire community of educators, either the school or district community, was not involved. There are reports of individual teachers and small groups of teachers who have made salutary progress, but translating changes

in one or a few classrooms into an effect on the entire student body simply has not been reported; we believe that the probability that it will be is low. Even very successful "add on" programs, such as "Reading Recovery" will not result in increased student learning throughout the school unless all faculty are involved in improving the learning of reading and writing.

4. *Goals and Inquiry.* Finally, goals and the understanding about how to achieve them were kept central. For example,

   • all have had specific student-learning goals in mind. None have had only general goals of the "to make test scores go up" variety.

   • all have measured learning outcomes on a formative and summative basis, collecting information about student gains on a regular basis rather than leaving evaluation to a yearly examination of post hoc information derived from standard tests only.

   • all have employed substantial amounts of staff-development in recognition that the initiative involved teacher and student learning of new procedures. The staff development targeted the content of the initiatives specifically. Data about the progress of imple-mentation were collected regularly and made available to project personnel.

Curriculum and instruction as content, adequate staff development with follow-up by the schools, and collective effort—the involvement of everyone—characterize these programs.

COMBINING CURRICULUM, INSTRUCTION, AND TUTORING: SUCCESS FOR ALL

The Center for Research on Effective Schooling for Disadvantaged Students at Johns Hopkins University (Slavin et al., 1990; Slavin et al., 1991) is studying its efforts to improve primary education in inner-city schools. The Success for All program is a complex initiative that combines an intensive reading curriculum with close-order diagnosis of learning problems, immediate intervention with tutoring aimed directly at the problems, cooperative learning, and family support teams. The staff development program continues throughout the year, with heavy emphasis on follow-up for implementation. The focus is on preventing the onset of the downward spiral that so often begins during the primary years and leaves the students unable to cope with the ordinary demands of the upper grades. While the program is expected to have its largest effects cumulatively over time, the product of the first year is achievement that is average for the nation, rather than the dismal picture that generally ensues. (The program developers aim at bringing *all* students to satisfactory levels and not accepting the losses that occur when usually distributed achievement occurs.) It is interesting that the largest effects from the first-year program occurred in the third grade, leading to optimism about what can be done with the somewhat more mature learners who have accumulated learning deficits from the earlier grades.

The multi-year effects of the program are very positive. Retention in grade has been reduced greatly (from about 40 percent to 10 percent in some project schools and to nearly zero in the schools receiving the most intensive attention). Gains in reading are considerable across a variety of tests, and, as achievement rises, fewer students are qualifying for special education services (Slavin et al., 1990). Success for All has worked quite well in multicultural and multilingual settings and, with intensive efforts, has reached all but a handful of the students judged to be most "at risk."

The complex Success for All intervention is reminiscent of Spaulding's (1970) program for a similar population in North Carolina. Spauling's most important academic goal was to raise aptitude to learn as measured by tests of ability or intelligence. He also used a combination of careful diagnosis, direct and immediate intervention, intensive reading instruction, and several well-tested models of teaching, including social learning theory, simulations, role-playing, and cooperative study. The ability indices of the average student in Spaulding's initiative rose about one-half of a standard deviation after three years. As in the case of Success for All, the results indicate that curriculum and instruction can be aimed directly at learning capacity.

Success for All demonstrates what can be done with the intensive implementation of the available tools for teaching. While many districts agonize over the number of students who fail to learn adequately, the straightforward, "relentless" approach gets the job done with a combination of careful design and provision of support for the school personnel to work through the stages of implementation.

INTENSIVE, INSTRUCTION-ORIENTED STAFF DEVELOPMENT: THE SCHENLEY PROJECT

In Pittsburgh a side effect of the development of an extensive districtwide staff development program was a test of what can happen if some of the most highly regarded teachers in a large district are concentrated in a high school whose lower SES population has been far below the national average. The Schenley School became a staff development center where outstanding teachers were brought together. Other district teachers rotated into the school, spending several weeks observing those teachers and studying instruction (Wallace et al., 1984; Wallace, LeMahieu, & Bickel, 1990). There was an immediate rise in achievement measured with standardized tests in eight of nine curriculum areas. In terms of the percentage of students scoring at or above the national average, the rise in total language results was from 27 percent to 61 percent, in reading from 28 percent to 45 percent, in physical science from 21 percent to 63 percent, in biology from 13 percent to 41 percent, and in algebra from 29 percent to 73 percent. The gains were maintained or increased during the second year.

As interesting as are the sizes of those improvements, it is equally interesting that they were so immediate. High schools need not feel hopeless about students with poor learning histories. The gifted Schenley teachers, working in an environment that intensified the study of instruction, transformed the learning environment of their school immediately. The students responded by allowing their intelligence to become focused on eliminating their deficits and, in the main, looking more able at graduation than many of their counterparts who had not suffered cumulative deficits in their past education.

The Baltimore and Pittsburgh programs both make a statement about how powerful schools can be with respect to all students. The one showed that the school can eliminate the concept of "at risk" for primary schools and the other that, despite years of failure, students can succeed, *and succeed immediately,* in the high school. Staff development/school improvement programs that are oriented toward student learning can make a dramatic difference. A side effect is the raising of the teachers' morale. Nothing can make teachers feel better, or more quickly raise educators' professional status, than learning to help students succeed who would have failed! Unless, of course, it is learning how to help all students learn more. And more. And more. And begin life after school knowing they can teach themselves what they need to live a high-quality life and make a high-quality contribution to their families and their society.

COLLABORATIVE ORGANIZATION AND INTENSIVE STAFF DEVELOPMENT ON MODELS OF TEACHING: THE AUGUSTA PROJECT

The Richmond County (Georgia) School Improvement Program was focused on instruction, staff development, and organizing faculties for collaborative action. Schools entered the program as units. A condition was that 80 percent of each faculty had voted to participate and the majority decision was binding on the entire faculty. Within the program all teachers in each participating school studied a set of well-tested models of teaching selected to increase the learning capacity of their students. The faculties were organized into study groups and elected councils whose responsibility was to examine information about the health of the school and plan school improvement initiatives (Joyce, Murphy, Showers, & Murphy, 1989).

In some of the schools, the need for school improvement was urgent. For example, in one of the middle schools the students had such poor learning histories that only 30 percent of the students achieved promotion at the end of the year before the project began. Scores on standard tests revealed that the average student in the school had gained only about six months' achievement for each year in school. (Ten months is average.) The school district had made a number of initiatives to alleviate the situation, including special programs for "at risk" students, lowered class size, and increased counseling services, all with little effect. However, as the teachers learned to use models of teaching designed to increase cooperative activity, teach concepts, teach students to work inductively and to memorize information, the learning rates of the students began to improve dramatically. By the end of the first year 70 percent of the students in the middle school achieved the standards required for promotion and 95 percent earned promotion at the end of the second year. Judging from the standardized tests administered at the end of the second year, the average students in the school were achieving at a normal rate, that is, gaining ten months of learning for ten months of effort when compared to the United States population as a whole. Time lost in disciplinary action decreased dramatically, to about one-fifth of the amount lost before the program began. Probably, helping the students learn a variety of learning strategies which enabled them to educate themselves more successfully reduced the incidence of punitive discipline; students who experience success in the classroom have less reason (and less time) to express their dissatisfaction with school in socially inappropriate ways.

After faculties of the first three schools were trained by consultants, a cadre of teachers disseminated the teaching strategies to other schools in the district. Results for the first nine schools on the Iowa Test of Basic Skills were substantial. Each of the nine schools completed eight tests for a total of 72 test scores. Forty of the 72 scores reflected gains of greater than four months over the previous year's results, and 20 of the scores reflected gains of between two and four months. It is important to note that faculties taught by a cadre of their peers learned new models of teaching as thoroughly, implemented them as frequently, and gained equally large student outcomes as faculties taught by outside consultants.

As in the case of Success for All and the Schenley program, large effects on student learning occurred rapidly—in the first year of implementation—once again demonstrating the efficacy of the schools that make changes in curriculum and instruction. Many educators believe that school improvement efforts will not have demonstrable effects on students for several years, but the evidence points toward quite a different conclusion. Students respond right away to changes in instruction and begin to accelerate their rates of learning provided that the educational environment is designed to do just that—teach the students to learn more effectively.

CURRICULUM AND SOCIAL CLIMATE
WITH COMMUNITY INVOLVEMENT:
JUST READ AND WRITE

Another program is a curriculum initiative where the social climate of the school was the critical factor (Joyce & Wolf, 1992). In the Panama Region of the Department of Defense Dependents Schools' initiative, Operation Just Read and Write, the staff studied how much the average student was reading independent of school assignments. Throughout the initiative, whereby all of the 12 schools and the district central office promoted at-home independent reading with extensive parent involvement, reading and writing quantity and quality were studied. The fifth-grade data illustrate the changes that were typical in all the schools and at all grade levels. Before the initiation of the project, the average fifth-grade student read about seven books per year out of school, a figure considerably above the national average! In the second year of the project, the average fifth-grade student read 44 books during the school year, an increase of more than six times. The lowest number of titles recorded was three times the average recorded as baseline when the program was initiated. The average first-grade student read 175 books during the second year of the project compared to 50 during the baseline period.

A side effect is that quality of learning improved substantially and the tests of reading comprehension administered by the district showed substantial gains (e.g., fifth-grade students gained 11 months during 6 months of instruction, as measured pre and post by the Comprehensive Test of Basic Skills).

Just Read was a curriculum-augmentation initiative that involved the community. Implementation required substantial "nurturant" staff development to help teachers, students, and parents learn to collect data on reading and celebrate accomplishments.

Just Read has been employed by a number of other districts since it was developed in Panama and, as with the case there, building a community of readers has been the primary goal, which means, among other things, reducing or eliminating a phenomenon of "not reading" independently at home. In the fall of 1993 three schools in the Newport/Costa Mesa Unified School District in California collected their baseline data and then began their community-involvement projects. One school, in a community where many of the children were just learning English, moved from a baseline average of only 1 book per child per month to over 11 books per child per month. A second, in a neighborhood of affluent families, discovered that more than half of their students were not reading at home at all! By March, that number had been reduced to 15 percent as the school doubled the number of books read per week. A third school, also in an affluent neighborhood, tripled the at-home reading in the first four months and nearly eliminated non-reading at home. Between November and June, the 500 children in that school read 70,000 books. Prior to the projects, all the students in each school had been in schools where one or more of the conventional programs to increase interest in reading were operating.

In Ames, Iowa, the average student in the district's elementary schools now reads about 100 books a year, independent of assigned reading, and, perhaps as important, the kindergarten students now share about 150 books per year in the "read-to" or "read-with" mode. At an inner-city primary school, K–2 parents have been reading an average of a book a day to or with their children or listening to their children's reading daily with the result that those children are virtually indistinguishable, in standard test terms in reading or mathematics, from "suburban" children.

The message from these efforts is fairly straightforward. Carefully chosen content, carefully planned implementation, the study of implementation, and the study of student learning characterize all of them. The Baltimore and Schenley programs focused on "inner city" schools, the Richmond County program dealt largely with schools whose populations were traditionally low-achieving children who were also racial minorities, and the Panama program was developed in a district that, while not low-achieving by any means, contains a very large minority population.

A MULTIPLE-DIMENSIONED EFFORT:
THE AMES, IOWA, PROGRAM

We are often asked whether the same strategies can have substantial effects in suburban schools where there are few "minority" students and where achievement has always been relatively high.

A recently reported program (Joyce et al., 1994) in the 11-school district of Ames, Iowa, where, traditionally, standard test scores have placed the district in the top 5 percent nationally, involved all teachers and students in all nine elementary schools. The program is unusual in the wide range of support provided by its staff development program.

The district has created strong and balanced support for staff development generated by teachers as individuals, by school faculties in the action-research mode, and by the district as a unit. Individually generated staff development acknowledges the division of the workplace into units (classrooms) where individual teachers need to use their perceptions and strategies to create innovations to which they can be committed. Whole-faculty-generated action research is supported because the curricular and social climate of the school can be addressed in a way not possible through individual action alone. Further, schoolwide action research directly addresses the goal of developing shared-governance modes and increasing the capacity of the faculty to inquire into and solve problems requiring concerted, democratic action. The districtwide initiatives emphasize the importance of curricular coherence and the development of faculties who embrace professional citizenship in the larger sense of belonging to a community whose children deserve equity in educational opportunity and a common core of knowledge and skills. In this section, we will deal primarily with the districtwide initiative. The others will be discussed later in the book as we discuss governance and its effects on staff development programs.

The district initiatives include the study of models of teaching applied to curriculum changes in the language arts that favor literature-based approaches with close connections between reading and writing. In addition, Just Read was begun to increase the amounts and quality of independent reading by students. (Teacher-administrator coordination and support teams were formed to articulate the curriculum and to arrange support.) The two models of teaching selected for initial study were "inductive thinking in cooperative groups" and "concept attainment," both basic approaches to teach students to build concepts, in this case, concepts that enhance reading comprehension and, through the reading-writing connection, comprehension of strategies for writing.

The focus here is on quality of writing, which was assessed by scoring sets of writing prompts given to the students in the fall and spring of the school year 1992–93, when all dimensions of the program were in full swing. Particular attention was given to expository writing, which has proved to be so difficult to teach from a national perspective (Applebee et al., 1990). The results were compared with a baseline derived from comparisons of fall and spring writing the year before and with the average gains indicated by the National Assessment of Writing Progress for the nation as a whole. Here we will use part of the grade four assessment, dealing with other comparisons later in the book.

Table 4.1 compares the means for the two periods (fall, 1992, and spring, 1993) for the three dimensions for which quality was assessed (Focus/Organization, Support, and Grammar and Mechanics). Altogether, the scores for 95 students were compared.

In the fall, coefficients of correlation between focus and support and grammar were .56 and .61 respectively and between support and grammar was .63. In the spring, these were .84, .65, and .74 respectively.

Effect sizes computed between fall and spring scores were, for focus, 2.18, for support, 1.53, and for grammar, 1.37.

All these are several times the effect sizes of the national sample and of the baseline gains determined from the 1991–1992 analyses.

To illustrate the magnitude of the difference, Table 4.2 compares the mean results for the spring fourth-grade assessment to the sixth-grade fall results.

The gains here indicate that, in the area of writing, it is possible to increase gains per year to several times the average gain, even in a district with a tradition of very high achievement. One can not tell what portion of the effects came from any one of the three dimensions of this full-service staff development program, but that is not particularly important. What is important is the magnitude of the gains.

Although making large differences in student achievement through school improvement programs is hardly routine, the number of reports and variety of

TABLE 4.1   Mean grade four scores on expository writing for fall, 1992 and spring, 1993

	Dimensions		
Period	*Focus/Organization*	*Support*	*Grammar/Mech.*
Fall			
Mean	1.6	2.2	2.11
SD	0.55	0.65	0.65
Spring			
Mean	2.8	3.2	3.0
SD	0.94	0.96	0.97

TABLE 4.2 Mean grade four spring, 1993, scores on expository writing compared with the mean grade six scores from fall, 1992

	Dimensions		
Period	Focus/Organization	Support	Grammar/Mech.
Grade Four Spring			
Mean	2.8	3.2	3.0
SD	0.94	0.96	0.97
Grade Six Fall			
Mean	2.11	2.90	2.87
SD	0.62	0.91	0.92

programs having considerable success suggests that the technology for making rapid and significant change exists. The ones mentioned above are just a few. Others include effective implementation of "Mastery Learning" programs (Block, 1971; Bloom, 1971), DISTAR (Becker, 1978; Becker & Gersten, 1982), teaching skills in mathematics (Good, Grouws, & Ebmeier, 1983), and broadcast television development such as the products of the Children's Television Workshop (Ball & Bogatz, 1970). Additionally, Levine and Lezotte (1990) have discussed the effects of helping schools study the results of studies of demonstrably effective schools, and Calderon (1994) and her colleagues have successfully involved large groups of teachers in the improvement of bilingual teaching with a very high criterion for measuring success.

STAYING WITH THE PROXIMAL

All the large-scale programs are remarkably straightforward. They focused their efforts on proximal areas (i.e., those that directly affect the students) and set about organizing everyone to achieve implementation, the effects of which they then studied. All of them recognized the importance of providing time for staff development and making collective decisions. In a structural sense, they changed the workplace.

Some very popular large-scale innovations have had very weak or no effects; some have actually made things worse. We believe that a major reason is that they have concentrated energy on the more distal variables—ones that are a distance from the environment of the child. Examples include:

Site-Based School Improvement

Both in the literature and in councils of policymakers, a considerable amount of attention is paid to the encouragement of faculties to study the school climate and the states of growth of the students and, based on the findings, to generate initiatives to improve the school. In many settings, site-based school improvement efforts are far more difficult to manage than many persons have assumed.

Several studies have examined how school faculties respond to the challenge. Rosenholtz (1989) found that most faculties become what she termed "stuck" in the process, unable to agree on direction or to take action. David and Peterson (1984) studied efforts, some heavily funded, where volunteer schools were granted discretionary resources to engage in the process of self-renewal. They, too, found that most of those schools were also "stuck," in terms of effects on students, despite the grants. Most of those who were less stuck had not made initiatives in curriculum implementation or instruction, but had generated changes in scheduling, parent involvement, disciplinary codes, and other areas believed to be important but which did not require changes in what is taught or how it is taught.

Calhoun's studies (1991, 1992) of school faculties learning to engage in schoolwide action research indicate that nearly all schools need facilitation and technical assistance if they are to progress to unified action that affects instruction and student learning (see also David, 1989; Sizer, 1991; Timar, 1989). *For many schools, extensive technical assistance* is needed if the site-based approach is to yield improved education for all students (Muncey & McQuillan, 1993). The reason why sites need assistance is that the action research process depends on the development of norms of collegiality, and the process of developing collective decision making and collective action collides with the norms of privatism and autonomy that have for so long characterized the workplace (Lortie, 1975). In addition, many faculties begin by focusing on the distal—policies governing discipline, methods of reporting, assessment, and such, rather than focusing on how well students are learning and what changes need to be made in curriculum, instruction, technology, and social climate. Focusing on the distal does not violate the norms of privatism (you can change discipline policy or assessment without learning to teach differently). We believe that faculties who engage in improving education at their site need to know, when they begin, that they are going to have to focus on the proximal variables sooner or later and that effects on students will not be likely to occur until they get to the proximal.

The Voucher Plans

Various forms of the "voucher" are being touted by the federal government and are getting support from many segments of the population. What is little known is that, 20 years ago the same government supported, at considerable cost, a series of projects to test the worth of various voucher plans (Cohen & Farrar, 1977). The results were indifferent in terms of student achievement. Perhaps more important, the evaluation tested one of the central theses of the voucher: that competition for students would cause schools to generate improvement efforts. Schools did *not* respond to the voucher by engaging in innovative activity in order to become more attractive to their clients. The evaluators concluded that if the government wanted innovations to occur, it should fund them directly rather than hoping that they would be a natural consequence of competition (see Cohen & Farrar, 1977; Jencks et al., 1970; Rand Corporation, 1981).

Voucher plans are an example of emphasis on the distal rather than the proximal. Whether there are vouchers or not, school improvement requires changes in the learning environment of the students and that is unlikely to occur without staff development that focuses on teaching students to learn better.

Magnet Schools

Some other forms of "choice" programs, such as magnet high schools, have been of questionable value in improving the achievement of students admitted to them and, moreover, have been hurtful to students not admitted to them. Moore and Davenport's (1989) analysis of the effects of magnet school programs on the nonadmitted indicates that, in the large eastern cities, they are a virtual social disaster. Removing the better students from their peers will not help the more effective learners unless their learning environment changes for the better, and segregating by ability does not accomplish that. The learners who are left behind are damaged severely by the segregation. Aside from the moral issues involved, it is technically possible to make all schools powerful ones, but the more we segregate by learning ability, the greater the tasks of school improvement and the more staff development will be required.

Pressure through Standards

Several common ways of putting pressure on schools, such as increasing the intensity of testing programs and changing standards for promotion and graduation, do not appear to stimulate change or to have an effect on student learning. Instead, some of these tactics to improve "quality" have actually increased retention and dropouts (see Gamoran & Berends, 1987; Potter & Wall, 1992; Slavin, 1987; 1991). Changing standards is *distal* and apparently does not affect the *proximal*.

Essentially, these "indirect" approaches to school improvement, focusing on the context of instruction rather than on the learning environment, have not worked very well, despite their common sense appeal. Worse, they have had some very unpleasant side effects.

Several other currently popular movements may face similar problems if they do not pay attention to the proximal. Integrated curriculum plans, although they may be worthwhile for other good reasons, are poor bets unless instruction changes. "Non-grading," like other plans for grouping, can create a setting more congenial to school improvement, but will not by itself affect student learning greatly. Management plans, whether "TQM" "systemic reform," or "strategic planning," are low probabilities, also, unless it is understood right at the beginning that a staff development system needs to be developed as part of the planning process and much of the content will have to generate changes in the learning environment.

THE CHALLENGE OF CONTENT

In the next chapter, we will discuss instructional practices that help students learn more effectively and the magnitude of effects we can expect from them. The messages of the large-scale programs described above are fairly clear as to structure and process. They also constitute a challenge to all to ensure that the limited resources now being devoted to staff development are focused on content that is likely to pay off. In our personal work we find the challenge relentless and exciting. Can we find better and better content? Can we ensure that combinations of content are productive for a particular setting? Can everyone keep working together to make the studying of new ways of learning and teaching an inquiry both into how students feel, think, and learn and also whether we are stretching them as best we can in this moment?

And in the next moment, too, we hope always a little better.

SUMMARY

The messages from the successful programs are becoming clear in that they emphasize the proximal and make changes in curriculum and instruction by providing adequate and focused staff development. Initiatives that skirt the learning environment or don't support change with strong staff development generally fall short of their goals and actually can consume much energy and increase frustration.

chapter 5

The Continued Search for Content That Has Student Effects

Proposition: With little time or resources available for staff development, it is of particular importance that we find content that will pay off for students. A number of teaching strategies and curriculum designs have solid and positive research behind them—as candidates they have good credentials as content for staff development. They set a standard by which to judge other candidates.

Proposition: There are three curricula in the system. One is defined by individuals and their reflective colleagues and is person- and situation-specific; the second is defined by faculties and focused on the creation of vital schools; the third is defined by district faculties and centers on broad program renovation. All three can draw on research on teaching, curriculum, and technology for content matured through the process of research.

The search by individuals, faculties, and district personnel for content that has been tested by research enhances reflection and leads to choices with a high probability of increasing student learning. Drawing on the results of research should not conflict with personal knowledge about teaching and learning—knowing research should enhance individual and collegial vision. Also, the state of the art is not such that any specific curricular or instructional models can solve *all* problems of student learning. We are sometimes disturbed when a school, individual, or district picks one strategy and believes that it will accomplish more than it can. Knowledge about curriculum and instruction is quite specific with respect to the effects that can be expected.

It could be argued that the benefits to personnel and organization are by themselves a sufficient rationale for the development of a strong staff development system and that increased student learning might be something "nice if we can have it, too." However, in this chapter we will continue to concentrate on the kinds of benefits that can accrue directly to students from the study of teaching, curriculum, school improvement, and technology. We feel that staff development that skirts student learning is hollow in terms of professional relationships. Our work is interacting with students so that learning and development occur, and student learning is at the heart of professional interaction. Our study time together should concentrate on how we can make our work more effective. The focus on student learning needs to be a mix of our perceptions from our interaction with students and from the literature.

Also very important, program planning can be greatly enhanced by a knowledge of the storehouse that has been developed through research. Too often, program offerings are developed from something "at hand" or from something currently promoted by professional organizations or consultants with excessive claims about what can be expected. There is a lot of good stuff out there, and an enlarged vision can lead to better selection about what will actually serve the students in a given situation.

During the last 35 years there has been a great expansion of the number of research and development personnel in education and applied psychology with a consequent enlargement of the output of educational research that can be applied to practice. Although there has been a great effort to make this information available to school personnel (Walberg, 1986; Wang, Haertel, & Walberg, 1993; Joyce, Weil, & Showers, 1992), many staff development workshops in today's programs still contain content that is unlikely to pay off. Small wonder that teachers attending those workshops complain that "workshops don't make any difference." At this time educational research provides an array of serious candidates for content that can increase student learning. Much of it is suitable for study by individuals and faculties or as a focus for district initiatives.

In the pages that follow we present a selective review of some of the areas that show promise with particular emphasis on the amounts and types of achievement that can be expected from careful implementation.

SOURCES OF PROMISING PRACTICES

The concept of validated educational practice defines one of the most promising areas for bringing educational research and practice together (Joyce, Showers, Dalton, & Beaton, 1985). If research can identify effective teaching skills and they can be incorporated as the objectives of pre-service and in-service teacher education programs, the distance between the activities of scholars and practitioners can be greatly reduced (Gage, 1978; Medley, 1977; Brophy & Good, 1986). The yield from four distinct lines of inquiry has now accumulated to the point where we can assess the findings and begin to organize the results in a form that can be useful for program planning. The four lines of inquiry are:

Models of Teaching—studies of theories of curriculum and instruction

Studies of curriculum and curriculum implementation

Studies of schools thought to be effective

Studies of teachers thought to be effective

When these are considered together, the body of research is substantial. Each broadens the concept of educational practice by illuminating different aspects of the work of teachers.

MODELS OF TEACHING

From psychology, social psychology, philosophy, therapy, and other disciplines have come experiments designed to learn whether theoretically derived patterns of teaching produce the distinctive effects for which they were designed (Joyce, Weil & Showers, 1992). Most models of teaching are designed for specific purposes—the teaching of information, concepts, ways of thinking, the study of social values, etc.—by asking students to engage in cognitive and social tasks that are unlikely to occur in many classrooms. The testing of these teaching models generally begins with a thesis describing an educational environment, its presumed effects, and a rationale that links the environment and its intended effects—develop concepts or learn them, build theories, memorize information, solve problems, learn skills. Some center on delivery by the instructor while others develop as the learners respond to tasks, and the student is regarded as a partner in the educational enterprise. However, all mature educational models emphasize how to help students learn to construct knowledge—learning how to learn—including learning from sources that are often stereotyped as passive, as learning from lectures, films, reading assignments, and such.

Testing instructional models requires training teachers to use them. The first step in theory-driven research is often the collection of baseline data about how the teachers normally teach. Then, the teachers are prepared to use the new teaching behaviors. Implementation of the new behavior is monitored, either in the regular classroom or in a laboratory setting, and theory-relevant student behaviors or outcomes are measured. Experimental classrooms are often compared with traditional classrooms to determine the presence, direction, and magnitude of change. In a very few studies, combinations of theories have been intensively employed to attempt to influence intelligence and personality (Spaulding, 1970). Since nearly all teachers use the "recitation" or "lecture-recitation" as the primary mode of teaching (Goodlad, 1984; Goodlad & Klein, 1970; Hoetker & Ahlbrand, 1969; Sirotnik, 1983), training in new strategies must often be intensive. In lines of programmatic research, such as those conducted by Pressley, Levin, and their colleagues on mnemonics (Levin and Levin, 1990) and those by Sharan (1990, 1992) and his colleagues on complex cooperative learning models, repeated studies attempt to engineer increasingly effective ways of helping students learn. One way of looking at this type of research is that the development of a model of teaching is the process of submitting an educational idea to repeated testing and refinement until the idea has *matured* to the point where fairly precise predictions can be made about how to use it and the effects to be expected if it is implemented well. Some models of teaching have been studied several hundred times. The effort involved in examining them is rewarding, because some of the developed practices are powerful and many address areas that schools have found difficult, such as helping students study values and their own self-concepts. The resulting teaching skills are an interesting blend of the cognitive and the interactive.

In most cases the intellective component needed to use the teaching skills is fairly substantial: One needs to master the theory of the model and learn to apply it to academic substance and instructional materials. (This aspects requires far and away the largest amount of learning energy.) One also has to learn how to create the social system appropriate to the model, induce the students to engage in the cognitive and social tasks of the model, and modulate those according to the responses of the students. In nearly all cases, the mastery of a model by the students is the key to effectiveness—the students have to learn how to engage in the particular learning process emphasized by that model.

In this review, we will concentrate on a few quite different models as illustrations, following the framework proposed by Joyce, Weil, & Showers (1992) that classifies models according to the most prominent kinds of learning strategies they emphasize: personal, social, information-processing, or behavioral systems. In some cases researchers have concentrated on specific, "model-relevant" outcomes, whereas in other cases a broad spectrum of school outcomes have been examined.

The Effects of Selected Social Models of Teaching

There have been three lines of research on ways of helping students study and learn together, one lead by David and Roger Johnson, a second by Robert Slavin, and the third by Shlomo and Yael Sharan and Rachel Hertz-Lazarowitz in Israel.

Among other things, the Johnsons (1990) and their colleagues (1979; 1981) have studied the effects of cooperative task and reward structures on learning. The Johnsons' (1975; 1981) work on peers-teaching-peers has provided information about the effects of cooperative behavior on both traditional learning tasks and the effects on values and intergroup behavior and attitudes. Their models emphasize the development of what they call "positive interdependence," or cooperation where collective action also celebrates individual differences. Slavin's extensive 1983 review includes the study of a variety of approaches where he manipulates the complexity of the social tasks and experiments with various types of groupings. He reported success with the use of heterogeneous groups with tasks requiring coordination of group members both on academic learning and intergroup relations, and has generated a variety of strategies that employ extrinsic and intrinsic reward structures. The Israeli team has concentrated on Group Investigation, the most complex of the social models of teaching. It begins with a confrontation with a puzzling situation. The students react to the situation and examine the nature of their common and different reactions. They determine what kinds of information they need to approach the problem and proceed to collect relevant data. They generate hypotheses and gather the information needed to test them. They evaluate their products and continue their inquiry or begin a new line of inquiry (Thelen, 1960; Sharan & Hertz-Lazarowitz, 1980; Sharan & Shachar, 1988; Hertz-Lazarowitz, 1993). The central teaching skills build the cooperative social environment and teach students the skills of negotiation and conflict resolution necessary for democratic problem solving. In addition, the teacher needs to guide the students in methods of data collection and analysis, help them frame testable hypotheses, and decide what would constitute a reasonable test of a hypothesis. Because groups vary considerably in their need for structure (Hunt, 1971) and their cohesiveness (Thelen, 1967), the teacher cannot behave mechanically but must "read" the students' social and academic behavior and provide the assistance that keeps the inquiry moving without squelching it. The research that underlies the models consists in part of tests of the general thesis of the social family—that cooperative activity generates synergistic energy that advances learning—and in part directly tests the model itself—that group investigation builds democratic-process skills, increases social cohesion, and results in the learning of information, concepts, and the processes of academic inquiry. Sharan and his associates (1982) studied the effects of different degrees of implementation. Results showed that the stronger the implementation, the greater the effects on both lower-order and higher-order academic learning, with the largest effects, as predicted, on higher-order outcomes. The children also learned the skills required by the model, and group cohesion and intergroup attitudes were affected positively. Sharan's group, through their careful study of implementation, documented the need for extensive training and for the formation of a community of teachers who could help one another perfect their use of this complex model (see chapters 6, 7, and 8).

What is the magnitude of effects that we can expect when teachers learn to use the cooperative learning strategies effectively? In Rolheiser-Bennett's (1986) review, she compared the effects of the degrees of cooperative structure required by the several approaches, the group investigation model being the most extreme (Joyce, Showers, & Rolheiser-Bennett, 1987). On standardized tests in the basic curriculum areas (such as reading and mathematics), the highly structured approaches to teaching students who work together generated effect sizes of an average 0.28 with some studies approaching one-half a standard deviation. On criterion-referenced tests the average was 0.48 with some of the best implementations reaching an effect of about one standard deviation.

The somewhat more elaborate cooperative-learning models generated an average effect size of somewhat more than one standard deviation, with some exceeding two standard deviations. (The average student was above the 90th percentile student in the control group.) The effects on higher-order thinking were even greater, with an average effect of about 1.25 standard-deviations and effects in some studies as high as three standard deviations. Taken as a whole, research on cooperative learning is overwhelmingly positive—nearly every study has had from modest to very high effects. Moreover, the cooperative approaches are effective over a range of achievement measures. The more intensely cooperative the environment, the greater the effects, and the more complex the outcomes (higher-order processing of information, problem solving), the greater the effects.

The cooperative environment engendered by these models has had substantial effects on the cooperative behavior of the students, increasing feelings of empathy for others, reducing intergroup tensions and aggressive and antisocial behavior, improving moral judgment, and building positive feelings toward others, including those of other ethnic groups. Many of these effect sizes are substantial—one or two standard deviations is not uncommon and one is as high as eight. Hertz-Lazarowitz (1993) recently used one of the models to create integrative interaction between Israeli and Arab students in the West Bank! Margarita Calderon has worked with Lazarowitz and Jusefina Tinajero to adapt a cooperative integrated reading and composition program for bilingual students with some very nice results (Calderon, Hertz-Lazarowitz, & Tinajero, 1991). An adaptation in higher education that organizes students into cooperative study groups reduced a dropout rate in engineering from 40 percent to about 5 percent (Bonsangue, 1993).

The long lines of careful research establish a number of cooperative learning models as candidates for study where academic, personal, and social learning outcomes are desired. As we will see, they are not the only candidates.

Effects from Selected
Information-Processing Models

Quite a number of models of teaching are designed to increase students' ability to process information more powerfully. These include methods that assist memorization and teach students how to organize information for mastery, models to teach students to collect and organize information conceptually (such as the ones described in the study of inductive thinking, above), and systems to teach students to use the methods of the disciplines, to engage in causal reasoning, and to master concepts (Joyce, Weil, & Showers, 1992).

Many of these models have extensive recent research literature (the number of pertinent studies per model ranges from about a dozen to more than 300). Here, we will discuss Advance Organizers, approaches to mnemonics, and other information-processing models, although research relevant to the disciplines-oriented inductive approach will be included in the discussion of the effects of curricula, below.

Advance Organizers.   David Ausubel's formulation (1963) that there would be greater retention of materials from presentation and reading if the material was accompanied by organizing ideas has generated more than 200 studies. Essentially, lectures, assignments of reading and research, and courses are accompanied by presentations of concepts that help the student increase intellectual activity during and after exposure to information. The early studies involved much experimentation with ways of formulating and delivering organizers. Because of modest findings, some reviewers asserted that the line of work was not paying off (Barnes & Clausen, 1975). The technique advanced quite a bit during the 1970s, however, and current reviewers are quite positive (Lawton & Wanska, 1977, 1979; Luiten, Ames, & Ackerson, 1980). Rolheiser-Bennett's (1986) review of 18 recent investigations turned up an average effect size of lower-order achievement (such as the recall of information and concepts) of 1.35. (With such an effect the average student studying with the aid of organizers learned about as much as the 90th percentile student studying the same material without the assistance of the organizing ideas.) The effects on higher-order thinking (transfer of concepts to new material, etc.) averaged 0.42. Longer-term studies obtained somewhat better results than did short-term studies, presumably because the organizing ideas became better anchored in the minds of the students and had greater facilitating effect.

Stone's (1983) analysis indicated that organizers are effective across ages—being somewhat more effective for students at the stage of concrete operations, when students may need more assistance formulating abstract ideas to anchor content—and across curriculum areas. Illustrations add to the effectiveness of organizers and the impact is increased when they lead to activities and generalizations. While they affect several kinds of outcomes, recall of facts and formulas are most affected. The prediction that can be made is that teachers who accompany presentations and written assignments with organizers will have consistent, although sometimes modest, effects on the learning of information and concepts. Because readings and lectures repeatedly reach so many learners, the cumulative potential is great. Also, structuring a course around organizers, organizing presentations and assignments within the course, tying the organizers to activities that require their application, and illustrating them can have effects as high as two standard deviations. (With an effect of that size the lowest achieving students are about where the average student would be when studying without the help of organizers. The rest of the distribution is comparably above the control.)

The primary skills required by teachers if they are to use organizers are cognitive in nature. To frame organizers one needs to study the material the students are to study and generate ideas that can provide for the learner what Ausubel calls an "intellectual scaffolding" that can hold the information and concepts to be learned. The formulation of the organizers is difficult, as indicated by the modest results in much of the early research, but recently much-improved guidelines have emerged. The presentation of organizers is not difficult, and the time to prepare illustrations with appropriate media appears to pay off substantially. Clearly the advance organizer technology is a candidate for staff development activities.

Mnemonics (Systems to Improve Memorization).   Although research on memorization and mnemonic strategies has been conducted for more than one hundred years, until a few years ago most of the yield offered few and very general guidelines for instruction, such as advice about when to concentrate instruction and when to distribute it. Little research had been conducted on the learning of school subjects. In the mid-1970s, a productive line of work was begun by Atkinson at Stanford University which has been greatly extended by Pressley and Levin at the Universities of Western Ontario and Wisconsin. They have developed a series of systems for organizing information to promote memory and have given particular, although not exclusive attention to one known as the "link-word" method. Atkinson applied the method during experiments with computer-assisted instruction in which he was attempting to increase students' learning of initial foreign-language vocabularies. He experimented with what he called "acoustic" and "imagery" links. The first was designed to make associations between foreign pronunciations and the sounds of known English words. The second was used to make the connection vivid (Atkinson, 1975). In one early study the link-word method produced as much learning in two trials as the conventional method did in three. The experimental group learned about half as many words more than the control group and maintained the advantage after several weeks. He also found that the method was enhanced when the students supplied their own imagery.

Further developmental work included experiments with children of various ages and across subjects. Using a link-word system in Spanish vocabulary learning, second- and fifth-grade children learned about twice the words as did children using rote and rehearsal methods (Pressley, 1977). In later work with Levin and Miller (1981a), Pressley employed a "pictured action" variant of the method with first- and sixth-grade children, who acquired three times as much vocabulary as did control groups. With Dennis-Rounds (1980) he extended the strategy to social studies information (products and cities) and learned that students could transfer the method to other learning tasks with instruction. Pressley, Levin, and McCormick (1980) found that primary school students could generate sentences to enhance memorization. The results were three times as great as for students using their own methods. Similar results were found with kindergarten and preschool children (Pressley, Samuel, et al., 1981). With Levin and Miller (1981b), the work was successfully extended to vocabulary with abstract meanings. Levin and his colleagues (1983) have also extended the application to abstract prose.

It was important to learn whether better "natural" memorizers, with practice, develop their own equivalent methods. Pressley, Levin, and Ghatala (1984) asked whether students, with age and practice, would spontaneously develop elaborated methods for memorizing material and found that very few did. The better performers had, however, developed more elaborate methods than the majority, who used rote-rehearsal methods alone. However, the newly developed mnemonic methods enhanced learning across the range. Hence, it appears that the method or an equivalent one can be very beneficial for most students. The consistency of the findings is impressive. The link-word method appears to have general applicability across subject matters and ages of children (Pressley, Levin, & Delaney, 1982) and can be used by teachers and taught to children.

The effect sizes reached by many of the studies are quite high. The *average* for transfer tasks (where the material learned was to be applied in another setting) was 1.91. Recall of attributes of items (such as towns, cities, minerals) was 1.5. Foreign language acquisition was 1.3, with many studies reporting very high outcomes. Delayed recall generally maintained the gains, indicating that the mnemonics strategies have a lasting effect.

The teaching skills required to use these methods with students are largely cognitive. Generating the links is the chief activity. Once they have been generated and the materials prepared, the presentation to the students is easily done, whether through worksheets, computer, media, or presentation by the teacher. The results on transfer of the method to other tasks is particularly important. A possible application is for all teachers and students to study how to memorize and to learn how to use mnemonics generally in teaching and learning activities. The study of meta-cognitive processes, whereby students become more aware of the processes of learning and guide their behavior accordingly, has important implications for the conduct of education in general.

Other Information-Processing Models.   Models taken directly from the sciences have been the basis for curricula for both elementary and high school children. A description of the teaching skills and the effects of the science-based curricula is included in a later section of this chapter. The results of the research indicate that the scientific method can be taught and has positive effects on the acquisition of information, concepts, and attitudes. More narrowly defined studies have been made on inductive teaching and inquiry training. Beginning with Taba's (1966) exploration of an inductive social studies curriculum, periodic small-scale studies have probed the area. In 1968 Worthen provided evidence to support one of its central theses—that induced concepts would facilitate long-term recall. Feeley (1972) reviewed the social science studies and reported that differences in terminology hampered the accumulation of research but that the inductive methods generally lived up to expectations, generating concept development and positive attitudes. Research on Suchman's (1964) model for teaching causal reasoning directly supported the proposition that inquiry training can be employed with both elementary and high school children. Schrenker (1976) reported that inquiry training resulted in increased understanding of science, greater productivity in critical thinking, and skills for obtaining and analyzing information. He reported that it made little difference in the mastery of information, per se, but that it was as efficient as didactic methods or the didactic cum laboratory methods generally employed to teach science. Ivany (1969) and Collins (1969) examined variants in the kinds of confrontations and materials used and reported that the strength of the confrontation as a stimulus to inquiry was important and that richness in instructional materials was a significant factor. Elefant (1980) successfully carried out the strategy with deaf children in an intriguing study that has implications for work with all children. Voss's (1982) general review includes an annotation of a variety of studies that are generally supportive of the approach. The skills of these models apparently require intensive training. Teachers need to study the substance of a lesson, unit, or curriculum and develop a rich array of instructional materials that can be explored by the children. They have to guide concept formation activities and help the students become more sophisticated in the making of categories and inferences. The flow of instruction emerges, depending on the thinking of the students, and the environment has to be adjusted to the developing lesson. Knowledge of both the substance and process appears to be critical.

Reviews (Sternberg, 1986; Sternberg & Bahna, 1986) of some of the recently developed packages for teaching elements of analytic reasoning to students have reported modest effects for some of them. Bereiter (1984) produced a fine analysis of various approaches to the teaching of thinking in which he concluded that the teaching of thinking is far better undertaken in a fashion that is integrated with the curriculum areas than in a "separate-skills" approach.

For staff development policy, an important implication of the research on the inductive and inquiry-oriented models of teaching is that the processes of inductive and analytic reasoning can be taught effectively to students in the context of curricula in the basic school subjects. To do so on a wide scale requires that teachers learn the substance and the teaching technologies that will enable them to design and implement lessons, units, and courses around these models.

Personal Models of Teaching

Student-centered models are numerous and controversial. From a scientific point of view, it is unfortunate that the literature is so rhetorical and that so many personalists have devoted energy to diatribes against traditional methods or even against the work of theorists of other persuasions. Only in the last 20 years has considerable energy been devoted to research to explore the dynamics of these methods in school settings and to deal directly with the serious concern of their critics—that person-centered education may neglect the development of academic outcomes.

An interesting exception is the work with synectics (Gordon & Poze, 1971), which is designed both to enhance personal flexibility and creativity and to teach another of the higher-order thinking skills, specifically the ability to think divergently and generate alternative and relevant solutions to difficult problems and alternative perspectives on important concepts and values.

Research on synectics indicates that it achieves its "model-relevant" purposes, increasing student generation of ideas, divergent solutions to problems, and fluency in expressing ideas. (Effect sizes average 1.5 for generation of ideas and problem solving.) By helping students develop more multidimensional perspectives, it also increases recall of material from written passages by an effect size of 2.0 and the information is retained at an even higher level.

For policy in most school districts, what will be of most interest is that teaching students to think creatively is positively related to the learning and retention of information and can increase the lower-order outcomes to a substantial degree.

Nondirective Teaching. Carl Rogers' *Freedom to Learn in the Eighties* (1982) includes a chapter summarizing much of the research from the humanistic perspective. Aspy and Roebuck (1973) and Roebuck, Buhler, and Aspy (1976) have been very productive over the last 15 years. They have explored several of the theses of the personal family of models, particularly that building self-directed, empathetic communities of learners will have positive effects on students' feelings about themselves and others and, consequently, will free energy for learning. Roebuck, Buhler, and Aspy's (1976) study with students identified as having learning difficulties produced positive effects on self-concept, inter-group attitudes and interaction patterns, achievement in reading and mathematics, and increased scores on tests of intelligence. In studies of classroom teachers, they have documented the need for extensive training (Aspy et al., 1974). The students of teachers who had learned the model thoroughly achieved more, felt better about themselves, had better attendance records, and improved their interpersonal skills. The model of nondirective teaching is very complex. Teachers have to develop egalitarian relationships with the students, create a cooperative group of students who respect one another's differences in personality and ability, help those students develop programs of study (including goals and the means for achieving them), provide feedback about performance and behavior, teach the students to reflect on one another's behavior and performance, help individuals and groups evaluate progress, and maintain an affirmative social climate. We think that the research personnel from the personalistic school of thought have answered their critics, and have developed a teachable technology. That technology requires a thorough knowledge of the theory of the approach and how to use it in the development of the educational environment. Because more than ordinary behaviors are necessary to implement the personalistic models, extensive training and practice are required.

Behavioral Systems Models

This family, based on the work of B. F. Skinner and the cybernetic training psychologists (K. Smith & M. Smith, 1966) has the largest body of literature. Studies range from programmed instruction to simulations and include training models (Joyce & Showers, 1983) and methods derived directly from therapy (Wolpe & Lazarus, 1966). There is a great deal of research on the application of social learning theory to instruction (Becker & Gersten, 1982), training (K. Smith & M. Smith, 1966), and simulations (Boocock & Schild, 1968). The behavioral technologists have demonstrated that they can design programs for both specific and general goals (Becker & Gersten, 1982) and also that the effective application of those techniques requires extensive cognitive activity and precise interactive skills (Spaulding, 1970).

A recent analysis by White (1986) examined the results of studies on the application of the DISTAR version of social learning theory to special education. The average effect sizes for mathematics and reading ranged from about one-half to one standard deviation. The effects for moderately and severely handicapped students were similar. Perhaps most important, there were a few studies in which the effects on aptitude (measures of intellectual ability) were included and, where the DISTAR program was implemented for several years, the effect sizes were 1.0 or above, representing an increase of about 10 points in the standard IQ ratio.

Summary of Research on Teaching Models

Have the developers of theory proven that they can design effective approaches to teaching? We think they have. With modification, most of them have applicability across the gamut of subjects and grades although some of them have been developed for particular subjects or ages. For example, the jurisprudential model was created specifically to prepare secondary school students to analyze public policy questions. Does the application of the theory-driven models endanger the traditional goals of the school? By no means. On the contrary, they enhance the traditional goals of the school. What is the nature of the teaching skills necessary for use of these models? We think that the cognitive and interactive aspects are intertwined. Effective implementation of each requires a thorough understanding of the theory and the means to provide to students cognitive and social tasks that are presently unusual in the classroom.

Specific Teaching Practices Applicable across Models and Styles

A number of research and development teams have developed ideas about aspects of the instructional act that reasonably might facilitate student achievement and feelings of self-worth if they are used regularly, regardless of the model of instruction that is used or the stylistic preferences of the instructors. We will deal with just two of these here, one, the concept of "wait-time," because of its long research history and the second, "Teacher Expectations and Student Achievement" (TESA), because its wide dissemination in workshops sponsored by the Phi Delta Kappa organization has made it one of the most-used offerings in staff development programs across the country.

The concept of wait-time was formulated by Professor Mary Budd Rowe (1969, 1974) who has long had a concern with the relationship between instructor behavior and the intellectual and affective engagement by the students. On first encountering the concept, it seems simple and uncomplicated enough. Rowe had observed, as had other students of teaching, that many classrooms are characterized by brief statements or questions by teachers and students that are densely packed into the time period. (In one study by the present authors there were as many as 250 utterances between teacher and students in an average *hour* of instruction—the average communication lasting only about two seconds!) She theorized that such density fragments thought processes, not allowing students enough time to process the information contained in one communication before another is upon them. The teacher, controlling the interaction in a staccato fashion, also left the students cognitively and socially powerless—if a student thought for a few seconds and had something important to say, the time would have passed with the discourse several communications down the road. Rowe speculated that if instructors slowed down the pace by *waiting more between communications*, then the students would be enabled to think over what was being discussed, would have more to say, would become more involved, and would be empowered to bring their cognitions into the discourse to a higher degree. Also, they would be more inclined to listen to one another and to comment on one another's ideas. In other words, she expected that the practice of waiting between communications would affect many other aspects of classroom interaction.

A study by Kenneth Tobin (1986) lends the best support thus far to Rowe's theory. He successfully trained teachers to teach units in mathematics and language arts lessons and found a number of interesting effects. Among these were that the students were more often able to respond to questions (presumably because they had time to think about them and formulate their responses), their utterances became longer, and they were more likely to respond to one another. The teachers became more positive and in language arts asked more questions that dealt with comprehension rather than simple recall of what had been read. The differences were actually manifested in student achievement with a modest effect size (about 0.2). That the effect is modest should not disqualify it from being considered as a candidate for a staff development program. The practice is clear and easy to understand, teachers can acquire the requisite behaviors quickly, and they are appropriate for many situations. A modest behavioral change that improves the quality of classroom discourse and is likely to increase student involvement and pay off regularly in achievement-related terms is, from our perspective, a fine candidate for our attempts to improve our teaching.

Sam Kerman (1979) and his associates developed the Teacher Expectations and Student Achievement program from their observation that students in the same classroom are often treated differently, frequently without the teacher being aware of the differences, in ways that can affect their engagement and achievement. Specifically, students with the poorer learning histories are often called on less, giving them less opportunity for involvement, and often their responses are treated more negatively. Gradually the students become less involved and feel less valued. In discussions with teachers, Kerman found that many had rational explanations for the differential treatment, citing a desire not to embarrass the low achievers and also to allow the higher achievers to talk more to bring out better and more correct ideas. Hence, procedures were developed to help teachers, through observation and feedback, to get a picture of the distribution and nature of the communications in their classroom and provide them with ideas about how to involve all the students affirmatively. A large body of research on teaching was used as sources of ideas for helping students respond, treating varieties of responses, maintaining a high level of respect and courtesy in the classroom, and so on. Their training has been successful and their formal studies indicate that the increased involvement by all students has an effect on student learning of about the same magnitude as wait-time.

Again, they have provided a very direct avenue to helping teachers produce what most observers would agree is a more desirable classroom climate, an avenue that can be followed with modest amounts of training and which promised general educational benefits in the personal, social, and academic domains.

Constructivism

In recent years there has been a new "call to arms" to help students learn to construct knowledge (Brooks & Brooks, 1993). Three types of student learning are discussed: One is the students' attempts to discover the world from their own perspectives; the second is the work by groups of students to inquire together and construct ideas about the world; the third is inquiry based on the academic disciplines, where students try on the ideas and approaches to inquiry of the disciplines. Each of these three can be facilitated by the different families of models of teaching. Although the purpose is not to increase student learning in the traditional sense of "improving test scores," the assumption that if students construct knowledge student learning will increase is borne out by most of the research. Whether it is the "inquiry" approaches to language learning (Hillocks, 1987), the inductive approaches to science (Bredderman, 1983), or the development of group investigation in social science (or any other curriculum area), the various themes of constructivism pay off, not only in helping students learn to reason and gain conceptual control over academic substance, but in the learning of information and skills as well.

STUDIES OF CURRICULUM

Initiatives to improve curriculum areas or to establish new ones are especially important to the systemic and collective components of the staff development system. It has been well established that curriculum implementation is demanding of staff development—essentially, without strong staff development programs that are appropriately designed, a very low level of implementation occurs (Fullan & Pomfret, 1977; Fullan & Stiegelbauer, 1991).

The curriculum of schools—what is taught and how it is taught—obviously affects what students learn as a product of their engagement in schooling. Over the years much of the content that students are exposed to in the common curriculum areas has been relatively standardized. Nearly everyone can describe the content of elementary school arithmetic courses, for example, and almost any high school science teacher has a fairly good idea of the major topics that are likely to be covered in physics courses or advanced-placement chemistry courses. Yet there are differences between schools and school districts. In elementary school language arts programs, for example, the amount of attention to writing and literature differs quite a bit. In science the amount of time devoted to laboratory work varies.

Over the years variants on the standard courses have developed so that it is possible for quite a variety to be used, both with respect to content and teaching process. The important question to be dealt with here is how much difference there is when different materials, teaching processes, and content are implemented. We stress *implemented*, because a different plan will not by itself give us differences. In a sense, the fundamental question is whether we possess a technology that offers the prospect of more powerful curricula, so that districts have serious choices both in what is selected and in whether they will devote the staff development energy to implementing the curricula they choose. A second important question is whether faculties can learn to use them. A third is whether conditions can be developed in schools to stabilize the curricula so that they can have effects. If the answers to these questions are affirmative, then teaching skills derived from formulations of curriculum can legitimately be employed as the objectives of teacher education.

Currently the clearest evidence about the potential effects on students comes from the study of the academically oriented curricula in science and mathematics that were developed and used during the 20-year period from 1955 to 1975 and from the experience with elementary curricula in a variety of subject areas (Becker & Gersten, 1982; Rhine, ed., 1981). The theory of the academic curricula was relatively straightforward. The essence of the position was stated in *The Process of Education* (Bruner, 1961) and Schwab and Brandwein's *The Teaching of Science* (1962). The teaching of science should be as much as possible a simulation of the scientific process itself. The concepts of the disciplines should be studied rigorously in relation to their knowledge base. Thus science would be learned as inquiry. Further, the information thus learned would be retained well because it would be embedded in a meaningful framework and the student would possess the interrelated concepts that make up the structure of the disciplines.

In the academic reform movement of the 1950s and 1960s, entire curricula in the sciences (e.g., BSCS Biology), social studies (e.g., Man, A Course of Study), mathematics (e.g., School Mathematics Study Group), and language (e.g., the linguistic approaches) were developed and introduced to the schools. These curricula had in common their designers' beliefs that academic subjects should be studied with the tools of their respective disciplines. Most of these curricula therefore required that students learn the modes of inquiry employed by the disciplines as well as factual material. Process was valued equally with content and many of these curricula became characterized as "inquiry oriented." In addition, general approaches to early-childhood education (e.g., Headstart and Follow Through) and the education of older children (Individually-Prescribed Instruction and DISTAR), studies of curricula mediated through television and computer-mediated and assisted curricula make their contribution—even though some of them investigate the role of the human training agent in settings other than the classroom.

Much curriculum research resembles the experimental studies of teaching, but the unit under study is a configuration of content, teaching methods, instructional materials and technologies, and organizational forms. In the experiments any one of the elements of curriculum may be studied separately or in combination with the others, and the yield is expressed in terms of whether a curriculum produces predicted effects. Research on curriculum depends heavily on training in the content of the curriculum and the teaching strategies needed to implement it. Following training, implementation is monitored, either by classroom observation or interviews. Effects are determined by comparing student outcomes in experimental and control classrooms. In a few studies (e.g., Almy, 1970), combinations of curricula are employed to determine effects on cognitive development and intelligence.

In both the academic reform movement and the early-childhood programs, elaborate curriculum materials were prepared to support the teaching/learning activities. The evaluation of the curricula was difficult once it was learned that implementation was more arduous than had initially been thought. Only partial implementation occurred in many settings (Goodlad & Klein, 1970; Goodlad, 1984; Fullan & Pomfret, 1977). In the early stages, research was meager and evaluation was poorly funded. However, eventually quite a number of studies were completed in sites with fairly high levels of implementation. El-Nemr (1979) concentrated his analysis on the teaching of biology as inquiry in high schools and colleges. He looked at the effects on achievement of information, on the development of process skills, and on attitudes toward science. The experimentally oriented biology curricula achieved positive effects on all three outcomes. The average effect sizes were largest for process skills (0.44 at the high school level and 0.62 at the college level). For achievement they were 0.27 and 0.11 respectively, and for attitudes, 0.22 and 0.51. Bredderman's (1983) analysis included a broader range of science programs and included the elementary grades. He also reported positive effects for information (0.10), creativity (0.13), science process (0.52), and, in addition, reported effects on intelligence tests where they were included (0.50). From these and other studies, we can conclude that it is possible to develop curricula that will achieve model-relevant effects and also will increase learning of information and concepts. Also, vigorous curricula in one area appear to stimulate growth in other, apparently unconnected areas. For example, Smith's (1980) analysis of aesthetics curricula shows that the implementation of the arts-oriented curricula was accompanied by gains in the basic skills areas. Possibly an active and effective curriculum in one area has energizing effects on the entire school program. Hillocks (1987) review of the teaching of reading and writing produced similar effects. His conclusion indicated just how closely how we teach is connected with what we teach. Essentially, the inductive approaches to the teaching of reading and writing produced average effect sizes of about .60 compared to treatments that covered the same material, but without the inductive approaches to the teaching/learning process.

From the evidence in science and several other subject areas, we conclude that curricula can be constructed that can increase student learning. Also, they can be implemented, although not as easily as was believed 20 years ago. On the other hand, research on training has progressed substantially, so that we now know that we can engineer conditions that will implement the curricula much more efficiently than was the case 20 years ago. The nature of the teaching skills is a blend of the interactive and the intellectual. Many require a high degree of skill in a variety of models of teaching. (See the skills described above in the review of theory-driven research.) Many also require mastery of an academic discipline. Fullan's (1982) analysis argues persuasively that implementation requires a "deep understanding" of the curriculum itself—its rationale, process, structure, and materials.

There is little question that skills to use these curricula require far more than ordinary knowledge and skills and, therefore, imply extensive training and practice. Spaulding's (1970) study asked important questions about the ability of teachers to implement a curriculum based on several theory-driven models of teaching well enough to achieve both general and model-relevant effects. The curriculum was designed for economically poor, socially disruptive, low-achieving elementary school students. It required teachers to master four teaching models and employ them selectively to achieve a complex set of goals. Social learning theory was employed to induce independent learning and socially integrative behavior. Inductive instructional methods were moderated by a cognitive-development frame of reference to define the learning tasks. The teachers had to comprehend and use social learning theory, inductive theory, and Piagetian cognitive psychology. Over a three-year period, the students achieved greater personal control, integrative behavior, academic achievement; and even measures of intelligence responded to the treatment. Spaulding's work underlines the skills of implementing a complex, theory-derived curriculum. The teachers had to be able to employ several theoretical frameworks. They had to be able to discriminate students on the basis of independence, social integration, achievement, and cognitive development. They had to be able to teach inductively, helping students gather, categorize, and label sets of data and to modify the processes of induction in accord with the characteristics of the students. Spaulding demonstrated that the teachers could acquire those skills and use them powerfully enough to reach a variety of goals.

For staff development policy in school districts, the important message is that curricula can make a difference and that some have been engineered and implemented that have made a large difference to students. Without a strong program in content, materials, and teaching process a poor level of implementation is likely to result (Hall, 1986; Hall & Loucks, 1977), which we will deal with in the following chapters.

STUDIES OF SCHOOLS THOUGHT TO BE EFFECTIVE

Research that compares schools has gone on for some time. In the early years, these studies were designed on a planned variation model, where schools operating from different stances toward education were compared with one another. For example, 50 years ago, an "eight-year study" (Chamberlin & Chamberlin, 1943), technically designed with great virtuosity, submitted the theses of the Progressive Movement to a serious (and generally successful) test and defended it against the suggestion that social and personal models of education were dangerous to the academic health of students. Twenty years ago the Coleman et al. study (1966) ushered in an era of investigation that continues, with the focus on naturalistic studies in which schools with unusually high achievement are compared with others. This study was widely interpreted as indicating that variations between schools had little effect on student success because the ability and socioeconomic background of the students themselves were such powerful factors. Recent research on the differential effectiveness of schools (Brookover et al., 1978; Edmonds, 1979; Rutter et al., 1979) has called into question the findings of the Coleman study and advanced the methodology for studying schools. Although the study of effective schools has been criticized (Ralph & Fennessey, 1983; Rowen, Bossert, & Dwyer, 1983; Purkey & Smith, 1983) both on methodological grounds (studying the social and curricular organization of a school is complex and unwieldy) and in terms of its interpretation (whether we can use the characteristics of an outstanding school to make another school better), the research continues and is making available to the field a much clearer set of hypotheses about how to approach the problem of increasing the positive impact of the school environment.

Research on effective schools is fueled by the belief that the realization of education goals is achieved both by the organizational settings in which learning occurs as well as by the quality of specific curricula and individual teachers. The focus is on the social organization of the school (the social climate) and curricular and instructional practices. Schools are first differentiated on a criterion of effectiveness, generally those aspects of academic achievement that are measured by mass administrations of commercially available tests. The researcher studies the schools and attempts to find out what accounts for the differences in productivity. Currently this work is evolving toward attempts to find causal connections by changing schools and trying to learn whether the changes are accompanied by changes in student achievement. The really fine work by Lezotte (Levine & Lezotte, 1990) and Levine (1991) has led the way in this area.

Several technical difficulties have confronted researchers studying schools for their effects on students. Little is known about the stability of either effectiveness or environments. Instrumentation is difficult and the logistics are even more complicated than the study of the classroom as a unit. However, recent investigations (Weil et al., 1984) have attacked these problems by studying schools that have been unusually effective for several years, comparing them with typical schools, and improving the reliability of instruments. The data base is new but promising. The first step is to learn how some schools achieve more than ordinary effects. The second is to learn how faculties, operating as a unit, can create energizing environments at the school level. These behaviors will compete for their place in preservice and inservice programs.

Many of the studies that have followed those by Brookover, Rutter, and their associates have oriented their search around the early findings. The result has been a body of studies that confirms many of the early results, which is useful because it suggests that the differences are in fact systematic. However, it is quite possible that there could be improvement in the definition of the variables or that other factors would emerge were they studied differently. Also, very little of the research has been oriented toward the potentially relevant concepts that are available from social psychology and organizational theory. Inclusion of these frames of reference might be worthwhile. The findings are emerging. Currently they fall in the following three areas:

> School Learning Climate, including expectations and standards, clarity of mission, curricular organization, the monitoring of student progress, the

reward structure, connectedness with the parents, and the provision of opportunities to learn

School Social Climate, including a sense of community, student involvement in governance, orientation of the peer group, and provisions for orderliness and safety

School Organizational Climate, including administrators, active instructional leadership, and collaborative decision making

Although research on effective schools has a soft focus on the teacher behaviors that produce the conditions believed to be associated with effective school climates, we believe that they have to be taken seriously for a number of reasons. One is the size of the unit in question. Although the effect sizes are often small (about 0.10 in Weil's study), the number of students affected is very large. Second is the potential for interaction between school climate and many of the behaviors identified in the other lines of research. The power of curriculum and teaching may well be magnified by the climate of the school. Third, some of the conditions described in this research are very similar to those described by other lines of inquiry. (The production of an orderly, affirmative climate with clearly articulated goals and curriculum is an example.) Finally, the implementation of the skills derived from the other lines may well depend on the organizational factors that are emerging from the study of effective schools (Levine & Lezotte, 1990).

The research on models of teaching can provide direct assistance in defining relevant skills more clearly. The social and behavioral theories certainly promise methods for building social systems, methods that can be incorporated into preservice and inservice programs. Clearly the study of how to build effective school climates needs to be undertaken to define teachable skills further. Progress may be made relatively quickly if the messages of the current literature on educational change and training are brought to bear. It may be that a major part of the skill in improving the educational climate may be in the management of educational change and the learning of new skills for implementing effective models of teaching. For the present the skills of working cooperatively to select the missions of the school and to think out how to create orderly yet stimulating environments appear to be essential. These skills are manifested in the role as faculty member rather than the role of instructor.

STUDIES OF TEACHERS THOUGHT TO BE EFFECTIVE

The Anderson-Brewer (1939) studies are generally acknowledged to mark the beginning of the modern era of investigations that employ the paradigm where descriptions of teacher behavior (process) are collected and correlated with a measure of desired student behavior (product). They studied dominant and integrative behavior in early childhood settings and measured the effect of the actions of the teacher on the social behavior of the students. Their research was important both because it established that teachers' social behavior does influence their students and also because it made clear how subtle and intricate are the relationships between teachers and students. In the classrooms where teachers were more integrative, the students found ways of behaving more integratively with their peers. In the classrooms where teachers were more dominating, the students learned how to be more dominative toward one another. Over the years many frames of reference have been used to describe teacher-student interaction and a wide range of types of student learning have been included (Flanders, 1970; Medley, 1977; Medley & Mitzel, 1963; Rosenshine, 1971; Spaulding, 1970; & Stallings, 1979).

What distinguishes this research is the focus on naturally occurring class-room behaviors. The research begins with the measurement of student academic achievement or other categories of student learning (growth in self-concept, independence, etc.). The researcher may elect to study teachers whose students are at the high, middle, or low sectors of the distribution. An alternative is to study a fairly large sample of teachers and expect that variation in student achievement will occur naturally. The next step is to study teacher and/or student behavior in the instructional setting—usually the classroom. Classrooms manifesting different levels of achievement are then compared and the frequencies of teacher and student behavior are correlated with the measures of learning. The findings emerge from this analysis. If teacher behaviors are identified that appear to differentiate levels of student learning, the investigators may then proceed (Good, Grouws, & Ebmeier, 1983; Stallings, Needels, & Stayrook, 1979) to an experimental mode. Teacher behaviors associated with higher rates of student achievement will be taught to teachers whose students typically manifest low or moderate achievement, in order to determine whether acquiring the ability to manifest the behaviors will raise student learning. If the results of the experimental phase are positive, the teacher behaviors that differentiate the more from less effective teachers qualify as candidates for teachable teaching skills.

The naturalistic studies can be difficult to carry out. Access to the teachers and students has to be arranged and substantial amounts of classroom observation are necessary. The problem of stability both of effectiveness (Brophy & Evertson, 1974; Medley, Soar, & Coker, 1984) and behavior (Shavelson & Dempsey-Atwood, 1976) has been vexing. From year to year, teachers have their ups and downs in terms of the achievement that occurs in their students, and the researcher has to be careful because the apparently successful teacher in one year may be associated with only modest results the next. (Stability coefficients average only about .20.) Similarly, teachers' patterns of behavior change, causing us to modify our conception of what worked for those teachers. Also, what works for one may not always work for another.

From the standpoint of management, successful research often requires entry to the classrooms of very ineffective teachers, many of whom may experience acute discipline problems. The incidence of discipline problems also confronts the researcher with the problem of differentiating those aspects of teacher behavior that are related to the discipline problems from those that may be associated with the effectiveness of instruction per se. However, the paradigm for the research is straightforward and provides a relatively clear path to the findings, and the problems have not prevented energetic and well-organized researchers from carrying out some large and complex studies, and the results are providing some promising avenues for staff development. It is important to note that all of the studies that have successfully differentiated more and less effective teachers have reported that effectiveness is the product of a complex set of behaviors, rather than the use of a few practices. As we will see, some of the behaviors are relatively easy for teachers to learn and others appear to be much more difficult. Because of the complexity of the research and its yield, we will need to deal with a number of investigations in order to get a useful picture of the findings.

The focus of naturalistic research on teaching is based on what teachers do in regular classrooms. Many of the studies focus on the management of instruction—what teachers do to prevent discipline problems and how they respond to them when they do occur, the arrangement and organization of materials, the time allotted to various activities and subjects, etc.—as much as on the means of instruction—the kinds of information provided and questions asked, the types of activities provided. The patterns of management and teaching employed by more successful teachers, that is, by teachers whose students score higher on standardized achievement tests, are often then collected into prescriptions or treatments and tested in experimental studies of teaching effectiveness.

Many of the naturalistic studies have been conducted in low-SES, primary classrooms (Stallings & Kaskowitz, 1972–73; Soar, 1973) and elementary classrooms (Good, Grouws, & Ebmeier, 1983; Anderson, Evertson & Brophy, 1979; Crawford et al., 1978; Evertson et al., 1980; Fisher et al., 1980; McDonald & Elias, 1976). There are a few studies in junior high classrooms (Evertson et al., 1980; Good, Grouws, & Ebmeier, 1983) and a handful with high school teachers of remedial subjects (Stallings, Needels, & Stayrook, 1979).

The teacher behaviors, practices, and skills that emerged from naturalistic studies of teaching generally relate more to the management of instruction than to actual instructional behaviors, although an important finding concerns the *amount* of instructional behavior used in teaching episodes. (Some of the less effective teachers apparently provide little instruction and rely on "seatwork" and other assignments to do the instructing for them.) Teacher practices recommended by several investigators (Brophy & Evertson, 1974; Good, Grouws, & Ebmeier, 1983; Fisher et al., 1980; Soar, 1973; Stallings & Kaskowitz, 1972–73) included the teaching of students in large groups, allocation of time to academic tasks, the maintenance of highly structured learning environments that reduced student off-task behaviors, the supervision or monitoring of seatwork, and the regular assigning of homework. The pattern of teaching represented by this cluster of behaviors is often referred to as "direct instruction," which generally implies a clear presentation of goals, instruction over those goals, the provision of practice in the classroom and/or in assignments to be accomplished out of school, and the monitoring of that practice with direct corrective feedback over work to be accomplished. There have been some fairly consistent findings for teacher practices with young, low-SES students. Stallings and Kaskowitz (1972-73), in their correlational study of Follow Through first- and third-grade classrooms, found higher reading and math scores associated with structured, systematic instruction patterns (e.g., longer amounts of time spent on reading and math, direct instruction from teacher with praise and/or feedback). More flexible, less structured classrooms had somewhat lower scores in reading and math, although students in those classrooms had higher attendance rates, exhibited more independence, scored higher on problem-solving tests, and were more likely to take responsibility for their successes. The less structured classrooms were characterized by less direct instruction from teachers. Teachers in these classrooms spent greater amounts of time organizing the instructional environment with which students interacted, and in one-to-one interactions with children. Not every investigator has produced confirming results. For example, Flanders (1970) reported that the less structured, more "indirect" classrooms generated better results in both achievement and social behavior.

Some investigators have differentiated among types of student achievement. In another study of Follow Through kindergarten and first-grade classrooms, Soar (1973) examined teacher behaviors with two types of student learning, which he called complex-abstract and simple-concrete. Simple-concrete gains were positively associated with teachers' direct time on academic activities, the asking of direct, narrow questions, large group instruction, initiation of verbal interactions, and provision of praise and positive feedback. Soar also noted, however, a curvilinear relationship between teacher behavior and types of learning outcomes. He found moderately high levels of freedom facilitated complex growth while greater teacher direction increased simple learning. Both Soar and Stallings conducted extensive classroom observations with quite different observation instruments. Although results from the Beginning Teacher Evaluation Study (Phase II) (McDonald & Elias, 1976) were mixed, BTES (Phase III) (Fisher et al., 1980) replicated Stallings's and Soar's Follow Through findings in grades 2 and 5. Teacher behaviors or practices associated with greater student achievement in reading and math included teacher accuracy in diagnosis, prescription of tasks related to student achievement level, substantive (academic) interaction with students, academic feedback, structuring, and clear directions.

As some of the investigators identified teacher practices that appeared to be associated with the achievement of low-SES students in reading and mathematics, they proceeded with experiments to see if they could help teachers increase student achievement by using those practices. Two examples of this experimental work are Anderson, Evertson, and Brophy's (1979) experiment in first-grade reading and Good, Grouws, and Ebmeier's (1983) experiment in fourth-grade mathematics.

The Anderson, Evertson, and Brophy (1979) experimental study in first-grade reading was conducted over a period of months with middle-class students. A manual describing 22 principles of instruction thought to be effective for small-group instruction in the early grades was distributed to the 17 treatment teachers. The manual was described to teachers as a "set of guidelines for teacher management of reading group instruction" (p. 195). No additional training was provided the experimental group. The principles dealt with management of the group as a whole and the responses that teachers gave in feedback to students' answers. Mean reading scores at the end of the experiment for the observed and unobserved treatment groups were 57.09 and 59.81 as compared with a mean score of 50.90 for the control groups. The superior performance of treatment teachers' students was attributed to teacher process variables, some of which could be attributed to the experimental treatment (e.g., efficient transitions, appropriate seating, use of overviews, minimizing choral responses, using ordered turns to select respondents, moderate and specific use of praise). Practices most likely to be implemented were those that "specifically described the skills . . . , focused on behaviors that were familiar to the teachers . . . , and had a rationale based on other classroom processes or student outcomes that made sense to teachers" (p. 219).

Good, Grouws, and Ebmeier (1983) did a series of experiments. The first, in the teaching of fourth-grade math, was conducted with relatively low-SES students. Twenty-one teachers read a manual that described the treatment practices (e.g., daily review, development of new content, seatwork, homework) that had been identified as contributing to student learning in the naturalistic study. Two 90-minute sessions were held with teachers to assure that they understood the recommended practices. Implementation by treatment teachers was high, with the exception of the "development" behavior advocated for 20 minutes per session. At the end of the two-and-one-half-month experiment, students of experimental teachers performed significantly better than control teachers' students on math computation and showed no difference in problem solving. In some subsequent studies few effects were observed.

We believe that some of the practices identified by the naturalistic studies of teaching do not require extensive training. Others do. Although Stallings's work with secondary teachers is an exception, treatments have often consisted of providing teachers with a manual explaining the desired behaviors and in some cases a brief discussion of those behaviors (e.g., Good, Grouws, & Ebmeier, 1983; Crawford et al., 1978). The ease of training and implementation of these behaviors should not be surprising, however, when remembering that the behaviors were first identified among the practices of many classroom teachers teaching as they normally taught. The most difficult skills for teachers to acquire are those involving instruction to the whole class or small groups. Teachers who use the "truncated" recitation, that is, who rely heavily on seatwork and instructional materials to do the teaching, have a relatively difficult time learning how to conduct instruction.

The naturalistic study of teaching has provided a rich storehouse of effective practices for the management of instruction and student behavior, and has demonstrated the relative ease of instructing teachers to use these practices. Future work in this area will need to address the generalizability of these findings to older and higher SES students in areas other than reading and math. And this work has already begun, with promising results with older students. Perhaps more productive may be the wedding of this work to that of the theory-based instruction researchers, who have concentrated heavily on the process and content of instruction for multiple purposes.

Most of the naturalistic studies have provided guidelines about how to conduct instruction in classrooms where the most frequent teaching episode has clear objectives; the teacher presents material and has the students either practice skills or study the material and then discuss it or recite it under the guidance of the teacher. This constitutes what we have called the basic recitation mode of teaching.

The more effective teachers:

teach the classroom as a whole (they group the students for activities stemming from the foci that are developed).

present information or skills clearly and animatedly.

keep the teaching sessions task-oriented.

are nonevaluative and keep instruction relaxed.

have high expectations for achievement (give more homework, pace lessons faster, create alertness).

relate comfortably to the students, with the consequence that they have fewer behavior problems.

These behaviors are similar to those advocated by Hunter (1980), whose ITIP program stresses clear goals, affirmation toward students, closely monitored practice and homework, and direct, objectives-related feedback.

It is important to understand that the practices identified through the naturalistic research paradigm are those already used by the more effective teachers. Those more effective teachers do not need training in those practices, since they already use them. The greatest benefit will accrue when the least effective teachers, perhaps 25 or 30 percent, receive training in these practices. Even then, the assumption that student achievement will automatically rise cannot be made. An intensive three-year program to teach teachers a range of practices that appear supported by the naturalistic studies recently resulted in little or no effect on student achievement. In fact, the untreated control group actually exceeded the experimental group by the end of the third year (Slavin, 1986). Also, implementation is very important. Changing teacher behavior is a delicate matter and increasing the frequency of use of certain practices may not have much effect unless they are employed appropriately and powerfully (Mandeville & Rivers, 1991).

The interpretation of the results also has to be made carefully. As data analysis becomes more sophisticated some of the early findings are being reinterpreted by some researchers. For example, Lara and Medley (1987) noticed that most naturalistic studies have used class means as the measure of student achievement. Essentially, classes are tested before and after the period of observation and the average gain is computed. Lara and Medley hypothesized that the same behaviors might have different effects on high- and low-achieving students, and they added to their analysis a comparison of students more than a standard deviation above and below the mean. Their results are striking. A number of behaviors helped either high or low achievers but had no or even a *negative* effect on the other group. For example, the provision of clear, explicit instructions helped low achievers but had no effect on high achievers. Praise and rewards, which are often associated with moderate class mean gains, was *negatively* correlated with both high and low achievers. Their analysis adds clear evidence that the interaction between teachers and students is very complex. Conceivably the *most* effective teachers may turn out to be those who do not simply use certain practices regularly, but those who modulate those practices in such a way that they create more energy for learning across the spectrum of individual differences. We need to be careful that we do not advocate practices that appear to raise the average but which actually disadvantage certain categories of students.

Also, although effective practice appeals to some program planners because, on the surface, it appears "simpler" to help learn discrete strategies than what appear to be the more complex teaching strategies and curriculum patterns, such is not the case. Some large-scale programs have found very poor implementation. Training apparently has to be as carefully designed to get implementation of teaching practices as it does for the apparently more complex content (Mandeville & Rivers, 1991). However, we estimate that if a thoroughgoing program were implemented that helped the teachers in the bottom 20 percent to take on the practices that the top 20 percent use in common, the effect size could be as much as .50.

SUMMARY

The message of this chapter is that quite a number of educational practices— ranging across ways of managing students and learning environments, teaching strategies or models of teaching, curriculum designs, dimensions of the learning environments of schools, and the use of technologies—can affect student learning. In our opinion, this array of tested alternatives should be part of the substance of staff development. The improvement of student achievement should always receive major attention within the system. We also stress that very few practitioners currently have mastered and, therefore, can use many of the practices described above. We are frequently surprised when we find that district policymakers believe that somehow, without training, teachers and administrators have developed a wide range of strategies. Rather, a good many teachers use a very narrow range of practices (Sirotnik, 1983; Goodlad & Klein, 1970; Medley, 1977) and expand that repertoire only when substantial and carefully designed training is provided. However, they can accomplish that quite easily when good conditions are provided.

part **III**

The Technology of Student Achievement through Staff Development

In chapters 6, 7, 8, and 9, we deal with the "technology" of staff development—the knowledge, procedures, and skills necessary for designing and managing school improvement initiatives.

To engage in intensive, continuous staff development requires not only sound policy decisions at all levels of the education enterprise and understanding/appreciation of the culture of the school but bodies of knowledge and skill to actually put in place a pervasive, dynamic system of professional growth. We envision a human resource development system embedded in every aspect of the school and completely enmeshed in the cycle of problem identification and problem solving.

The technical body of knowledge for staff development includes data collection and analysis for problem identification, location and evaluation of content to address identified needs, designing training, monitoring implementation, and conducting formative evaluation. In chapter 6, we examine the identification of needs and the selection of content for staff development programs, illustrating the process with examples of needs that various schools have identified for their student populations. In chapter 7, we look at the design of training and the organization of the workplace that makes it possible to put new content (curriculum, instruction, technology) in place. In chapter 8, we explore the procedures most likely to ensure implementation of new content—the "change" that is intended to address student needs. Lastly, in chapter 9, we discuss the design of formative evaluation systems that will provide timely feedback on effects of new programs and information to staffs for their ongoing decision-making processes.

chapter 6

Identifying Needs, Selecting Content

Proposition: Nearly all content should deal with the learning environment and take the form of an *inquiry* to improve it.

In this chapter we will focus on the selection of content for schoolwide
improvement initiatives, dealing with the individual and systemic more briefly.
As we deal with the process of selecting content, we make the assumption that
the organizational structures suggested in chapters 2 and 3 are in place. That
is, all teachers are members of study groups and, within those, can engage in
collaborative study, planning, and development with other members of
the groups. Within each school, the group leaders are organized in a school
improvement committee, and within the district, or clusters of schools in the
case of large districts, representatives from each school improvement council
are organized in a district or cluster staff development council. Within this
organizational structure the content for each of the substantive components—
individual, collective, and systemic—is selected and the programs are brought
into existence.

An important duty of the district committee is to engage in the study of
alternatives—the kinds of initiatives we have just discussed in chapters 4 and
5—and bring information to school councils and, through them, to study groups.
As our process unfolds, informed decision making will be critical. As this is
written, many teachers, schools, and school districts are not studying alternatives
that would have great promise for them simply because the information about
those alternatives has not been made available.

As many districts move to site-based management of school improvement,
district committees may want to allocate staff development funds in accordance

with district policy, with the largest percentage going to sites and lesser percentages allocated to the individual and district components of the staff development system.

CONTENT FOR THE INDIVIDUAL COMPONENT

The individual component is made up of an array of workshops and courses that teachers will select on the basis of their perception about what will benefit them and, through them, their students. The decision-making process needs to identify substantive candidates for the array and to make selections, get them operating, and enable teachers to enroll for them.

We suggest that three procedures be employed concurrently to generate the candidates for new content to be studied: those that tap teachers' perceptions of substance that will benefit them, those that teachers and other staff have the capability of offering to one another, and those created through research and development activities of the types described in chapters 4 and 5.

Perceptions of Need or Potential Benefit

These are obtained through the procedure that has become known throughout the profession as the "needs survey." Essentially, each teacher is asked to examine their curricular and instructional practices (what they teach, how they teach, and the instructional materials they use) and indicate whether there is content, teaching skills and strategies, or materials that they would like to study because they believe it would improve the quality of their instruction. It is important that people take a hard look at *all* the courses and curriculum areas they teach and that they consider content needs as well as needs for teaching and materials. In responding, each teacher looks at their content areas (for elementary teachers, content will include all of the basic curriculum areas—language arts, math, science, social studies) and answers the questions, "Can I think of any materials, knowledge of content, or instructional skills that would help me do a better job in this area? Which ones would have the highest priority for me?"

The study group leaders organize the product and take it to the school council, which further organizes it and forwards it to the district or cluster committee. That committee now has the task of sorting out the items that have been suggested and formulating what we will call the Teacher Request List.

Potential Providers

This procedure centers on identifying potential providers of service—teaching and administrative personnel and persons from local universities, teacher centers, intermediate agencies, and professional organizations. The personnel are asked if they are prepared to offer service to others and what it might be. They are asked to recommend others who might offer service. University departments, not only in education but in academic areas, are asked if they would like to provide service. The district committee asks school councils to canvass their personnel and approaches the other agencies and departments in the district for their ideas. The resulting product is added to the Teacher Request List and they are compared as well to determine which of the requests from the survey of perceived needs can be matched with a potential provider.

Suggestions from Research and Development

The study by the district council of alternatives from research and development should result in a third list of possibilities that can be compared with the other lists. The result will enable us to compare suggestions from the three sources and correlate them.

For example, it is useful to learn how potential providers line up with suggested content and with researched alternatives, for it allows us to see the feasibility of matching perceived needs with high-impact options for which potential staff are available.

The entire organized list is now sent back to the teachers to ascertain their perception of priorities. In addition to items that an individual has contributed in the early round of expression of needs and wants, each person now examines what has been suggested by others, potential providers, and the district committee. At this stage each person is asked to indicate what has the greatest appeal to them as individuals.

With that information in hand the council sets to work to assemble the offerings that will be made. Some popular items may have to be shelved because providers are not available. The council will consider whether to locate providers in some of those areas for the future, or to develop trainers by finding interested teachers and obtaining training for them. Time is a consideration—some promising ideas may require more time than can be feasibly arranged or some of the more extensive items may have to be saved for another year.

The eventual array of choices should be balanced among the study of teaching skills and strategies, content, and the exploration of instructional materials. Some items should be included that help people enhance their existing repertoire and some items should provide the opportunity for the learning of new material. Many districts reserve some places for items of personal interest (such as stress reduction or wellness programs) and possibilities of attendance at interesting conferences.

SELECTING CONTENT FOR
THE COLLECTIVE COMPONENT

Choosing content for a collaborative-change effort is a critical step in the school improvement process because, once it is selected, many people are committed to learning and implementing the new content. Whereas an individual can fairly easily change course in midstream if the content chosen is not addressing an identified need, for an entire staff to abandon a change effort can be both costly and damaging. The major difference between selecting content for individuals and a schoolwide or collective effort is a heavier reliance on data for decision making. Also, the distinction between individuals and school needs to be clear. In the past, we have observed districts where resources have been provided to schools but used as if individual preferences were the key, generating opportunities for individuals as volunteers rather than common directions with a commitment by all.

The selection of content is dictated by the need for change that a faculty perceives. The targets for change or improvement vary tremendously among schools, depending on the process a faculty employs to identify needs and to set priorities for addressing those needs. Generally faculties use a combination of perceptions ("What do we feel are our most pressing needs?") and data ("What do our test scores tell us?") to select targets for improvement. If the process results in a list of needs in which all items have equal weight, the list may grow to 15 or 20 items and include everything from reading and math achievement to parent involvement and neighborhood gang activity. If the faculty then proceeds to select content or "treatments" to address all identified needs, the resulting plethora of change programs makes it virtually impossible to mount a coherent, facultywide approach to any single problem. If, on the other hand, a faculty can focus on a top priority in a way that simultaneously acknowledges both the presence and importance of everything on the list and the near impossibility of addressing all of them effectively at one time, it is much better positioned to succeed in changing something.

In our experience, the selection of content to address identified needs frequently receives much less attention than other parts of the school improvement process. Perhaps faculties, with limited time for collaborative planning and decision making, inadvertently use most of their time in reaching a decision about what needs to be addressed and have little time left to examine their options. Or perhaps, by this time in the process, people are tired of talking and eager to begin doing something.

Beliefs immediately come into play when staffs begin the process of collecting data to determine needed improvements and/or changes in a school's educational program. Faculties (as well as individuals) have beliefs and theories about causation of perceived problems that direct both the data collection and analysis as well as the eventual selection of content to address problems.

For example, in School A, state reading tests show the mean of the school to be below the twentieth percentile of all students taking the test. Faculty concern for poor reading test performance is fueled by perceived pressure from the community and state to improve test scores. Faculty feel their competence and effectiveness are judged by these scores, and although they acknowledge that their students are reading at levels far below what they would like to see, they believe that the test unfairly penalizes schools with their particular demographic characteristics. The staff of School A elects to collect no further data at the site before choosing a program to address the identified need. The need, however, is identified as "reading test scores" rather than "reading." Consequently, the content selected is an individualized computer program in which each child spends a specified time weekly on specific skills presented and tested in the state test format. The computer lab is operated by an instructional aide who carefully keeps track of each child's progress through the battery of mini-tests until he/she has successfully completed/mastered all the skills components of the program. Meanwhile, reading instruction in the class-room proceeds unchanged.

School B, in the same district, also scored poorly on the state reading tests. School B's faculty likewise felt community and district pressure to improve test scores but believed that, although their students certainly entered school with little reading readiness, good readers would perform well on the state reading test (or on any reading test, for that matter). Their beliefs led them to identify their problem as "reading" rather than "test taking skills" or "test content," which led them to seek additional information about their students' reading behavior. Individualized reading tests administered to a sample of students provided considerable diagnostic information. A study of successful programs yielded useful information about processes that appeared to help beginning readers become independent readers. Recommendations about the amount of independent reading students should be doing out of school were studied. As a result of their additional data collection and study of options, this faculty adopted content for their staff development program that included: 1) instruction in the teaching of reading for all teachers, 2) the training of tutors for an after-school program, and 3) the adoption of a program to increase out of school reading.

In another district, secondary schools were asked to collect data on their failure rates and discipline referrals in an effort to stem the tide of dropouts. All secondary schools collected the data requested (actually, schools already had data on both discipline referrals and grade distributions but had not analyzed it as a source of information for determining directions for school improvement). Data on failure rates, discipline referrals, and dropout rates were similar for all secondary schools in the district (e.g., all had high rates of failure, discipline problems and dropouts). Depending on each school's interpretation of this data, however, the identified needs varied dramatically. One school, for example, wrote a grant proposal requesting funds for additional security apparatus and personnel; the school's identified problem was the high-crime neighborhood in which it resided. A second school embarked upon a parent-involvement program that entailed notifying parents immediately if students were absent or tardy; and a third school adopted a cooperative instructional strategy, reasoning that class-room practices that decreased the isolation and pressure experienced by students and increased their chances for success in the classroom would reduce discipline referrals in the classroom.

Clearly, from very similar data faculties can draw quite disparate conclusions about the causes of identified problems, and these collective attributions dictate the "content" that will be selected to address identified needs.

These examples illustrate some of the complexity schools face when determining content appropriate for their identified needs. Selecting content for school improvement initiatives is not a simple process of matching problems with solutions. Rather it is a complex dynamic in which the school culture filters data through its norms, values, beliefs, and theories to define problems and attribute causation; thus, a school determines the types of content that might appropriately address the problems as understood and agreed upon by a staff.

Our recommendations for selecting content begin with the proposal that staffs identify competing hypotheses regarding causation for identified problems and thus alternative solutions. If a staff identifies its primary problem as "discipline" without exploring the actual occurrences of student misbehavior and possible causes for it, the choice of interventions will necessarily be narrowed. Once data at the site have been examined and needs identified and discussed, the search for appropriate content can begin. Again, the search for content is somewhat more heavily reliant on "objective" sources of data than when selecting content for individual needs. If an entire staff is to expend time and energy in a collective effort to address a school need, it should have some confidence that the content selected has a fairly high probability of accomplishing its objective. The district committee can serve as a resource to the school committee as they search for content and providers that align with their specific needs. In some cases, the district committee is able to coordinate efforts among schools that have similar needs for training.

Some of the options we have observed include:

The Renovation of a Curriculum Area

In elementary schools the generalist teacher provides most of the instruction in the basic areas and it can be argued that some area should always be in a process of renovation. Reading, language arts and literature, social studies, science, arithmetic, and the other areas are candidates. Generally the curriculum areas are not in equally good shape, and it is not difficult to find one that could bear improvement. In secondary schools the offerings by grade are often convenient foci. For example, in one year freshman courses might be considered; in another, advanced placement courses; in another, the articulation of courses within a subject. Cross-subject strategies are also feasible. Reading and writing in the content areas has been a popular staff development focus for some faculties.

Teaching and Learning Strategies

A faculty can take a strategy, such as cooperative learning, mnemonics, or one of the other models discussed in chapter 5, and study and learn to use it together. Some faculties are currently studying ways of teaching every subject in such a way that the thinking ability of the students is improved (Perkins, 1984; Costa, 1985). It is feasible for people to add one or two teaching strategies to their repertoires in any given year and the possibilities are great enough to provide food for instructional improvement for many years.

Technology

We have already mentioned the computer. The use of videotape and broadcast television are other applications of technology to instruction. Some schools have positively impacted their instructional programs by incorporating resource-based offerings for their students, thus enabling the study of topics and courses that cannot be offered by the faculty. In small high schools, for example, the number of offerings is necessarily limited and resource-based courses provide many additional opportunities.

Attending to Special Populations

Population-oriented initiatives for school improvement have become popular in recent years as the states and the federal government have provided resources for students having special needs (generally known as "special education"), students of varying cultural backgrounds, students believed to have special talents, bilingual students, and so on. Most of these initiatives are difficult to implement properly. "Pull-out" programs, in which students are removed from "regular" class for special attention, have been particularly unsatisfactory, because they disrupt continuity and often generate fragmented programs for the students in question. Many of these programs need attention.

The school council needs to lead the faculty to a narrowing of the list of possibilities and the selection of the one or two areas that will receive attention during any given year. It is *very* important for the focus to be narrowed. There is a tendency to get too many projects going at once, with the result that none gets done well.

As each school settles on its candidates for improvement efforts, it should forward them to the district committee, which then has the task of trying to find staff development support for the initiatives. They need to search for consultants and instructional personnel from the same sources as are tapped for the individual component. Possibly teachers from some of the schools can obtain training, which they can bring back to their faculties. Possibly the district cadre needs to consider some of the suggested areas. The committee also must assess costs and decide how much assistance can be given to particular schools. The eventual decisions need to be a result of negotiation.

THE SYSTEMIC COMPONENT

Most districts have not been organized to accompany systemwide initiatives in curriculum, instruction, or technology with the staff development to ensure a healthy implementation (Crandall et al., 1982; Fullan & Pomfret, 1977; Fullan &

Park, 1981; Huberman & Miles, 1986; Joyce, Hersh, & McKibbin, 1983). In the area of curriculum, for example, it has been thoroughly demonstrated that district committees can produce curriculum guides and order and deliver textbooks and other materials to classrooms; however, implementation, including the use of new textbooks in many cases, often doesn't occur because the staff development component has not been extensive enough. There are two reasons for this state of affairs: One is that educators have simply not understood the amounts and types of study that are necessary for people to learn how to employ new procedures and new content in the classroom (see chapters 7 and 8). The second is that it is difficult to make the hard decisions to narrow the district focus in any given period. Ideas for school improvement abound and it is not uncommon for districts to have a dozen or two dozen initiatives going at one time, none of them supported substantially enough for a systemic implementation. Coordination has been a problem. We have observed all too many districts where a large number of departments or other organizational units generate initiatives without the knowledge that their counterparts are generating similar ones. Thus the curriculum units, departments of elementary, secondary, and special education, staff development offices, the department serving the gifted and talented, and many others generate initiatives and communicate them to schools and teachers haphazardly.

The answer we propose is to replicate the process we have described above for identifying the focus of school-based initiatives but with the purpose of identifying the one or two important initiatives that will have center stage in the district for a year or two. Teachers, study groups, schools, and committee members need to put forth their candidates. Lists must be developed and culled. The committee needs to ask whether the district has unfinished business with past initiatives or has committed to expenditures for facilities and equipment that will not be used well without staff development. Have videotape machines been purchased for schools? How is the computer doing? Have additions been made to the library or has it acquired access to electronic libraries or become stocked with self-instructional programs? It is even possible that the district initiative for a given year will be the same as that selected by one or more schools in the district.

Essentially the list we generated when thinking about the possibilities for schools can serve the same purpose when thinking about the district. Curriculum, technology, and teaching skills and strategies can all become a focus in the larger organization.

It is within the schools that the district initiatives will have their implementation, so communication is essential during the decision-making process and in the planning of implementation. For example, were a teaching strategy like cooperative learning to become a district focus, the result would be training for a large number of people in many sites and much hard work in every school to implement the strategy. Or, if school social climate became the focus, then all school faculties would have to learn to examine their social climates and make plans for improvements. It may be that many districts would be wise to plan their initiatives no less than a year in advance so that they can develop the strong cadres that will be necessary to support the training.

SUMMARY

Content for the clinical, collective, and systemic components of staff development programs may be similar; that is, curriculum, instruction, or technology might serve as the substance of study for individuals, school faculties or entire districts. Decision-making processes for the various components, however, will vary with their goals. Individuals will be evaluating personal needs while schools and districts will determine needs for groups of students. Adequate training will be the key to the success of all three components. Hence, let us turn our attention to the design of training and to the research that now enables us to plan staff development programs that have a very high probability of succeeding.

chapter 7

The Design of Training and Peer Coaching

Proposition: All teachers can learn just about any teaching strategy or practice that anyone has thus far developed.

In the early 1980s, we published a review of research on training design and a set of hypotheses relating to transfer of new content/behavior to classroom practice (Joyce & Showers, 1980). In the 15 years since, two notable changes have occurred in the field of staff development: First, the duration and intensity of many training events have greatly increased, including various forms of follow-up and continuing technical support; and second, one-shot events tend to be carefully prefaced with "This session is for 'awareness' only." In other words, greater clarity has been achieved between objectives that entail the acquisition of information and those that include changes in educational practice.

We also have experienced substantial changes in our conception of and orientation to staff development in the years since this book first appeared. Influenced by the work of organizational and change theorists (Fullan, 1990; Huberman, 1992; Seashore-Louis & Miles, 1990) and by our own numerous attempts to work with districts, schools, teams of teachers, and individuals to increase student growth in all its manifestations (Joyce et al., 1989; Joyce et al., 1994; Showers, 1989), we have come to view the school as the organizational unit most capable of facilitating student growth; and we have struggled with ways of impacting that organization to achieve its desired student outcomes. In the process, we have continued to refine a training design that enables teachers to learn and use new knowledge and behaviors that translate into success for more students. The colleagueship of many gifted teachers has been invaluable in this pursuit as we have studied and experimented together to make training more productive. We have also evolved in our thinking about the role and function of collaboration in service of school improvement. At this point, training and peer coaching have become so inseparable in our minds and our practice that we have treated them together in a single chapter in this edition.

PROVIDING THE CONDITIONS FOR LEARNING

Our first goal is the design of training that enables people to learn knowledge and skills new to them and transfer that knowledge and skill to active classroom practice; this means identifying principles for designing programs that will result in a high level of skill and its implementation. The second goal is a search for ways of conducting training so that it increases the aptitude for learning skills more easily and effectively. In other words, we want to design training so that people learn to become more effective learners. The review in this chapter is oriented around those two goals. As we did in chapters 4 and 5, we will often report results in effect sizes (standard deviation units) to make comparisons between treatments clearer.

Training Design

What do we expect good training to accomplish? Aside from the content—academic knowledge, approaches to curriculum and instruction, how students develop and learn, technologies, etc.—what is the nature of the behavior necessary to put that content to work in the classroom?

Content.   Figure 7.1 illustrates the range of possibilities for selecting objectives. The left side of the figure identifies types of training outcomes and the top right side of the figure describes the content of the training in relation to the teachers' existing repertoire. If the content consists of knowledge and skill that teachers generally possess to some extent but which need refinement for optimal classroom use, decisionmakers will be working in the left side of the matrix. For example, training that focuses on teacher praise and encouragement of student work or on time allowed for students to respond to questions would be classified as "refining of existing skill." Presumably, teachers already provide verbal encouragement to students for their efforts and ask questions during classroom recitations. The object of training becomes a more appropriate use of existing behaviors.

If, on the other hand, the content represents for teachers an addition to their repertoire—knowledge and skill not currently known about or practiced in their instruction—the right side of the matrix will be used. Obviously, "new repertoire" must be defined in relation to the knowledge and skills of individuals—what is new to one person may exist in the repertoire of another. Research on classroom teaching, however, has fairly well described how most teachers teach and we can be fairly certain that few teachers use the curricular

Training Outcomes	Content			
	Redefining of Existing Knowledge and Skills		Addition to Repertoire	
	Simple	Complex	Simple	Complex
Awareness/Knowledge: Theories, Practices, Curricula				
Attitude Change: Self, Children, Academic Content				
Skill Development: Discrete Behaviors, Stategies				
Transfer of Training: Consistent Use, Appropriate Use				

FIGURE 7.1 Decision-making matrix: Selecting objectives

and instructional models described in chapter 5—such as the more complex varieties of cooperative learning and group investigation, key-word and link-word memory strategies, synectics, and inductive thinking (Sirotnik, 1983; Medley, 1977; Goodlad & Klein 1970; Good, Grouws, & Ebmeier, 1983, etc.). On the other hand, most teachers praise students, correct them, orient students to lessons, provide practice in class and assign homework; so training that concentrates on those practices is for most persons an elaboration and strengthening of existing practices.

In addition to deciding whether content will be a refining of existing knowledge and skill or an addition to repertoire, designers should also estimate the difficulty level of knowledge and skills to be learned. Placing content on a simple/complex continuum will clarify later decisions about the intensity and duration of training experiences.

Types of Outcomes. The outcomes expected of training have implications both for the design and evaluation of training. Potential outcomes are:

1. the knowledge or awareness of educational theories and practices, new curricula, or academic content;
2. changes in attitudes toward self (role perception changes), children (minorities, handicapped, gifted), academic content (science, English as a second language, math);

3. development of skill (the ability to perform discrete behaviors, such as designing and delivering questions of various cognitive levels, or the ability to perform clusters of skills in specific patterns, as in a synectics exercise); or

4. transfer of training and "executive control" (the consistent and appropriate use of new skills and strategies for classroom instruction).

Given the objectives of any element of a program, the next task is to design training for maximum probability that the desired effects will be achieved.

Training Components.   Several elements are at our disposal. The first component is an exploration of theory through discussions, readings, lectures, etc.; this is necessary for an understanding of the rationale behind a skill or strategy and the principles that govern its use. Study of theory facilitates skill acquisition by increasing one's discrimination of the demonstrations, by providing a mental image to guide practice and clarify feedback, and by promoting the attainment of executive control.

The demonstration or modeling of skill is the second component; it greatly facilitates learning. Skills can be demonstrated in settings that simulate the workplace, either mediated through film or videotape, or conducted live in the training setting. Demonstrations can be mixed with explanation; the theory and modeling components need not be conducted separately. In fact, they have reciprocal effects. Mastery of the rationale of the skill facilitates discrimination, and modeling facilitates the understanding of underlying theories by illustrating them in action.

The third component is the practice of skill under simulated conditions. The closer the training setting approximates the workplace the more transfer is facilitated. Considerable amounts of skill can be developed, however, in settings far removed from and different from the workplace. "Peer teaching" (practice with other teachers) even has advantages. It provides experience as a "student," enables trainees to profit from one another's ideas and skill, and clarifies mistakes. Peer teaching and practice with small groups of children are safer settings for exploration than a full classroom. How much practice is needed depends, of course, on the complexity of the skill. To bring a model of teaching of medium complexity under control requires 20 or 25 trials in the classroom over a period of about eight or ten weeks. The more simple skills, or those more similar to previously developed ones, will require less practice to develop and consolidate than those that are more complex or different from the teachers' current repertoire.

Peer coaching, the fourth component, is the collaborative work of teachers to solve the problems/questions that arise during implementation; it begins in training settings and continues in the workplace following initial training. Peer coaching provides both support for the community of teachers attempting to master new skills and the time for planning and lesson development so essential to changes in curriculum and instruction.

RESEARCH ON TRAINING

Training, of course, does not exist outside a context. As described in earlier chapters, a process must be in place to decide what will be the substance of the training, who will provide training, when and where the training will be held and for what duration. The norms of the workplace impinge on the receptivity of participants to various configurations of training experiences, as do labor-relations histories and interpersonal relationships among participants. We have less data on the impact of many of these environmental and governance variables on the effectiveness of training than we have on actual training components. However, we recommend the participatory governance modes described in chapters 2, 3, and 6 to increase understanding of both the content and why it was selected for each component.

Also, as we discussed in chapter 3, we believe that cohesiveness and strong leadership in the school are critical to the success of training. The best trainers, working with the most relevant and powerful content, will find little success or receptivity in poor organizational climates. However, good climates and high motivation will not substitute for well-designed training. Fortunately, we can assert that research and experience have reached the point where we can state that, for specific training outcomes, certain training components or combinations of components provide optimal conditions for learning. Essentially, nearly all teachers can master a wide range of teaching skills and strategies provided that the training is well-designed and the climate of the school facilitates and promotes cooperative study and practice.

Hence, designers of training must answer several questions before planning any training experience. For whom is the training intended and what is expected to result from the training? Is follow-up to training built into schools as a permanent structure or must follow-up be planned and delivered as part of the training package? Does the content of the training represent new learning for participants or is it an attempt to refine existing knowledge and skills?

Also, designers need to decide which training components will be used and how they will be combined. These components include the presentation of information or theory about the topic of the training, live and mediated demonstration or modeling of new skills and teaching models, and opportunities for practice of new skills and strategies in the training setting as well as in the workplace. Peer coaching of new skills and strategies, which largely occurs in the workplace, ideally is taught and practiced in the training setting as well.

Research on training provides some interesting insights into the efficacy of various training components and, particularly, combinations of them (Bennett, 1987; Showers, Joyce, & Bennett, 1987) (see Table 7.1). Information or theory-only treatments increase knowledge by an effect size of about .50 between them (one-half of a standard deviation on a normal curve), whereas theory combined with demonstrations, practice, and feedback results in an effect size of 1.31 for knowledge, compared with about .63 if presentations alone are employed (Bennett, 1987).

TABLE 7.1   Effect sizes for training outcomes by training components

Training Components and Combinations	Training Outcomes		
	Knowledge	*Skill*	*Transfer of Training*
Information	.63	.35	.00
Theory	.15	.50	.00
Demonstration	1.65	.26	.00
Theory Demonstration	.66	.86	.00
Theory Practice	1.15		.00
Theory Demonstration Practice		.72	.00
Theory Demonstration Practice Feedback	1.31	1.18	.39
Theory Demonstration Practice Feedback Coaching	2.71	1.25	1.68

When skill is the desired outcome of training, the advantage of the combinations is equally clear. Theory or demonstration alone results in effect sizes for skill of around .5 and .26 respectively for refining existing skills, lower for new skills. Theory, demonstration, and practice combined result in an effect size of approximately .7 for skill, whereas theory, demonstration, practice, and feedback combined result in an effect size of 1.18. When in-class coaching is added to the theory, demonstration, practice, and feedback, skill continues to rise.

Strangely, the question of transfer of training has been asked much less frequently in research on training than has the question regarding skill acquisition. Consequently, many fewer studies of training have measured transfer effects than have measured skill acquisition. Perhaps the assumption has been that skill, once developed, would automatically be used in classroom instruction. Recent analyses of the literature on training confirm what many trainers, teacher educators, and supervisors have long suspected—transfer of learned knowledge and skill is by no means a sure bet. In studies that have asked transfer questions (e.g., did participants use new skills in the classroom, did they use them appropriately, did they integrate new skills with existing repertoire, and was there long-term retention of the products of training?), several findings emerge. First, the gradual addition of training elements does not appear to impact transfer noticeably (effect size of .00 for information or theory; theory plus demonstration; theory, demonstration and feedback; effect size of .39 for theory, demonstration, practice, and feedback). However a large and dramatic increase in transfer of training—effect size 1.68—occurs when in-class coaching is added to an initial training experience comprised of theory explanation, demonstrations, and practice with feedback.

We have concluded from these data that teachers can acquire new knowledge and skill and use it in their instructional practice when provided with adequate opportunities to learn. We have hypothesized, further, that fully elaborated training systems develop a "learning to learn" aptitude and that, in fact, individuals learn more efficiently over the long-term by developing the metacognitions that enable self-teaching in settings where essential training elements are missing.

Implications for Staff Development Practice

We have drawn several conclusions from the research on training that have implications for staff development programs serving individuals, schools, and systems.

First, regardless of who initiates a training program, participants must have sufficient opportunity to develop skill that they can eventually practice in classroom settings.

Second, if the content of training is new to trainees, training will have to be more extensive than for substance that is relatively familiar.

Third, if transfer of training is the objective, training must include the facilitation and structure for collaborative relationships that enable teachers to solve the implementation problems.

SKILLS TEACHERS NEED AS LEARNERS TO MASTER NEW KNOWLEDGE AND SKILLS

As research on effective teaching yields more data, it becomes increasingly urgent that teachers be able to use the products of that research. Designing training that maximizes opportunities for mastery of new information and skills is an important task. Are there "learning-to-learn" skills which some teachers develop in or bring to the training setting, and if so, can they be developed in others? And what have we learned from training about conditions that nurture and develop "learning-to-learn" skills?

Ripple & Drinkwater (1981, p. 1949), in their review of research on transfer of learning, note the following about learning-to-learn:

> The concept of learning-to-learn implies that development of strategies or learning is a result of practice with a variety of problems. Preliminary practice on tasks that will transfer positively to performance on different criterion tasks is required for the development of learning-to-learn strategies.

From research on training and curriculum implementation, school improvement and change, and our personal training experiences, we have identified several practices, attitudes, and skills that appear to facilitate learning aptitude.

Persistence

Practice of new skills and behaviors increases both skill and comfort with the unfamiliar. The benefits of practice are well known to educators and are often reiterated in training settings. Yet many trainees try a new skill or practice only once or else never try it at all. The "driving through" initial trials in which performance is awkward and effectiveness appears to decrease rather than increase is one characteristic that appears to differentiate successful from unsuccessful learners. Avoidance of the difficult and awkward is not unique to teachers as learners, as golfers, skiers, and tennis players can attest. Changing one's own behavior is difficult, especially when one has fairly dependable strategies already fully developed.

Acknowledgment of the Transfer Problem

Mastery of new skills, especially when they differ substantially from existing skills, is rarely sufficient for implementation in classroom practice. Introducing a new procedure or teaching strategy into an existing repertoire of instructional behaviors generally creates dislocation and discomfort. Yet, considerable practice of new behaviors is required if teachers are not only to become technically proficient with them but also to integrate them sensibly and appropriately with existing behaviors. Teachers who understand the necessity for the additional effort required if new behaviors are to be merged with existing instructional practices and who expend the extra effort to think through where the new behaviors fit and for what they are effective are much more likely to implement an innovation than teachers who don't acknowledge and address this learning task. Understanding that transfer of training is a separate learning task is a metacognitive condition that appears to increase efficiency in skill acquisition as well as eventual transfer of learning. Both trainers and learners have tended to underestimate the cognitive aspects of implementation—teachers have assumed they have only to see something in order to use it skillfully and appropriately, and trainers have devoted little or no time during training to attacking the transfer problem.

Teaching New Behaviors to Students

Part of the difficulty in introducing new curricula or teaching processes into the classroom is student discomfort with change. Students quickly learn the rules of the classroom game and how to respond to the demands of the learning environment. Those who are successful with existing conditions may be particularly reluctant to have the rules changed. When new procedures are introduced, students may exert pressure on the teacher to return to the familiar patterns of behavior with which they are comfortable, or, if not comfortable, which they understand well. Consequently, if a teacher has typically run a brisk recitation in which students were asked rapid-fire recall questions over material they have previously read or been introduced to, students have learned how to signal they know the answers, how to avoid being called on when they don't know the answers, and what to expect in terms of feedback (e.g., immediate information regarding the correctness of responses, the message that there is a "right" answer). If this teacher then introduces an inquiry process into the classroom which shifts responsibility to students for collecting and analyzing data and setting and testing hypotheses, and knowledge is viewed as emergent and tentative, student discomfort with the new demands may encourage the teacher to abandon the new strategy after one or two trials. When this happens, neither teacher nor students develop sufficient expertise with the new strategy to evaluate potential benefits and uses.

Teachers who directly teach the requisite skills to students, including both the cognitive and social tasks required by specific innovations, are much more likely to integrate successfully the new behaviors with existing instructional repertoire.

Meeting the Cognitive Demands of Innovations

Teachers frequently have complained that their training has overemphasized "theory" and neglected the practical or clinical aspects of teaching. It is probable, however, that without a thorough grounding in the theory of an innovation, or what Fullan calls "deep understanding," that teachers will be unable to use new skills and strategies in any but a most superficial manner. Understanding of the theory underlying specific behaviors enables flexible and appropriate use of the behaviors in multiple situations and prevents the often ludicrous following of "recipes" for teaching. Thus, a teacher who wishes to organize presentations or entire courses with advance organizers must understand the conceptual framework of the material to be so organized and be able to extract and organize concepts into a hierarchy of ideas. The teacher who wishes to apply the linkword method to the acquisition of foreign language vocabulary must understand the research from cognitive psychology regarding the role of association in memory. And the teacher who wishes to implement a contingency management system must completely understand the nature of reinforcers and how they operate.

Teachers who master the theory undergirding new behaviors that they wish to use in their classrooms implement those behaviors in greater congruence with the researched and tested ideal and are more likely to replicate results obtained in research settings with their own students.

Productive Use of Peers

During the last few years, research on training has documented the benefits of peers helping peers in the implementation of innovations. Regular, structured interaction between or among peers over substantive content is one of the hallmarks of a profession and is viewed by other professionals as essential professional nourishment rather than a threat to autonomy. A family dentist does not hesitate to consult a root canal specialist in the midst of an examination if he or she feels the need, nor does a hairdresser feel constrained in getting a second opinion regarding the type of permanent needed for a particular head of hair. This propensity to seek the advice and assistance of other professionals was vividly illustrated when one of the leading cardiologists in the world explained to us his decision-making process in the operating room. Fifteen medical personnel (surgeons, anesthesiologists, cardiologists) discussed the pros and cons of reopening a patient's chest versus using drug therapy following by-pass surgery in which the patient's heart was fibrillating. Rather than feeling embarrassment that he had asked for other opinions, the cardiologist seemed to assume we would find comfort in the fact that he had consulted the other professionals on the spot.

Teachers also have begun to appreciate the benefits of mutual study and problem solving in relation to professional competence. The programs that build into training and follow-up of training opportunities for collegial work on the mastery and use of innovative practices and content contribute not only to the individual competence of teachers participating in them but also build their sense of membership in a profession. Furthermore, teachers who assume a proactive stance in relation to self-help peer relationships appear to gain much more from such programs than do teachers who merely "submit" to them. Observing other professionals work is a valuable learning experience in itself, and collaborative analysis of teaching and planning for appropriate use of an innovation usually results in more practice and more focused practice. Finally, the proactive teachers who can and will state what they need—what they understand and what they don't—rather than relying on the mind-reading capability of their peers are likely to benefit more from professional collegial study than teachers who are passive in the relationship.

Flexibility

Flexibility appears to be a highly functional attribute of teachers in training. During the first stage of learning when trainees are introduced to new content and/or processes, traditional thinking about curriculum and instruction may have to be reoriented. If training consists of learning an inductive thinking strategy, for example, current materials may have to be reorganized or supplemented in order to provide students with data rather than conclusions and generalizations. Teachers may also have to rethink their roles as instructors in the classroom. If they have conceived of their roles as information givers, instructional processes that transfer greater responsibility to students for their own learning may require rethinking of educational goals, ways, and means. In the transfer stage of learning, when teachers are attempting to use new content and processes appropriately in the instructional setting, a reorientation to students may be necessary. When new and different expectations are held for students, teachers must figure out what learning skills students possess and which must be directly taught in order for students to operate within different frameworks. Teacher flexibility in the learning process can be summed up as a spirit of inquiry, a willingness to experiment with their own behavior, and an openness to evidence that alternatives have something to offer.

COACHING

In general, training is expected to result in sufficient skill that practice can be sustained in the classroom and transferred into the working repertoires of teachers. While coaching programs can support the implementation of individual or system initiatives, their organization and institutionalization happen at the school level. As we continue to experiment with the design of coaching, the major purpose of peer-coaching programs remains the implementation of innovations to the extent that determination of effects on students is possible. In the past few years, we have become increasingly convinced that creating the conditions that nurture learning and growth requires a much greater organizational innovation than the creation of peer-coaching study teams alone. The organization cannot remain passive in relation to the study teams it shelters, but rather must actively support the norms of experimentation, collaborative planning and development, and implementation of content aimed at collective goals. A recent study of the functioning of peer-coaching study teams in schools where everyone is a member of a study team as compared with schools that have only one team operating as a microcosm within the larger organization (Murphy, 1992) suggests the need for shared effort as well as shared goals.

In the following pages we will revisit what we mean by peer-coaching study teams, their structure and function; compare and contrast them with other forms of "coaching"; and share what we believe are the next steps in the evolution of training and coaching most likely to increase the power of school improvement efforts.

The Evolution of Coaching

Understanding of how education personnel can help each other has come from a variety of sources. Only within the last 25 years, however, have the processes of training and implementation come under close scrutiny. By the early 1970s, it had become recognized that a great many efforts to improve schools, even when well funded and approved by the public, had encountered great difficulty and achieved very low levels of implementation. Since that time, innovators, organizational specialists, curriculum development personnel, and technologists concerned with such innovations as computers in the classroom have behaved much less naively. The nature of training, organizational climate, curriculum implementation, the processes by which teachers learn, and the organization of the school district itself have been attended to with much greater care. We draw on all of these for our knowledge about how all personnel can work together to ensure that skill development and the mastery of content result from training, and that personnel are skillful in the collaborative effort to transfer those products into active educational practice.

History, Pre–1980.   We acknowledge the work of many of our colleagues in the development of coaching programs for transfer of training. The concept of teachers as trainers has been explored by Bentzen (1974), Devaney and Thorn

(1975), and Sharon and Hertz-Lazarowitz (1982), among others. Berman and McLaughlin (1975) noted the importance of in-class assistance and teachers observing other teachers for effective educational change programs. Fullan and Pomfret (1977) cited the importance of training and administrative support in the implementation of curricula.

The work most similar to ours is that of Sharon and Hertz-Lazarowitz (1982). They provided extensive initial training (52 hours) to teachers learning a complex new teaching strategy and supported the initial training with consultant-assisted self-help teams composed of three or four teachers. The teams engaged in cooperative planning of teaching processes and content, mutual observation of teaching, and feedback by teammates to the teacher being observed. Their teacher self-help teams were developed on the basis of earlier work by Nelson (1971) and Roper, Deal, and Dornbusch (1976). In the second year of their project, 65 percent of the participating classroom teachers were using small group teaching (group investigation) regularly and appropriately.

As we studied the work of Sharan and his associates, we were struck by the thoroughness and duration of training, the consistency of in-class follow-up, and particularly by the help provided by peers to each other as they attempted to implement a teaching process quite different from their normal practice.

History, 1980–1995.   During the past 15 years, our understanding of how we learn new behaviors and put them into practice has continuously evolved, both as a result of work by colleagues in schools and universities and our own efforts with teachers and schools.

When we first advanced the notion of coaching (Joyce & Showers, 1980), we had just completed an exhaustive review of literature on training and presented our findings as a set of hypotheses about types of training likely to result in various levels of impact. The training components discussed in that early work were guided by what was then present in the literature, for example, presentation of theory, modeling or demonstration, practice, structured and open-ended feedback, and in-class assistance with transfer. Given the state of knowledge about training in 1980, we believed that when teachers were attempting to think about and refine their current practice, "modeling, practice under simulated conditions, and practice in the classroom, combined with feedback" (p. 384) would be the most productive training design. When teachers were attempting to master new curricula and approaches to teaching, we hypothesized that continued technical assistance of some form at the classroom level would be essential for adding new practices to existing repertoires.

In the early 1980s, we formally investigated the latter hypothesis in studies designed to explore the impact of coaching on long-term implementation, following initial training in new content (Showers, 1982; 1984). We found that continuing technical assistance, whether provided by an outside expert or by peer experts resulted in much greater classroom implementation than was achieved by teachers who shared initial training but did not have the long-term support of coaching. These early studies structured the coaching process by pairing teachers with an outside consultant or an expert peer, the assumption being that the coach would have to have greater expertise in the new content if the relationship were to be productive. We were heavily influenced by the literature on supervisory practices (Goldhammer, 1969; Hunter, 1980) and feedback (Bondi, 1970; Borg et al., 1969; Orme, 1966; Ronnestad, 1977) and struggled to create the kind of structured feedback that appeared to facilitate skill development.

We can divide the results of our early studies of coaching into two categories: 1) facilitation of transfer of training and 2) development of norms of collegiality and experimentation. Furthermore, coaching appeared to contribute to transfer of training in five ways.

1. Coached teachers generally practiced new strategies more frequently and developed greater skill in the actual moves of a new teaching strategy than did uncoached teachers who had experienced identical initial training (Showers, 1982). Apparently, the support and encouragement provided by peers while attempting new teaching strategies helps to sustain practice through the often awkward stages of implementing different teaching practices and teaching students how to respond to them. Even though uncoached teachers had shared 30 hours of training with coached teachers, they tended to practice the strategies little or not at all following training, despite their stated intentions to use the new models of teaching for classroom instruction.

2. Coached teachers used their newly learned strategies more appropriately than uncoached teachers in terms of their own instructional objectives and the theories of specific models of teaching (Showers, 1982; 1984). Coached teachers had opportunities to discuss with each other instructional objectives, the strategies that theoretically were best designed to accomplish those objectives, and the types of curricular materials that would be needed for specific strategies. Consequently, they experimented with new instructional strategies in their own curriculum areas more quickly than uncoached teachers and shared lessons and materials with each other early in the coaching process. Uncoached teachers, on the other hand, tended to practice in their classrooms using lessons they had seen as demonstrations or in peer practice during initial training sessions. Once they had exhausted those possibilities, they had difficulty finding appropriate occasions for use in their own curriculum areas and tended to quit practicing. Interestingly, however, regular interviews revealed their continuing intention to use the strategies as soon as they had time to think through their potential applications.

3. Coached teachers exhibited greater long-term retention of knowledge about and skill with strategies in which they had been coached and, as a group, increased the appropriateness of use of new teaching models over time (Baker & Showers, 1984). Six to nine months after training in several new models of teaching, coached teachers had retained, and in several instances, increased their technical mastery of the teaching strategies. Uncoached teachers, however, were in many cases unable to even demonstrate the new strategies after that period of time had elapsed. They were as surprised as we were by the loss of skill,

although in retrospect we all should have realized that disuse over a spring, summer, and fall time period would lead to skill loss.

4. In our study of peer coaching (Showers, 1984), coached teachers were much more likely than uncoached teachers to teach new models of teaching to their students, ensuring that students understood the purpose of the strategy and the behaviors expected of them when using the strategy. For example, students of coached teachers were more likely to understand the nature and definition of concepts, metaphors, and analogies and were therefore more able to operate independently with concept attainment and synectics teaching strategies. These students not only had more experience (practice) with the strategies but had been provided direct instruction in component model skills. Students of uncoached teachers, on the other hand, had insufficient practice with the strategies to develop skill and confidence with them. Therefore, when their teachers occasionally attempted one of the new strategies, the more outspoken students were likely to suggest that they not waste time with the new strategy but rather conduct the lesson in ways with which they were all familiar and, by implication, competent.

5. Finally, coached teachers in our studies exhibited clearer cognitions with regard to the purposes and uses of the new strategies, as revealed through interviews, lesson plans, and classroom performance than did uncoached teachers (Showers, 1982; 1984). The frequent peer discussions regarding appropriate use of strategies, objectives for which specific models were more suited, experiments with use of strategies in ways different from those studied in training, design of lessons and materials, etc. seemed to enable coached teachers to think with the new strategies in ways that the uncoached teachers never exhibited. Uncoached teachers who did occasionally use the trained models of teaching tended not to depart, at least consciously, from the exact forms and applications they had experienced in training. Therefore, if in training the synectics strategy was demonstrated as a pre-writing activity and organizer for writing, uncoached teachers were unlikely to apply synectics to problem-solving situations. Or, if an inquiry strategy was demonstrated with science content, uncoached teachers were less likely to apply the strategy to investigation of social policies or questions in anthropology and literature.

Current Practice.   In the mid-1980s, our attention turned to school improvement and the application of training and coaching technologies to schoolwide initiatives for change. These efforts presented quite different circumstances than work with groups of volunteer teachers pursuing their individual interests in curriculum and instruction. Working with entire schools necessitated collaboration with staffs to determine the most pressing needs of their students, to select content appropriate to their needs, to design training to enable the staff to learn the new content, and to study implementation of new content and its impact on students. Increasingly we find it necessary to discuss at length with staffs how we might work together and to request democratic decision making by faculties to determine if, indeed, the "school" wants to work with us. In terms of designing coaching, we have departed substantially from our initial designs. We refer to our evolved practice as "peer-coaching study teams" to differentiate it from our earlier forms as well as practices developed by other researchers.

First, when we work with entire faculties, all teachers agree to be members of peer-coaching study teams. The collective agreements governing the teams arc: 1) commitment to practice/use whatever change the faculty has decided to implement; 2) assistance and support of each other in the change process, including shared planning of instructional objectives and development of materials and lessons; and 3) collection of data, both on the implementation of their planned change and on student effects relevant to the school's identified target for student growth.

Second, we have omitted feedback as a coaching component. The primary activity of peer-coaching study teams is the collaborative planning and develop-ment of curriculum and instruction in pursuit of their shared goals. Especially when learning teaching strategies designed for higher-order outcomes, teachers need time to think through their overarching objectives as well as the specific objectives leading to them. Given the time required to plan sequences of lessons and units, collaborative planning is essential if teachers are to divide the labor of new development and use each other's products.

Remarkably, omitting feedback in the coaching process has not depressed implementation or student growth (Joyce et al., 1989; 1994; Showers, 1989), and the omission has greatly simplified the organization of peer-coaching teams in school settings. In retrospect, it is not difficult to understand this finding. Learning to provide technical feedback required extensive training (and time that might better have been used in planning and development) and was unnecessary after new behaviors were mastered. Peer coaches told us they found themselves slipping into "supervisory, evaluative comments" despite all their intentions to avoid them. Teachers shared with us their expectations that feedback tell them "first the good news, then the bad" because of their shared histories with various forms of clinical supervision, and admitted they often pressured their coaches to go beyond technical feedback and give them "the real scoop." To the extent that feedback actually was evaluative or was perceived to be evaluative, it was not meeting our original intention in any case.

Third, we have redefined the meaning of *coach;* when teachers observe each other, the one teaching is the coach and the one observing is the coached. Teachers who observe other teachers in their school who are attempting to implement new behaviors do so in order to learn from their colleagues' efforts with the innovation. There is no discussion of the observation in the "technical feedback" sense that we used in our earlier studies. Generally, brief conversations on the order of "Thanks for letting me watch you work. I picked up some good ideas on how to work with the students on 'X'" follow these observations.

Coaching appears to facilitate the professional and collegial relationships discussed by Little (1982; 1990), for example, development of a shared language and norms of experimentation. Our data about this process are somewhat less formal than that on skill acquisition and transfer. However, both anecdotal and interview data indicate that the effects of coaching are much more far reaching than the mastery and integration of new knowledge and skills by individual teachers. The development of school norms that support the continuous study and improvement of teaching apparently build capability for other kinds of change, whether it is adoption of a new curriculum, a schoolwide discipline policy, or the building of teaching repertoire. By building permanent structures for collegial relationships, schools organize themselves for improvement in multiple areas. We suspect that the practice of public teaching; focus on the clinical acts of teaching; development of common language and understanding; and sharing of lesson plans, materials, and problems contribute to school norms of collegiality and experimentation. However, we don't know exactly how coaching programs function to create such norms or if existing norms create favorable climates for coaching programs. On the other hand, we have, in the course of long-term relationships with school districts, conducted a number of informal studies on the learning-to-learn effect by asking coaching teams to teach themselves models of teaching through the print and video media alone—without the assistance of formal training—and they have been able to do so, which we attribute partly to their growing ability to learn and partly to the cohesion that has developed during the peer-coaching process.

Other Forms of Coaching

The term *coaching* has been used in multiple contexts in the last ten years. We will briefly discuss some of them in order to identify similarities and differences with the practice of coaching we now employ.

We have observed the terms *technical coaching, collegial coaching, challenge coaching, team coaching, cognitive coaching,* and *peer coaching* (as practiced in the traditional supervisory mode of pre-conference/observation/post-conference) (Garmston, 1987). All seem to share a concern that they not be confused with or used for evaluation of teachers. Technical coaching, team coaching and peer coaching have in common with our practice a concern for learning and implementing innovations in curriculum and instruction (Kent, 1985; Rogers, 1987; Showers, 1985; Neubert & Bratton, 1987), whereas collegial coaching and cognitive coaching appear to aim more at the improving of existing practice and repertoire (Garmston, Linder, & Whitaker, 1993; Costa & Garmston, 1985). With the exception of our current practice and team coaching, all utilize feedback procedures as a vehicle for improving or changing classroom practice.

Next Steps in the Evolution of Training and Coaching

A perennial question drives our work—how to best facilitate teachers in their efforts to teach students in ways that build intellectual independence, reasoning and problem-solving capability, competence in handling the explosion of information and data, and, with the help of technology, the ability to navigate the information age. We believe there are specific behaviors that staff developers can incorporate in training settings and in continuing technical assistance to assist educators in their efforts.

First, we can facilitate schools and teams of teachers in the redesign of their workplaces during training settings. Rather than simply advocating that work-places provide time for collaborative planning and problem solving related to a school's specific plans for change, during training we can begin to solve the problem of finding time for the analysis, discussion, and decision making necessary for collective change efforts. Raywid's (1993) article on finding time for collaboration provides one way to begin such a session.

Second, peer-coaching study teams can be formed on the first day of training if they are not already in place, so that teams have opportunities to experiment with ways of working together that are productive for them. When entire school faculties are engaged in training together, they have many options for forming teams, and staff developers can facilitate discussion of those options. When training continues over a period of days, teachers can try alternative formats in order to experience the relative costs and benefits of alternative plans. Schools that are trying to develop an integrated curriculum as part of their improvement plan may want to experiment with cross-subject or cross-grade teams. Schools with a focus on multicultural curriculum may want to balance teams by ensuring that faculty expertise on various cultures is spread among teams. However teams are formed, it is useful for them to have immediate practice in working together toward shared goals.

Third, we can provide examples of formats or structures for collaborative planning. Many teachers have shared with us the difficulty they experience in jointly performing an activity that traditionally they have done individually. A structured "walk-through" of a planning activity that allows teams to respond to questions within specific time frames provides practice in thinking aloud the things individuals want to accomplish and identifying the overlap with the agendas of colleagues. For example, a sequence might include:

1. Think about your year's "course"; what are your big, overarching goals for your students this year?
2. Now think about the first six weeks of school. What objectives will you need to accomplish during the first six weeks if you are to meet your year's goals? How much time can you spend in review and still meet your objectives?
3. What instructional strategies are most appropriate for the various objectives you have set for the first six weeks? Are they consistent with your year-end goals?
4. Given the overlap of objectives in your group, are there ways you can divide the labor and develop materials that others can use?

Fourth, peer-coaching study teams need time to plan how they will monitor their implementation of whatever initiative they have agreed to adopt, and how they will determine the impact of that initiative on their students. When whole schools have agreed on a specific change agenda (e.g., to learn and use cooperative strategies in conjunction with constructivist approaches to teaching), study teams may want to first address these issues in their small groups and then combine their ideas in a whole-school session; the faculty, then, can devise a plan for monitoring both their implementation and impact on students as a whole. Measuring the impact of planned changes in the educational program is of critical importance to any school improvement and change effort. The training setting is an optimal time to plan the "mini-studies" that teams can conduct throughout the year in order to know if all their efforts are having the desired effects.

We are aware that including these types of activities in training sessions increases the time, and thus the cost, of staff development activities. We are convinced that, to the extent such activities result in greater clarity about means and ends, more thorough implementation of planned changes, and more immediate information about student effects, the additional effort will be well worth the investment.

SUMMARY

From the research on training and studies of transfer of training as well as clinical experience over the last 30 years, we have identified teacher skills, under-standings and characteristics that appear to facilitate learning. The concern for identification of learning-to-learn skills stems from the contradictions that exist between skill learning and use of those skills in staff development programs. That teachers can learn a wide variety of skills, strategies and practices is well documented. That behaviors learned in training settings are less often implemented in classroom practice is also well documented, even though more intensive training programs that include follow-up training and employ peer self-help groups have much better implementation records than the field as a whole.

Snow (1982), commenting on three papers prepared for a symposium on "The Student's Role in Learning," notes that "learning is a function of the amount of active mental effort invested in the exercise of intelligence to accomplish cognitive work" (p. 5). He further asserts that "it is possible to train directly the cognitive and metacognitive processing skills involved in intelligent learning and it is possible to prompt intrinsically motivated learning by intelligent arrangement of educational conditions" (p. 10). If the skills and characteristics identified in this chapter do indeed help teachers learn from training oppor-tunities to the extent that they are better able to master and implement new content and instructional practices, we are a step closer to developing the conditions that enable teachers to master the necessary "cognitive and meta-cognitive processing skills."

From a career perspective, it may be that learning how to acquire good practices should take a place of substantively equal importance with the good practices themselves. The effectiveness of preservice teacher training programs may well depend on the skill of the trainees to navigate the consolidation phase in the variety of settings in which they will find themselves. The creation of effective inservice training programs may equally depend on the skills of the trainees to learn ever increasing knowledge and practices and how to consolidate them.

The addition of peer-coaching study teams to school improvement efforts is a substantial departure from the way schools often embark on change efforts. On the surface, it should be simple to implement—what could be more natural than teams of professional teachers working on content and skills? It is a complex innovation only because it requires a radical change in relationships between teachers and between teachers and administrative personnel.

Many believe that the essence of the coaching transaction is in the offering of advice to teachers following observations. It is not. Teachers learn from each other in the process of planning instruction, developing the materials to support it, watching each other work with students, and thinking together about the impact of their behavior on the learning of their students. The collaborative work of peer-coaching study teams is much broader than observations and conferences.

chapter 8

Implementation: The Great Challenge to Staff Development

Proposition: Implementation is where it all happens or falls apart. We have to keep growth central as we think about implementation. We don't want anyone to fail! And we care about whether the kids will have the chance to learn from powerful models of learning!

In the previous two chapters, we have examined change and improvement processes in the contexts of individuals, schools, and districts attempting to change themselves. Both in the identification of needs and selection of content, the design of training and peer-coaching study teams, we have focused greater attention on the school, having argued (see chapter 3) that the school is the unit with the greatest potential for producing substantial student growth. In this chapter, we will again focus on whole-school improvement and change efforts in our discussion of staff development and the importance of implementation, as well as the technology for monitoring it.

The failure to monitor implementation of curricula, instructional strategies, and other innovations has cost school improvement efforts dearly in the past, resulting in both inability to interpret student learning outcomes as well as spurious conclusions regarding the impact of change programs. The primary reason to monitor implementation of innovations is to enable interpretation of their impacts on students. This is true whether a single teacher is experimenting with changes in his/her instructional program or an entire school or district is attempting changes to accomplish a collective goal.

A second reason to monitor implementation of planned changes, whether for individuals, schools, or districts, is to determine objectively at what level of intensity or frequency students are experiencing a planned change, given the intentions. It is important for an individual teacher to determine if new content or practices are actually implemented in his/her classroom, given the initial purpose for the change. For schools, data on implementation serve as a gauge of the organizational capacity of the school to make a decision and act upon it. Districts vary considerably in their abilities to implement a change, whether in curriculum or technology. We suspect in some cases that the absence of implementation data from district personnel demonstrates their need for an implementation strategy. For example, we have observed several districts in which, following adoption of new reading texts and a three-hour orientation session for all teachers, it was assumed that the new curriculum was in place. The districts lacked the capacity to implement a new curriculum but, none-theless, proceeded with a strategy that could not possibly succeed. Our experience is that many districts engage in similar "adoption cycles" without a design that makes a difference. The teachers feel (and are) buffeted by initiatives that ask them to change without adequate support.

MONITORING IMPLEMENTATION

Setting a Target

Whether for individuals, schools, or districts, the first step in achieving an implementation of anything is defining what it will look like. If a school has decided to use cooperative learning strategies to address academic and social needs and arranged for training for the staff, how will they know when they have the new processes in place? If every teacher uses a cooperative strategy once a week, can the school expect the benefits to students that motivated them to learn the strategies in the first place? Will they need to use their new cooperative strategies very heavily in the initial weeks of implementation in order to teach students how to function productively in cooperative groups? These are questions that need to be discussed openly and revisited frequently.

Data Collection

Once targets have been set for use of whatever innovation has been selected, a process is needed for collecting information on actual use. This type of data collection represents both new behavior and a departure from norms for many school faculties. In the case of schoolwide initiatives in school improvement, it vividly focuses on the meaning of collective decision making, and when norms of privacy are threatened, there will generally be fallout. Assuming that the process and structure described in chapters 2, 3, and 6 are in place, the school or district committees can design procedures for collecting the necessary data and communicating to staffs the purpose and use of the data (e.g., these are our data and we need them for our own decision-making process).

The nature of the data collected will be determined by the type of change faculties are implementing. For example, if a school, as part of its writing program, has decided to increase the number of computers available to students and teach all students a word-processing program, faculty will want information on several aspects of their program. First, they will need to set a target—how often do they want students to write on their computers and why? (The Bangert-Drowns study [1993] found that students who composed three times a week on computers improved their writing skills much more than students who composed at the computer only once or twice a week.) Then they will want to know how many students currently compose at the computer? How often do they currently write at a computer? Do some students write on computers at home? How long does it take for students to become proficient with at least rudimentary word-processing skills? Once targets are set for frequency of student writing on computers and instruction in the use of word processing has begun, teachers will want information on actual computer use for word processing. They will also have questions about the impact of word processing on the quality of their students' writing (see chapter 9 for discussion of formative evaluation projects).

The adoption of science kits by an elementary school appears to be a simple implementation problem. As in all change efforts, the adoption of a new curriculum usually results from dissatisfaction with existing programs. Why was the new curriculum selected? What knowledge and skills do faculty want their students to acquire as a result of interaction with the science kits, and how often will they need to experience the new curriculum if these objectives are to be accomplished? Are there sufficient materials/equipment for all classrooms to meet the implementation targets set? Will the faculty simply monitor the number of units "used" by each classroom, or are they actually interested in the frequency of student behaviors like hypothesis setting, conducting of experiments, observation, data collection, analysis of findings, and drawing of conclusions? These questions must be answered before the faculty can set its targets for implementation and design a system for determining when they have their new science curriculum in place.

Once schools are clear on the questions they have with respect to implementation, the nature of the data to be collected is clear. If the target is thrice-weekly composition on a computer, students can simply file all writing assignments in a folder or write their names and dates on a chart that lists writing prompts to determine if the target is being met. If the object of implementation of a science curriculum is "hands-on" science and the exercise of systematic observation and analysis of phenomena, teachers can tally student experiences on a chart or collect students' written reports of science experiences.

Using the Data

Individuals, faculties, and districts use implementation data for several purposes. First is the fairly straightforward issue of accomplishing what was planned—"After extensive analysis of our students' needs, selection of content, training, and practice, have we put in place what we set out to do?" The ability to follow through on plans builds both individual and collective senses of efficacy and the confidence to explore future alternatives to current practice.

Second, in nearly all change efforts, obstacles to implementation arise. Good implementation data provide the basis for analysis of obstacles as well as their potential solutions. Is the implementation faltering because of insufficient equipment or materials? Are teachers discovering they need additional or different training to accomplish a thorough implementation? Is specific assistance or cooperation from parents necessary before targets can be realized? When data reveal that targets for implementation are not being met, immediate problem solving should address why and generate whatever assistance is needed. Discovering at the end of the year that a change was never put in place leaves everyone feeling discouraged and inefficacious.

Finally, information about the implementation of any change makes interpretation of student outcomes possible. Whenever we change current practice, we expect specific student benefits, either in behavior (fewer suspensions, greater involvement in learning opportunities), achievement (higher grades, improved test scores, increased reading comprehension), thinking skills (the ability to identify categories in large amounts of unorganized information, to hypothesize and synthesize), self-esteem, or whatever perceived need impelled us to change in the first place. Solid use of a planned change as well as variations in implementation enable us to understand the impact of our behavior on that of students and to plan next steps in the use of innovations.

STUDYING AN IMPLEMENTATION: THE AUGUSTA MODELS OF TEACHING PROJECT

The implementation study reported here was part of a districtwide, school improvement project aimed at increasing student achievement and restructuring the workplace of teachers (Joyce, Murphy, Showers, & Murphy, 1989; Showers, 1989). The purpose of this study was to examine the implementation of several alternative models of teaching by faculties engaged in schoolwide school improvement programs. Because entire faculties were organized into peer-coaching study teams designed to facilitate the appropriate and consistent use of alternative teaching strategies, the functioning of study teams was observed as well.

Specific implementation questions were:

1. Did the faculties implement the content of the training (e.g., What levels of use and what degrees of transfer of training were achieved with the models of teaching in which teachers were trained?)?
2. What factors affected variation in faculties' use of the models of teaching (e.g., Did cohesiveness of faculties and peer-coaching study teams, individual growth states, grade level, age, and experience affect implementation?)?
3. Did changes in the workplace occur as a result of whole-faculty participation in the project, specifically the development of the ability of the faculty and administration to set specific goals for school improvement?

Sample

One hundred and sixteen teachers and administrators—the faculties from the first three target schools—were involved in the project. Although data were collected on all of them, this report deals with case studies of a subset of 18 teachers—six from each of the three target schools—who were selected on a stratified random basis. The case study sample for each of the two elementary schools included one teacher from each grade level (K–5) and at the middle school, two teachers from each of grades 6, 7, and 8. A second-grade teacher was dropped from the sample because of an extended illness which required her early retirement.

Training

The content for the first summer's workshop included four models of teaching— cooperative learning (Johnson et al., 1981), inductive thinking and concept attainment (Bredderman, 1983; El Nemr, 1979), and mnemonic strategies (Pressley, Levin, & Delaney, 1982)—which were selected because of their research-based impact on student learning (Joyce, Weil, & Showers, 1992). Instruction followed the theory/demonstration/practice mode during the summer workshop. Participants planned lessons they would teach and shared the plans, and their skepticism about whether the plans were practical, with colleagues. When school opened, all participants were urged to practice their new strategies frequently with students during the first few weeks.

In September, administrators scheduled specific times for study groups to meet; together with counselors and supervisors, these groups practiced in classrooms with students. The study teams were asked to concentrate on teaching their students how to respond to the models of teaching they were learning. They had been told that, although the students could respond immediately to the new cognitive and social tasks presented by those models, it would take about 20 trials before they would become really proficient.

Procedures

Six times during the 1987–88 academic year, teachers in the sample were observed in their classrooms and informally interviewed regarding their use of models. Teachers were asked to maintain monthly logs detailing their use of the teaching models over which they had received training during the summer of 1987 and were videotaped near the end of the first project year to determine skill levels with various models of teaching. Videotapes were completed for 14 of the 17 sample teachers.

Formal interviews regarding teacher use and attitudes toward the teaching strategies, which were the objects of this implementation effort, were completed with all sample teachers in April 1988 and again in January 1989.

Sixteen of the sample teachers attended a second two-week training session during the summer of 1988 and were studied during their second year of implementation. The procedures for examining implementation were identical to year one of the project.

Data Collection

Practice.   Amount of practice was simply a tabulation of the number of trials per month reported by each teacher on their logs. Teachers varied somewhat in their response to the expectation that they turn in a monthly log recording practice with the new strategies. Some teachers recorded every lesson while others recorded only examples of different types of lessons. The six informal interviews recorded during the year, as well as the formal interviews, helped validate the information recorded on logs.

Levels of Transfer.   "Levels of Transfer" is a continuum from a score of 1 (low—imitative use) to 5 (high—executive control). Level 1 represents *imitative use,* that is, exact replication of lessons demonstrated in training settings. Furthermore, the types of lessons selected for imitation often represent only the most simple and concrete examples of a class of demonstrations. For example, if a cooperative numbered-heads activity were demonstrated with a list of spelling words during training, and teachers were subsequently observed to use numbered heads only with their spelling lists, their level of transfer would be judged to be imitative, although appropriate. Likewise, the fact that various forms of more complex cooperative activity had been demonstrated during training but were absent from early teacher practice would tend to place a teacher at Level 1 of transfer.

Level 2 indicates *mechanical use* (or horizontal transfer) in that the same teacher who was using numbered-heads activities only for spelling begins to use numbered heads for drills in reading vocabulary, addition and multiplication facts, etc. Practice increases at this level, but there is little variation in types of implementation. More complex examples of the models of teaching learned during training continue to be missing from teacher practice.

Level 3 is a *routine* level of transfer, in that certain activities, types of lessons, and objectives become identified with specific models of teaching. For example, as students learn the states and capitals of the United States, geographic features of regions of the country, and major land forms and oceans of the world, teachers routinely select mnemonic strategies to accomplish their objectives. Use of the strategies is frequent at this stage but alternative strategies are not considered at this point, nor are curriculum objectives thought of in other than a lower-order, concrete fashion.

Level 4 transfer is called *integrated use* and generally occurs for different models at different rates. For example, a teacher who has frequently used mnemonics strategies for learning concrete information in multiple subjects begins to understand that sequences of events in history, major points in a philosophy, policy issues faced by presidents and governors are also areas for application of mnemonic strategies. The proportion of imitative to innovative, subject-specific use has become quite small.

Finally, Level 5 transfer is designated as *executive control* of the content of training. Executive control is characterized by complete understanding of the theories underlying the various models learned, a comfortable level of appropriate use for varieties of models of teaching, and consequently the ability to select specific models and combinations of models for objectives within a unit as well as across subject areas. Integrated curriculum objectives as well as high-order objectives are frequently observable at this level. Thus, a teacher introducing a piece of literature to fifth-grade students might begin with objectives relating to understanding of the relationships that evolve between certain characters in the book. Although the teacher may employ inductive thinking, concept attainment, mnemonic and cooperative strategies to teach the necessary vocabulary and word attack skills to enable the students to read the story with comfort, major emphases will be on analysis of the relationships among characters through categorization, on interpretation of key passages from the piece, and on writing with analogies to examine the changing nature of evolving relationships.

Teachers' lesson plans, interviews, logs, and observations were analyzed to determine levels of transfer. For each of the teachers, all lessons reported on logs and six systematic observations during each year of the project provided data for determining transfer level. Interview data supplemented lesson plans and observations with self-reports on teachers' use of the models of teaching in their classrooms. Each lesson analyzed was assigned a level of 1 to 5 and means were computed for each teacher.

Factors Affecting Variation in Implementation

To examine factors that were hypothesized to affect variation in teachers' use of the models of teaching, States of Growth (an orientation to the external environment with respect to both the formal and informal opportunities for professional development) were calculated for each teacher. States of Growth data were derived from interviews and observations of study teams. Data on teachers' grade level, age, and experience were available from employment records housed both at the school and at the central office.

States of Growth.   McKibbin and Joyce (1980) derived the States of Growth measure in their study of staff development in California. Through a structured interview process they examined teachers' and administrators' responses to opportunities for professional development through the formal staff development system offered by universities, counties, state-sponsored agencies, and districts; the informal opportunities provided by peers; and the participation in non-professional but personal growth opportunities available in the general environment (books, film, theater, etc.). In the study reported by McKibbin and Joyce, teachers who participated fully in both formal and informal professional development activities also tended to have well-developed interests in the personal domain; that is, teachers who were actively reaching out for growth opportunities in their professional lives were generally engaged in growth. Furthermore, teachers characterized by high growth states were more likely to implement innovations for which they received training and to achieve transfer of those innovations into their active teaching repertoires.

In a recent study by Hopkins (1990), in which both States of Growth of individual teachers and climate ratings of the schools in which they taught were examined for their influence on teacher implementation of training, growth states was found to be a more powerful predictor of implementation than was school climate (although the latter was not without effect).

The States of Growth hierarchy is described in full in several sources (Joyce, Bush, & McKibbin, 1982; McKibbin & Joyce, 1980; Joyce & Showers, 1988) and in greater depth in chapter 11. Briefly, the categories are:

Gourmet Omnivores are individuals who not only reach out for opportunities in their environments but who generate or initiate those opportunities for themselves and others. These individuals are active participants in many growth opportunities but are discriminating about their choice of activities.

Active Consumers are similar to gourmet omnivores in that they continually scan their environments for growth opportunities and take advantage of those opportunities in both the professional and personal domains. They differ from gourmet omnivores in that they are less initiating and less likely to create opportunities and options where none exist.

Passive Consumers comprised about 70 percent of the initial sample in the California Staff Development Study (Joyce, Bush, & McKibbin, 1982). They are characterized as conforming and highly dependent on their immediate social context. They attended required staff development programs but seldom did anything with the content; and the activities engaged in outside the work setting depended very much on whether their families and friends initiated such activities.

Reticents actually avoid opportunities for growth. Consequently, reticents often perceive efforts by peers or administrators to effect change as forms of conspiracy designed to leave them less powerful and less efficacious.

Results

What was the state of implementation and what were the factors contributing to it?

Practice.   Knowing that skill development requires a certain amount of practice before fluid and appropriate use is possible, we encouraged teachers at the three project schools in the Augusta school district to practice their newly learned models of teaching frequently, especially at the beginning of the school year immediately following training. In earlier studies, teachers who had postponed practice found if difficult or impossible to use the content of training. We urged teachers to implement the simpler forms of cooperative learning immediately and pervasively during the first month of school in order to teach students how to work in cooperative groups and to ease the implementation of other models of teaching. Teachers were so successful in this effort that by the end of the first month, most of the elementary teachers were reporting a minimum of two cooperative sessions per day and the middle school teachers at least four per week. In fact, one elementary teacher reported 80 trials with cooperative learning during the four weeks of September! Teachers found it much more difficult to implement the Concept Attainment, Mnemonics, and Inductive Thinking strategies. We have eliminated reports of practice with cooperative learning from our totals and in Table 8.1 have simply starred the teachers who reported at least once daily or greater use of cooperative learning strategies.

Analysis of teacher logs for the 1987–88 academic year shows that for our random sample of teachers, the new models of teaching were practiced 14.48 times per month (for School A, 16.8; for School B, 11.1; and for School C, 14.98). During the second project year, the average monthly use of models was 22.73 (for School A, 14.8; for School B, 24.4; and for School C, 29).

As is apparent in Table 8.1 (on page 136), teachers on the whole practiced their new strategies fairly frequently. The question of greater concern to us, however, was the level of transfer of training to teachers' active repertoires—how appropriatcly were the new strategies being used? If teachers did not develop at least a routine level of transfer during the first year, would they ultimately develop integrated use and executive control with the models of teaching?

Table 8.2 (on page 137) summarizes the levels of transfer achieved by our sample during the project. Again, data on cooperative learning lessons were not included in transfer scores, as they artificially inflated the levels of transfer achieved in Concept Attainment, Mnemonics, and Inductive Thinking. For year one, the mean transfer of training score for our sample was 3.3 (routine use). Of the 17 teachers, three were will largely operating at the imitative stage of

TABLE 8.1 Average monthly practice by teacher with three models of teaching for two years*

School	Teacher	Average Monthly Practice*	
		1987–88	*1988–89*
A	A**	19.6	20
	B**	13.0	20
	C	11.0	8
	D**	23.0	—
	E	15.6	14
	F	18.6	12
B	A**	18.0	40
	B**	20.0	38
	C**	10.1	20
	D	3.6	10
	E	3.7	14
C	A**	14.3	36
	B**	12.0	28
	C**	12.8	24
	D**	13.6	28
	E	17.2	—
	F**	20.0	29
		$\overline{X}$ = 14.5	$\overline{X}$ = 22.73
		S.D. = 5.4	S.D. = 10.3

*Excluding cooperative learning lessons.
**Teachers who used cooperative learning one or more times per day.

transfer (level 1), three had reached a mechanical level (level 2) and the remaining 11 had developed routine or integrative use levels of transfer. Thus, while 15 of the 17 teachers were practicing frequently enough to develop skill in the new models of teaching, only 11 (65 percent) were using the strategies appropriately enough during the first project year to predict that their students would derive the intellectual, social, and personal benefits promised by research underlying the models.

In the second year of the project, 10 (67 percent) of the 15 remaining sample teachers had developed a routine or higher level of transfer with the models; two of the three schools had increased both their practices and levels of transfer with models of teaching, while the third school (School A) actually suffered losses in both areas. Possible school-level causes for both gains and losses will be discussed later in this chapter.

Frequency of practice with the models was correlated with level of transfer at r = .62 (Spearman Rank Correlation Coefficient) during year one of the project and at r = .75 during the second year. Clearly, as is apparent in Tables 8.1 and 8.2 no one reached high levels of transfer without frequent and consistent practice. However, several teachers continued practice of the new strategies

TABLE 8.2 Transfer of training by teachers with three models of teaching for two years

School	Teacher	Transfer of Training*	
		1987–88	*1988–89*
A	A	3.1	3.0
	B	4.0	4.5
	C	1.8	1.0
	D	4.7	—
	E	3.1	2.5
	F	3.8	3.0
B	A	4.3	4.5
	B	4.6	5.0
	C	3.5	3.5
	D	2.0	1.5
	E	1.9	2.5
C	A	3.6	3.5
	B	4.4	4.0
	C	2.5	3.0
	D	2.0	2.0
	E	1.9	—
	F	4.9	5.0

*Levels of Transfer: 1 = imitative use; 2 = mechanical use; 3 = routine use; 4 = integrated use; 5 = executive use.

without apparently developing greater understanding of their use. They continued to imitate lessons they had observed with trainers or peers and found it difficult to depart from their teacher's manuals to experiment with alternative strategies for achieving similar instructional objectives.

Factors Affecting Variation in Use and Transfer. This project involved the entire faculties of three schools in the training and implementation of an innovation for school improvement. We hypothesized that individual characteristics (States of Growth, years teaching experience), small group characteristics (functioning of study groups), and school variables (principal leadership, faculty cohesion) might all affect teachers' rates of implementation (see Table 8.3).

Individual Factors. States of Growth scores were computed for all teachers in our sample near the end of the first project year (see Table 8.3 on page 138). The mean growth state for our sample was 3.1 (S.D. = .96, range 1–5), with the mean for School A at 2.67, School B at 3.0, and School C at 3.5. As reported by both McKibbin and Joyce (1980) and Evans and Hopkins (1988), States of Growth has proved to be a powerful predictor of implementation of innovations, both in projects involving whole schools as well as those involving only

TABLE 8.3   Teacher states of growth and transfer of training of three models of teaching

School	Teacher	Growth States*	Transfer of Training**	
			1987–88	*1988–89*
A	A	3	3.1	3.0
	B	3	4.0	4.5
	C	1	1.8	1.0
	D	4	4.7	—
	E	2	3.1	2.5
	F	3	3.8	3.0
B	A	4	4.3	4.5
	B	4	4.6	5.0
	C	3	3.5	3.5
	D	2	2.0	1.5
	E	2	1.9	2.5
C	A	3	3.6	3.5
	B	4	4.4	4.0
	C	3	2.5	3.0
	D	3	2.0	2.0
	E	3	1.9	—
	F	5	4.9	5.0

*Growth States: 1 = Reticent (satisfaction of basic needs); 2 = Withdrawn (psychological safety); 3 = Passive Consumer (concerns for belonging and security); 4 = Active Consumer (achievement orientation); 5 = Gourmet Omnivore (self-actualizing).
**Levels of Transfer: 1 = imitative use; 2 = mechanical use; 3 = routine use; 4 = integrated use; 5 = executive use.

volunteers. In this project, in which entire faculties participated if 80 percent or greater of their teachers requested the program, States of Growth correlated .87 with transfer levels during year one and .88 during year two (Spearman Rank Correlation Coefficients).

A common belief among both professional educators and the general public is that young teachers (i.e., teachers just entering the profession) are more open to innovation than older, more experienced teachers who have presumably become tired and set in their ways. The Joyce, McKibbin, and Bush (1983) study found no relationship between years of teaching experience and the willingness and ability to engage in professional growth. The good news from their study was that mature, experienced teachers are often at the height of their professional powers, while the bad news was that some young teachers just entering the profession are actively pushing away growth opportunities—they have quit learning at age 22.

We examined the relationship between years of teaching experience and transfer of training for our sample and found an r of .13 for the first year of the project and .10 for the second year. (A high positive correlation would have favored mature teachers whereas a high negative correlation would have favored beginning teachers.) Thus, for our sample, years of teaching experience was unassociated with ability to transfer training into regular classroom practice.

Peer Group Influences. All teachers in the three project schools were members of peer-coaching study teams, which were organized during the initial two-week workshop to facilitate the implementation of models of teaching. Study teams met weekly at the school sites on schedules worked out by the members of the team in conjunction with their administrators. The charge to study teams was threefold and emphasized only activities that were believed to increase practice with and implementation of the newly learned teaching strategies: teachers were to share lessons and materials already used in case others could use the plans/materials and thus cut down on preparation time; they were to observe each other trying the new strategies to learn from each other and study student responses to the strategies; and they were to plan future applications of the strategies within their curriculum areas in an attempt to integrate models' use with existing repertoire and instructional objectives.

Study group function is conceived on a continuum from the merely pro forma—in which teachers meet as scheduled, verbally share experiences of lessons they have attempted with new models of teaching, and observe each other as scheduled—to enthusiastic participation—in which teachers share lessons they have taught, materials they have developed, and observe each other easily and frequently to learn from each other—to fully collegial groups, in which teachers move beyond enthusiastic participation to the setting of common goals and the development of lessons and units, which all or part of the group will use in the future.

In the first year, none of our sample teachers belonged to a fully collegial study group, although some of the groups occasionally worked in a fully collegial fashion for several weeks at a time. Twelve of our 17 sample teachers, however, belonged to enthusiastic groups which shared past lessons and materials freely and increasingly observed each other at unscheduled times because they enjoyed seeing each other try out lessons. The remaining five teachers belonged to pro forma groups and were passive members of those groups, neither complaining about the static nature of their meetings nor initiating more dynamic activities.

One is tempted to view the study group functioning as a glass half empty, given the shortfall between what was possible and what occurred. However, we view the glass as half full, given that, prior to the project, teachers in the project schools never saw each other work, rarely met to discuss matters of curriculum and instruction (unless one counts monthly faculty meetings), and with three exceptions, shared no lesson planning or materials development even though five or six teachers in a school might be teaching the same grade level or subject and using exactly the same texts. The implementation of study teams in the project schools did, in fact, greatly reduce the isolation in which most teachers formerly worked. Furthermore, the level of study team functioning correlated .61 with transfer of training during the first year of the project.

Study team functioning during the second year was much more mixed. The organization and facilitation of study teams requires active administrative support, not only for scheduling but for maintaining focus and purpose. One of the schools (School A) lost a very active administrator and gained a new (first-time) administrator. The same school, halfway through the second year, was "raided" by an administrator who was assembling faculty for a new school and thus the School A teachers knew that nine of their number had been selected for the new school and would be leaving at the end of the year. This combination of factors was reflected in less practice for School A, declining rates of transfer, and lower study team functioning during year two of the project. For sample teachers in the other two schools, two of the teams achieved fully collegial status, two alternated between enthusiastic and fully collegial functioning, four groups functioned at an enthusiastic level and two functioned at a pro forma level.

Study team functioning was influenced by the States of Growth of individual members. Teams were generally comprised of four to six teachers. The four most successful study teams all had leadership from active consumers or gourmet omnivores. The presence of an active, growth-oriented individual, however, was not sufficient to ensure fully collegial functioning if one or more members were reticent or withdrawn. Study teams comprised of passive consumers were often enthusiastic but needed occasional structure. For example, they would approach the project consultants and ask for ideas or development projects to work on. They would then work enjoyably on a new idea or a unit or materials development scheme until it was finished, then request more input.

On balance, we believe the study teams functioned to boost implementation of an innovation for our project schools and, in addition, to increase teacher interaction about curriculum and instruction and reduce the norms of privacy and isolation. We do not believe, however, that the organization and functioning of study teams alone can change the climate of a school and create fully collegial interactions where few or none existed before, at least not in two years. Perhaps given our history of school cultures in which teachers have had so little opportunity to work in collegial fashions and make collective decisions, time will be required to develop truly collegial patterns of work. Whether this means more experience over the years or more intensive time together in the first year is not clear to us at this point. We are convinced, however, that collegiality will develop only in conjunction with meaningful and challenging reasons for collaborative work, such as efforts to improve curriculum and instruction for increased student learning.

School Level Factors.   We have already mentioned the role of administrative leadership in the organization and functioning of study teams. Principals and assistant principals performed several other roles as well. First, they were instrumental in their school's participation in the project, since schools were not considered for inclusion unless 80 percent or more of the staff were interested and principals wrote letters of application. Second, they provided varying amounts of pressure and support with respect to practice of the new strategies. During the first year, administrators at Schools A and B not only regularly observed (separate from "formal evaluation" observations) and encouraged teachers as they tried the new strategies but also borrowed classes and practiced the new strategies themselves. Administrators at Schools A and B met with study groups, and administrators at School C designated two lead teachers to meet with study groups and assist them during the first few months of the project. At Schools A and B, administrators generated schoolwide implementation projects for specific models of teaching during the first year, and during the second year, this activity was continued and increased in Schools B and C. Since project consultants met regularly with administrators and encouraged their active leadership and participation, we cannot predict what the absence of administrative support would have meant to the project. However, the lessening of administrative support at School A during the second year and the concomitant losses there suggest that the support of administrators was crucial to project success.

Changes in the Workplace.   Structural changes in the ways teachers worked with each other have already been discussed in the section on study teams. Possible increases (or decreases) in general cohesion and problem-solving ability can best be illustrated by what happened at the end of the project. Schools B and C retained their study group formats, selected curriculum areas to focus on (schoolwide), set goals for student achievement in those areas, secured additional training from consultants in their respective curriculum areas foci, and began working on the integration of models of teaching with new training in content and materials. School A, at the close of the project, was struggling to retain its study group format and incorporate 11 new staff members who had not had training in models of teaching. The principal was talking of retiring and the new assistant principal was gamely trying to coordinate some sort of school improvement focus for the year but had no consensus from the staff two months into the school year.

It is difficult to determine how enduring even large structural and attitudinal changes will be at specific school sites. Clearly, stability of staff and administration are important, as are shared experiences in decision making and training. It is probable that norms of continual renewal for individuals and collectivities must extend beyond specific schools to entire districts and the profession at large before large-scale change efforts can have long-range prospects for durability.

Implementation of the content of training was achieved at all three sites, although individual differences occurred. Given the history of implementation of curricular and instructional innovations (Fullan & Pomfret, 1977; Joyce & Showers, 1983; 1988), the implementation of models of teaching by three school faculties for whom the models represented additions to repertoire was a considerable achievement. Sufficient training was provided so that all teachers were able to practice their newly acquired skills, and teachers and administrators were able to restructure the workplace to the extent that teachers could regularly work together on implementation questions. At the end of the first project year, 88 percent of the teachers were using the new strategies regularly and skillfully enough (a mechanical level of transfer or higher) that students had developed the requisite skills for learning within the models frameworks. Sixty-seven percent of the teachers had achieved a routine or better level of transfer and thus had very good prospects for integrating the new models into their regular teaching repertoires.

We were heartened by the overall success of the implementation effort and the benefits to students as a result of the project (for details of impact on students, see Joyce et al., 1989, and chapter 4).

SUMMARY

The implementation of planned changes is crucial to the success of staff development and, thus, school improvement efforts if increased student growth is the intended outcome of such changes. Monitoring of an implementation—including setting a target for implementation, collecting data on an ongoing basis to determine if the goal is being met, and using the data collected to identify obstacles to use of the planned changes—empowers staffs and builds confidence in their collective ability to accomplish what they set out to do.

As can be seen from the Augusta example, monitoring an implementation can include any variables staffs believe will influence use of innovations. Studying implementation is not technically difficult but represents a change in norms and behavior for many staffs. With the help of a consultant or facilitator, individuals, teams, and schools are quite capable of studying their implementation, and, as we will see in the next chapter, the impact of changes on their students.

The study of implementation should be an inclusive process—everyone can use it as the basis for an ongoing inquiry into their practices and effects. Rather than having a few persons responsible for the study, or contracting the study to outside agencies, or consultants, if the study of implementation becomes a normal part of the operation, there should be a spawning of micro "action research" projects by individual teachers, peer-coaching teams, schools, and the district as a whole. We will visit this possibility again in chapter 9. Note that collaborative study is the hallmark of the process.

chapter 9

The Evaluation of Staff Development

Proposition: Increase in student learning is the goal of the effective staff development system. Evaluation of staff development systems, however, must address two questions: Are students experiencing the planned change and, if they are, is the change resulting in increased learning?

We believe that evaluation is an inquiry, a process for asking questions and seeking answers so that a staff development program can be gradually improved. This position contrasts with the conception of "evaluation" as an end point, a judgment—"This program is successful; that teacher is effective." Rather, evaluation helps us study rather than judge. Therefore, we view evaluation as a way the system can provide information for itself about its efforts on an ongoing basis—a formative rather than summative mode. In the context of a staff development system, formative evaluation is a critical element that maintains focus, linking a vision of what schooling can be for students and the progress toward that vision. And because we imagine a system that is governed by everybody, everybody has a place in designing and executing the evaluation process, interpreting the results, and acting to improve things.

A determination of the extent to which new content and processes are implemented must occur before questions about student outcomes can be addressed. Assuming the change that was planned is implemented, however, the question of greatest interest to most teachers, administrators, and parents can be asked—how are the changes we have put in place affecting our students?

We acknowledge the difficulties inherent in evaluating staff development programs. We recognize that the implementation of each event and program is heavily influenced by its context. The energy and interest of the schools and

143

teachers amplifies or diminishes the effects of training events. Also, staff development influences its ultimate goal, student learning, through a chain of events. Content of high potential needs good training design if it is to come to life in the classroom and achieve its potential. Measuring response to a series of training events by, for example, determining how participants liked them or whether initial skill and knowledge were developed provides only a beginning. If the skills are not employed and skillfully enough that student learning is affected, the chain is broken. Additionally, the measurement of many of the important variables is technically difficult. Frequently tests of student behavior and learning have to be constructed—some of the most-used, commercially available instruments are not appropriate for all the objectives that we may have. Finally, cost limitations almost always result in designs where a sample rather than the entire population is studied. (We definitely favor the thorough study of a sample rather than a more superficial study of the entire population because the chain of events and moderating variables can only be tracked by the collection and analysis of high-quality data.)

Having acknowledged the difficulties, we believe (and that belief is supported by ample evidence from reports of action research) that individuals, schools, and districts are perfectly capable of conducting evaluations of the impact of changes on students as a consequence of staff development programs.

A FRAMEWORK FOR EVALUATING STAFF DEVELOPMENT PROGRAMS

Because it is not universally agreed that the purpose of staff development is ultimately student achievement, we reiterate our central thesis here: Student achievement is the intended outcome of staff development. Consequently, the evaluation of staff development systems examines student growth.

In the next few pages, we suggest a simple framework for evaluating staff development programs and provide examples of individuals, schools, and districts who have employed it.

Formulating Clear Questions

Once an individual, faculty, or district has determined primary needs or concerns with respect to student performance, selected a course of action to address those needs, engaged in training, and studied the implementation of the planned change, clear questions about the intended student outcomes must be formulated. What propelled the move to change or improve something about the instructional program, curriculum, climate, or policies of the class/school/district? Was the concern for reading comprehension, the quality of writing, or what? Was the problem the number of failures and retentions experienced by students? Whatever the problem or concern, the initial step in designing an evaluation is revisiting that beginning point and stating the problem in measurable terms. Questions such as

"Have students' reading comprehension increased?" and "Have the number of student suspensions decreased?" serve to maintain focus on the purpose of the entire enterprise and provide direction for the kinds of data to be collected.

To Sample or Not to Sample

Once a question or questions have been formulated that clearly reflect a teacher's or faculty's intentions with respect to student outcomes, decisions must be made about the number of students to be observed or measured or studied in order to answer the questions. If a school asks the question, "Has the frequency of student suspensions decreased?" there is no need to select a sample of students for study. Most schools already keep accurate records of the incidence and cause of student suspensions, and these simply need to be compiled and summarized. If, on the other hand, a faculty asks the question, "Has reading comprehension increased?" it will almost certainly want to select a sample of students to study in-depth. The nature of the question governs the type of information needed as well as the cost of collecting it and, thus, the choices about sampling.

Data Collection

The type of data to be collected is again dictated by the questions asked. Questions about reading comprehension indicate a need for tests of reading comprehension. In elementary schools, staffs will probably want to administer individualized tests to a stratified random sample of students, given their greater reliability for young children and their greater yield of diagnostic information. Questions about writing quality will require the use of a rubric to score the organization and coherence of compositions, the use of detail to support major points, and the mastery of the mechanics of writing (spelling, punctuation, capitalization). The type of data collected must align with the intended outcomes. When the primary target of an intervention is increased student self-esteem, evaluation of the effort must measure changes in self-esteem.

Studies of implementation are not surrogates for studies of student learning. If the original impetus for an intensive program of word processing was the quality of student writing, implementation data would likely monitor the frequency with which students composed at the computer and the types of writing prompts to which they responded. On the other hand, evaluation data would examine the quality of compositions composed at the computer and perhaps the frequency with which students produced compositions, as compared with a baseline measure.

A second issue of concern to evaluators is the quality of data collected. Is it valid and reliable? Have we measured what we set out to measure and do our data accurately reflect students' knowledge and skill? We recommend, whenever possible, that evaluators use developed measures with established track records for validity and reliability. For example, the variable of self-esteem or academic self-concept is frequently measured in school improvement projects. Creating a measure of self-esteem and testing it are costly and time-consuming activities and excellent measures already exist (e.g., for young children see Harter's [1982] "Perceived Competence Scale for Children" and for adolescents March and O'Neil's [1984] "Self-Description Questionnaire").

Teacher-made tests are certainly defensible sources of data as well. No one knows better what academic content students were asked to master and thus no one is better positioned to construct tests over that material. And, we would suggest that teachers follow their natural inclinations to make tests extensive rather than brief. Teachers are not interested, as are by necessity the makers of standardized tests, in just sampling the information their students have mastered. For example, they want students to know *all* addition and multiplication facts; knowing only certain facts is not productive, given the teacher's initial reason for wanting his/her students to master such material.

In addition to determining the type of data to be collected, evaluators must decide how frequently and at what intervals data are to be gathered. If grade distributors are the indicators selected to evaluate program effects, data will be collected four to six times during an academic year. If written compositions are to be collected and scored for a sample of students during a year, a teacher or staff may want feedback on progress every six to nine weeks. In the case of suspension data, information is collected continuously, or with every incidence of the behavior being monitored. And if reading comprehension is being studied, data might reasonably be collected three times during an academic year.

The primary tasks for evaluators are to ensure that the type of data collected relate to the intended outcome; the measures are appropriate (valid, reliable, accurate) for the outcomes of interest; and data are collected at appropriate intervals. Once these decisions are made, there are numerous resources to help practitioners identify measures and their appropriate use (Miles & Huberman, 1984; Sagor, 1992). Obvious categories of data collection tools include observations, interviews, questionnaires, document analysis, and tests.

Data Analysis

Fortunately, a degree in statistics is not required to sensibly analyze data. The purpose for collecting the data and the need to communicate findings to all interested parties, however, necessitate organizing the data into usable forms.

The first step is to return to your questions; they will usually provide clues to the most useful ways of organizing information. Second, think about the audience(s) for the information and the uses to which it will be put. If, for example, the change being implemented is intended to improve student behavior and reduce referrals and suspensions, data may be summarized in a weekly form that includes the number of and reasons for referrals and suspensions. When the audience is teachers, results might be graphed and updated on a weekly basis so that all can see that their behavior makes a difference. When the audience is parents, a graph for a four- to six-week period might be inserted in an article describing the school's concern and the action it has taken with respect to student referrals and suspensions.

A major purpose of formative evaluation is the provision of information that enables individuals and groups to adjust their behavior. Data are meant to be communicated, and the form data analysis takes needs to be governed primarily by its relevance to the questions asked and its clarity in communicating results.

Nothing is more satisfying than determining that effort and energy, whether individually or collectively expended, has resulted in positive outcomes for students. Such information justifies the effort and builds both individual and group efficacy, a sense of confidence and competence. On the other hand, if ongoing evaluation data suggest the desired outcomes are not being accomplished, it's better to know before enormous amounts of energy and resources have been expended. We would warn evaluators, however, to be cautious about eliminating programs before they have had a chance to work. Negative results can just as easily generate reexamination of the implementation of changes or adjustments to the program. Espccially when new content and processes have been selected because of their successful track records in other settings, beware of disposing of them too quickly.

Let's put all this together and see what it looks like with respect to the evaluation of the system and each of its components.

THE STUDY OF THE SYSTEM

We need to create an efficient, embedded program of evaluation tied to a continuous effort to make the staff development system work better. The study is an active inquiry into how people use the system and what is done with the content of the events, with the purpose of learning how to improve the system.

The dynamics of each of the three components (individual, collective, and district) differ sufficiently that each deserves special consideration. Let us assume a fully functioning, three-component system and explore some of the questions we might ask of each and how we might explore them.

THE INDIVIDUAL COMPONENT

Who Is Served and What Affects Participation?

Assuming that the component was offered a high-quality array of content, an easy task is to count participants and their characteristics by type of offering. An intermediate agency that we are familiar with used their data in some interesting ways. Their offerings for teachers, which were developed through a democratic process similar to the one we have been describing, but with representatives from the 40 districts they serve, were categorized as follows:

Personal need content—such as "stress management," "time management," "personal finances," etc.

Various approaches to classroom management

Various teaching strategies

Basic teaching skills, largely from the framework of Madeline Hunter

Curriculum area studies—approaches to the teaching of reading and writing, multicultural education, the teaching of mathematics, etc.

They discovered that the personal need content and classroom management workshops drew several times more participants than did the workshops in any of the other categories. However, the participants in the other categories tended to be "repeaters," having attended one event, they were likely to attend others. And, this small, loyal band reported great satisfaction, especially finding the content useful in their professional work.

The planners observed that the workshops on teaching and curriculum were much longer than the others and were scheduled so that sessions followed one another closely—sometimes as often as three evenings per week. Those workshops also were often attended by friendship groups or teams from schools.

Now, what to do next? They could have decided to offer more workshops of the more popular types and reduced the less well attended ones, but, rather, they decided to experiment with ways of increasing the popularity of those dealing with the study of curriculum and instruction. They scheduled them differently, particularly spacing the sessions farther apart. And, they began to advertise for teams from schools. Within a year, those workshops were attended to capacity. However, those increases were not at the expense of the other categories. The agency had increased its clientele.

The planners also worked to increase the effectiveness of all the categories. One example was in the area of classroom management. They noticed that the highly structured behavior-modification approaches drew more participants than the approaches derived from individual and group-centered therapies, such as the Classroom Meeting Model. They conducted a small interview study with the teachers of a nearby school and discovered that most of the teachers saw management from a highly structured perspective. The finding resulted in an introductory offering called "alternative models of classroom management" that turned out to be very popular and caused an increase in participants for the group-dynamics centered workshops.

The agency modified their program on the basis of simple "head count" data, thoughtfully analyzed and carefully interpreted.

What Happens to the Content?

How much of the content finds its way into practice, does the use persist, and what are the perceptions of its effects? Here the evaluation approaches the transfer question that is so vital to the effectiveness of the system. Sampling will become very important, for to try to study transfer by all the teachers attending a large smorgasbord of offerings would entail enormous effort.

Using the example above, suppose our agency begins by analyzing the objectives of the workshops and selects the ones that have content and skill objectives that are pertinent to instruction. Then, suppose they randomly select one workshop from each category and, further, randomly select six participants from each workshop for follow-up studies. Those persons are interviewed at intervals following the workshop, seeking information about use and types of use and perceptions of effects on students. The results will resemble those obtained in the Ames study described in chapter 12.

Because we know that it is possible, with good design, to have consistent levels of transfer of 90 percent or better, the question is how closely the results of the interviews approach that figure. If the use of content is low, then improving training design needs to be considered. For example, a district we know offerred ten days' of instruction in various forms of cooperative learning to several hundred of its teachers as volunteers, providing substitutes for participants or paying them for summer and Saturday study. Their interviews had two findings of particular interest. One was that only about 25 percent of the teachers used any of the varieties of cooperative learning following the ten days of training and nearly all of those who did used the simpler, highly structured forms. Hardly anyone used the more complex forms that had occupied most of the workshop time. The planning group faced a number of issues. One was whether to go to a "bring a friend" format and organize participants into peer-coaching teams and see if that would help. A second issue was whether the workshop was adequately designed. (It turned out that there were very few demonstrations!) A third was whether too much was being attempted in one package, which led them to consider having an introductory offering of the simpler, highly structured forms, working on implementation, and making other offerings of the more complex forms.

A simple evaluation design had provided plenty of information on which to improve their system. Note how the interview phase depended on sampling both offerings and people, making the process feasible in terms of cost and effort. Had they tried to interview all the participants in all their offerings the process would have broken down.

In our own work, we ask teachers to provide us with simple "logs of use" that include information about how the students are responding and what kinds of help the teachers feel they need, and we select a sample for more in-depth study to help us plan events tailored, as best we can, to their perceptions of their needs.

Are the Participants Studying the Effects on Their Students?

We now turn to a major process objective of staff development, which is to support reflective teaching and facilitate the "teacher as researcher." We assume now that the workshops include provision for discussing how participants will study the responses of their students and will provide them, when necessary, with classroom-relevant tools for doing so. Our search is for economical ways of helping people conduct studies in the context of teaching and learning what kinds of help they may need to do so.

One direct way is to schedule sessions where people share their studies, which helps build community and gives us a chance to see what they produce. In our own work, we have found that helping people study student responses is one of our most technically demanding tasks because of the wide range of preparation people have for this aspect of teaching.

Studying Effects from a Teaching Model.   An example comes from a workshop where we had been working with upper-grade teachers on mnemonic devices to help students learn and retain the number facts. Some teachers developed a pretest to ascertain what facts the students knew, then taught them how to use the mnemonics, and gave a posttest to find out how much they had learned. They were also interested in retention and gave additional tests at two-week intervals for a month, following each up with study sessions for their students. By that time all the students knew just about all the facts. They then scheduled a test two months later so they could study whether the information had transferred into long-term memory.

Some of the other teachers left out the pretest, so learning could not be ascertained, but gave delayed-recall tests. Several teachers reported they would not use pretests because "that was cheating. The kids would know what would be on the final test." Nonetheless, the sharing process helped all the teachers get a sense of how effective had been teaching the students the devices, and the discussions over the pretest problem was useful to all. The amount of information gained by the first group of teachers was impressive to nearly everybody, and helped prepare people for similar studies on the effects of other models of teaching.

A Texas Physics Teacher.   Rob Robins, a physics teacher in Marshall, Texas, participated in an instructional improvement program in which he learned several models of teaching (Inductive Thinking, Concept Attainment, Cooperative Learning). Prior to his participation in this teaching program, he had maintained records from the previous year on student grades for unit tests over specific concepts. His questions were specific to the concepts his students are expected to master in physics; for example, Did students taught with a combination of cooperative and constructivist models of teaching perform better than students in the previous year who were taught with a lecture and recitation model?

He did not select a sample but used all student scores from two classes. Measures were teacher-made tests which, though not identical from year to year, were comparable in the knowledge tested and tasks required.

Mr. Robins is the classic example of a teacher who experiments with his behavior and studies its impact on his students. During the 1993–94 school year, he experimented only with his physical science class (ninth and tenth grades) and taught his advanced students (honors physics) as usual. Although he did not have exactly comparable classes each year (his physical science class in 1992–93 was an honors class and in 1993–94 a "regular" class), he compared the two groups throughout the 1993–94 school year.

He began the 1993–94 year full of enthusiasm, trying his new strategies frequently in the first three weeks of school. On his first test (measurement, speed, velocity), his students performed poorly and he stopped all experimentation, convinced that he had harmed his students. Following the first "booster" training session, he agreed to try again. During the second six-week period, when the class was studying laws of motion, he experimented broadly with cooperative learning structures (even inventing some new ones) and gradually reintroduced inductive thinking processes. The mean grade for his physical science class increased by a full letter grade, and failure rates fell from 9 percent to 4 percent.

Despite this encouraging result, he again dropped all use of new strategies during the third six-week period, citing various time pressures as interfering with the development of new lessons. At the semester break, he reorganized his priorities and commitments and again implemented cooperative, inductive, and concept attainment strategies in his instruction. On one unit (kinds of chemical reactions), students mastered working with equations using reactants and products in two days' time, as opposed to the two weeks spent the year before with an honors class. The mean test grade for the honors class on this unit had been 70 out of a possible 100 whereas the regular class (1993–94) scored a mean of 90 out of a possible 100. The regular class also outscored the honors class on the very difficult "momentum" unit (mean scores of 78 compared with 72 the previous year). The mean grade for the regular physical science class at the end of the 1993–94 school year was 81 (B–) as compared with 77 (C+) for the honors class in the 1992–93 year.

Reflecting on what he had learned in experimenting with his teaching behavior, Mr. Robins has made several observations and decisions in preparation for his next school year. First, he notes that he didn't initially give the students enough time to learn to respond to the new strategies. During the second semester, when students had almost daily experience, they developed greater skill in cooperative behavior and, according to Mr. Robins, greater flexibility and willingness to experiment with new strategies. He also observed that during cooperative work, "some of the worst [in science] kids said some of the best 'wrong' things I have ever heard. Their thinking was phenomenal and their hypotheses, although incorrect, showed reasoning far beyond what I typically expect from 'regular' classes." Mr. Robins admitted that his "experimental" class became his favorite class of the day. Next year he will experiment with new teaching strategies in all his classes and collect data more systematically to target what is and isn't working.

Mr. Robins conducted this study for his own information. As a professional who continuously studies his craft and strives to improve his skills, he is naturally curious about the impact on his students when he experiments with his own behavior.

Here again, we are illustrating a simple device, incorporated as part of our long-term objective of helping teachers conduct classroom research, and from which we have gained a good deal of informal knowledge about how to strengthen that aspect of our work. We reiterate that this aspect of the work can be technically demanding. For example, helping people learn to assess quality of writing and study the effects of instruction on it is very complicated and time-consuming. However, some of the technically difficult work is very rewarding, as it was in the case of the Ames project (see chapter 12).

What Do People Think about Their Experiences?

When and how to sample opinion is the question. We want to move from an evaluation system that depends, as most staff development programs currently do, on opinionaires about events. Opinions are important, to be sure, but their measurement is trickier than sometimes assumed, and the overreliance on surveys of satisfaction is what we question.

One simple way to sample opinion is to incorporate it into the type of interview study discussed above. On the whole, interviews give more information than do questionnaires, especially about how to improve events, and ties the study of opinion to the study of use. If people liked an event but don't use the content, we need to know why. As Miles and Huberman (1984a) brought to the attention of the field, initial attitudes do not necessarily predict use, but as people become good at something, their attitude toward it improves dramatically. Thus, we recommend studying attitudes along with use. In the Augusta project described in chapter 8, the persons who developed "executive control" most rapidly became the most positive, even if they had started with lukewarm attitudes toward the content. The persons who were stuck for long periods of time at the level of routine use tended to become discouraged until they "broke through" and their learning curve went up.

Studying initial reactions to events is tricky, to say the least. Unless tied to the study of use, first opinions can be deceptive. In Hopkins's (1990) study, the participants in a lengthy workshop were very positive toward the process and the content, but subsequent use, even supported by periodic workshops and get-togethers, was very low for most teachers. Miles and Huberman's (1984a) extensive long-term studies found initial attitudes a very poor predictor of subsequent use, which is the bottom line of attitudes. We will make just a few technical comments on the use of questionnaires.

On the Nature of Items.   Closed-ended items need to be few and not redundant to one another. Asking people their opinion of the service provider (the "presenter" in common argot), their content, and the process generally produces highly correlated responses. If one item will do, why use three? Mixing items on different aspects of events tends to confuse respondents. Asking opinions about room arrangements, refreshments, audio-visual aids, materials, providers, content, and process all at once can generate deceiving results. If the room is uncomfortable and opinion is asked about that, there is likely to be an effect on opinions expressed about the people and content. We favor sticking with a few items about content and process and asking people directly what they think about the nuts-and-bolts aspects.

We strongly resist the use of omnibus questionnaires of the "this questionnaire can be used to evaluate any event" type, primarily because they are almost impossible to design. Just how hard it is was illustrated recently in the results of surveys of opinions of events at a conference by a national organization. For a simple example, a one-hour talk that was applauded repeatedly by an audience of nearly one thousand people was accompanied by a form asking "was adequate time provided for interaction among the participants" (none) and "what was the quality of the 'handouts'" (there were none). Even though such a form may provide a place for "not applicable" the fact that it is asked implies some degree of appropriateness and can confuse responses. If we want to find out how people feel, we can take the time to tailor our instrument to the event.

Charming the Response.   When we're asked our opinions, can we sort out our reactions to the content and process from a strand of the event designed to get us to produce favorable responses? In other words, can service providers lead us to "want" to give their events high marks?

You bet they can. An excellent review of the literature on the subject (Abrams, 1984) includes studies where responses were manipulated spectacularly. It stands to reason that most experienced service providers have, perhaps unconsciously, learned to get good if not excellent ratings, which makes interpretation difficult. We don't worry much about this except that inexperienced providers sometimes show up badly, and we don't want a situation where young and new talent is not nourished. When building the cadres of teacher-trainers mentioned so frequently in the book, a major task is helping talented teachers transition to the role of giving service to their peers. The job is not technically difficult, but many teachers fear that their peers will not respond positively to them in the new role. We believe much of the fear comes because they know intuitively that, without experience, they will not yet have learned how to ensure positive response. We are uncomfortable when they are submitted to a questionnaire evaluation right after their first workshop and are compared to "the old smoothies."

Charm is real.

A Basic System for Looking at the Individual Component

We have suggested addressing four questions:

Who participates in what?
What happens to the content?

Are participants studying the effects on their students?

What do people think about their experiences?

The evaluation is run as an inquiry into how to improve the system, where participants in decision making, service providers, and participants join together to improve the component. Evaluation needs to be both embedded and economical, with sampling used when possible, and everyone should share in the idea and the process of working together to improve the system. We avoid collecting data that are not needed or will not be used (those heaps of files of questionnaires), and implementation becomes the fulcrum of the process.

THE COLLECTIVE COMPONENT

The collective component serves schools in two ways. One is by providing facilitation to schools as they analyze what they teach, how they teach, the social climate of the school, and, consequently, make initiatives to improve it. The second is staff development in support of the schoolwide initiatives in curriculum, instruction, and technology. We will concentrate on the assessment of facilitation first and discuss the effects of staff development when we discuss the study of the district initiatives, for the process for studying staff development for schools is very similar to studying the process for the district initiatives.

Studying the Effects of Facilitation

Studying process effects is not easy and can be very time-consuming if the questions are not sharply defined. Essentially, the questions center around the faculty's ability to organize themselves, engage in focused study, and generate initiatives and, most important for the system, whether facilitation needs to be modified which, given the history of the area, is almost certain to be the case.

Let us imagine a district with a dozen schools. (More or less will not affect what we have to say. Size affects organization, but not the process of evaluation itself.) The district has organized an action research facilitation team with members from each school faculty. The team has studied approaches for recreating schools as self-renewing organizations. Their job is to help the schools move forward and to facilitate the development of the organization more or less along the lines we described in chapters 1 to 3. The evaluation begins by looking at the condition of the structure for collective actions.

Are the schools organized into peer-coaching teams in preparation for learning new things?

Has time been provided for team and faculty meetings?

Are data being collected on the "vital signs" of the school: grades, other indicators of achievement, disciplinary action, connection of the school with parents and other community members?

Has a process for collective decision making been established?

The facilitators can collect and share these data by organizing the faculties to, periodically, prepare summaries of progress. Thus, the pictures they paint for one another are products of the faculties they are facilitating.

If progress is being made, all to the good. If it is not, the facilitators and committee, including the principals, need to think about how to change how they are handling the facilitation. Generally speaking, schools who cannot establish these or equivalent structures will have a difficult time developing initiatives (Joyce, Wolf, & Calhoun, 1993). If there are signs of sticking at this level, the facilitators can interview teachers to obtain their perceptions about what is wrong and how to fix it. The results can be shared and further decisions made about how to change the facilitation process.

The evaluation proceeds by exploring the kinds of initiatives the schools are developing. The initiatives the schools develop are the fulcrum of the site-based school renewal process. What are the student learning objectives and why? What kinds of staff development are planned? How will implementation be studied? How will effects on students be studied? What is the level of commitment to the initiatives?

Again, the facilitators can lead the schools to respond to these questions and the answers can be shared with an eye to improving the process and the initiatives themselves.

Having identified the presence and nature of initiatives, the evaluation can proceed to explore the product of the initiatives in terms of implementation and effects. The same questions can be asked and types of data collected as in the discussion of the individual component, but now are collected and shared by the faculties. The facilitators share the information, again plan how to improve facilitation, and get ready to continue the cycle.

Next Time Around

The cycle is repeated. The process should be easier the second time around. With experience, the facilitators should become more expert. The need for study and improvement will continue. The goal is that every school will be able to enter and complete the process as a part of normal operations.

THE DISTRICT COMPONENT

Now we turn to districtwide initiatives in curriculum, instruction, and technology, governed as we described in chapters 1 to 3 and will discuss further in chapter 12. These initiatives have substantial student-learning goals and are designed to track implementation and effects on students so that the initiatives can be improved. In other sections of the book, we have described the way the Richmond County, Georgia, schools and Ames, Iowa, schools went about the process of evaluating their distictwide initiatives. Here we will illustrate the process by turning to another districtwide initiative that was studied in-depth (Joyce & Wolf, 1992).

Just Read

The Just Read program (discussed in chapter 4) was a response to concerns about student reading and writing performance. Research on the connection between reading (skill as well as quantity) and the quality of writing as well as reports of how little American students read independently outside of school (NAEP, 1992) provided the impetus for Just Read.

The program, described here for the eight elementary schools, was designed to greatly increase students' out-of-school reading (and presumably, therefore, to decrease the hours spent watching television). The effort was broadly publicized, implementation data were collected daily (students kept logs of their independent reading), successes were celebrated, and the program was, in fact, extremely successful in increasing the numbers of books read by students outside of class (see chapter 4).

The questions generated for the evaluation of the project were: Has reading comprehension increased more than would be predicted by a normal year's growth? If reading comprehension has increased, has it done so in correlation with the greater amounts of independent reading? Has writing competence improved? Are improvements in writing correlated with amounts of independent reading?

Standardized tests of reading comprehension were administered to all district students as part of the district testing program (CTBS), and writing samples were collected from all students. A sample, however, was selected for intense study and analysis. All district fifth-grade classes comprised the sample. Fifth grade was chosen for special scrutiny because, at the end of elementary school, reading competence is so essential before progressing to middle school and the demands of more challenging academic material.

While all students were tested in March of 1991, fifth-grade students were administered an equivalent form of the CTBS reading test in September of 1990. Fifth-graders also responded to three identical writing prompts during the 1990–91 school year—the first in September, the second in January, and the third in May. Writing samples were scored with the system used in the National Assessment of Educational Progress (Quellmalz & Burry, 1983) to allow comparison of Panama DODDS students with a national sample.

The first question addressed was reading comprehension. The mean grade-level-equivalent for fifth-graders in September (pretest) was 5.7 and in March (posttest), seven months later, 6.8. Not only were students at fifth grade exceeding their prior rates of growth in reading comprehension, as a group they were scoring a year above grade level. Next, reading score gains were examined in conjunction with how much students had read outside of school. Schools were classified as "high implementation" or "low implementation," depending on the mean number of books fifth-grade students had read during the year. Four schools were high-implementation schools (mean number of books read by students was 64, 62, 55, and 52 respectively for the four schools) and five schools were low-implementation schools (mean number of books read by students was 43, 38, 30, 28, and 27.)

TABLE 9.1 Reading gain by implementation level: Panama DODDS "Just Read" (5th grade)

CTBS	High Implementation	Low Implementation
Pretest (9/15/90)	5.5 GLE	5.9 GLE
Posttest (3/15/91)	6.8 GLE	6.2 GLE
GAIN	1.3 GLE	.3

Reading comprehension scores were then grouped by school and means were computed for high- and low-implementation schools (see Table 9.1). Reading gains were, in fact, much greater for high-implementation schools and the evaluation data enabled teachers, parents, and administrators to draw some conclusions about the impact of students' independent reading on their ability to comprehend what was read. And because teachers and parents cooperated to encourage and reward students for out-of-class reading, the success of their joint efforts was important for future collaborative efforts in school improvement.

Writing samples were scored with the Analytic Scales for Assessing Students' Expository and Narrative Writing Skills (Quellmalz & Burry, 1983), a six-point scale on which levels one and two are clearly substandard, levels three and four are minimally competent, and levels five and six are good to excellent quality. The National Assessment of Educational Progress (Applebee et al., 1990) uses the scale at grades 4, 8, and 12, with the expectation that, by grade 12, students should be scoring four or higher on the scale.

Fifth-graders in the Panama "Just Read" project made substantial gains during the 1990–91 school year in writing competence, and again, the results for students in high-implementation schools (that is, schools in which students greatly increased the amount of independent reading done out of school) were much greater than for students in low-implementation schools (see Table 9.2).

TABLE 9.2 Writing quality for fifth-graders in Panama "Just Read" program

	High Implementation	Low Implementation
Pretest (means)	2.7	2.6
Posttest (means)	3.3	2.9
GAIN	.6	.3

Compared with the average yearly gain of students examined by NAEP, students in high-implementation schools gained more than three standard deviations (an effect size of 3.4) and those in low-implementation schools exceeded the national mean gain by an effect size of 1.2. In all fairness, it should be noted that, according to the *National Report Card* (NAEP, 1992), the average fourth-grade student reads only about seven books a year, so even the low-implementation schools greatly exceeded that number.

Teachers, parents, principals, and central office staff worked diligently to increase the amounts of reading done by their students. Building leadership teams at each site coordinated school efforts, and central office staff compiled data for districtwide reporting. The continuous documentation of progress toward goals and the positive evaluation findings were gratifying to all involved, including the students.

The evaluation design involved every student in the study of books read, every school in books read by their students, and the development of the picture for the district. Then, the effects on reading comprehension and quality of writing were studied.

THE AUGUSTA PROJECT

In chapter 4, we discussed the Augusta Project as an example of successful school improvement, and in chapter 8, we described the study of implementation for that project. Here, we revisit the Augusta Project and its evaluation design. Student outcomes of interest at the middle schools were grades (which formed the basis for promotion or retention), behavior (as reflected in suspensions), and for both elementary and middle schools, standardized achievement scores (for this district, the Iowa Test of Basic Skills [ITBS]).

For the middle school represented in the first three project schools, grades improved during year one of the project such that 70 percent earned promotion at the end of the first year and 95 percent earned promotion by the end of the second year. In the year before the project, only 30 percent of the students were earning promotion, based on their grades.

As grades improved, discipline problems decreased. In the year before the project began, the middle school reported 300 suspensions; during the first year of the project, that number fell to 70.

Growth was also reflected in standardized test scores. Prior to the project, the average student in the middle school was gaining six months for every ten months of instruction. By the end of the first project year, the average student was gaining ten months growth for ten months instruction, although students in high-implementation classrooms were gaining approximately 20 months growth for 10 months instruction. By the end of the third year of the project, when a cadre of teachers had trained an additional six schools, ITBS scores were showing general improvement. For the first nine project schools, each of which administered eight ITBS subtests to their students, a total of 72 tests were reported. Forty of the 72 tests showed gains of four months or greater, while 20 of the 72 tests showed gains of from two to four months. Because implementation was so carefully studied, project planners were able to identify patterns of high implementation with greater gains in ITBS scores.

SUMMARY

The evaluation of staff development programs is an inquiry involving all personnel in an analysis of the fruits of their labors. Evaluations should serve as feedback as individuals and groups reflect on their behavior and plan next steps in the growth and improvement cycle.

Evaluation requires a clear question as a beginning point, a question that plainly investigates the intended student outcomes of any change effort. Whether it is necessary to select a sample of students in order to answer the question adequately varies from setting to setting, as was evident from the examples described above. The types of data collected will be determined by the nature of the questions asked, as will the analysis of the measurements taken. Data should be summarized in simple and direct forms that clearly relate to the questions addressed and are easily communicated to all interested parties.

The examples of evaluations provided in this and other chapters illustrate simple and direct designs for inquiring into the links between teaching and learning. Although the information yielded in each case was invaluable to the individuals and groups conducting the studies, the benefits of such activity go far beyond the obvious advantages to students. A major benefit to teachers and administrators is the increased sense of efficacy that results from planning changes in what is taught and how it is taught, and seeing the results of those efforts.

part IV

The Intersection of Personal, Social, and Political Forces

Chapters 10 through 12 deal with the people who make up the structure of education. Chapter 10 examines ways of reorganizing the patterns of the structure in order to let our social and personal selves become more productive. Chapter 11 deals with research on individual variability and how variety affects us and can be capitalized on. Chapter 12 presents a somewhat prescriptive plan for governance.

People and Culture

Proposition: Because the structures of our organization affect our behavior so much, part of our ability to achieve freedom for ourselves and our students is to learn about those structures and how to change them.

We all have unique personalities and perceive the world through our unique conceptual lenses. We interact in small groups, and we, as personalities, interact with the other personalities to create a social system. These social systems have structures and normative patterns of behavior that affect us. We live in a larger society where the philosophical traditions of our culture and the issues and ways of resolving them place us in a larger social context.

From all of these perspectives we find that we live in a world of both tendency (our predilections) and variability (our adaptability). As personalities, we have consistency—we are recognizable from situation to situation—and yet we adjust, partly from inner feelings (some days we feel confident and integrative while on others we feel less secure and less adaptive to others) and partly from adaptation (in a group of assertive people we may behave differently than in a group of relatively reticent folks). Thus, our personalities interact with the social contexts in which we find ourselves. In the larger sense, we are recognizably consistent but we find ourselves pulled by varying normative patterns.

To make things just a bit more complicated, we are influenced by the structural conditions of organizations. One of the chief messages in Senge's (1990) *The Fifth Discipline* is that the structures of organizations affect our behavior in ways that are often opaque to us. The organizational structures seem to draw our behavior down channels that seem inevitably to be trod. Awareness of the fact that those avenues are products of the structure is very difficult to come by. Also, as Peter Drucker points out (as in Drucker, 1988), organizations pull energy toward the maintenance of the organization rather than toward changing it. In other words, the structures are inherently stabilizing. The creation of a "homeostasis of change" (Joyce, Hersh, & McKibbin, 1983) is, despite its oxymoronic character, one of the necessary solutions. Essentially, finding stability in productive adaptation is extremely important.

The pessimism manifested by Sarason (1982, 1990) and Cuban (1990) about school reform efforts arises from their recognition that the very structures of American organizations (they write specifically about the school) are designated to maintain rather than to adapt. The pivotal question is whether we can create enough awareness for ourselves that we can "back off" from our routines and generate organizational relationships that enable us to study our practice and make productive changes in it.

PEOPLE, SOCIAL NORMS, AND ORGANIZATIONAL STRUCTURES: STRUCTURES AND PROCESSES FOR PRODUCTIVE CHANGE

Some of the implications of "the way we are" have to do with structure and others with the process of creating and maintaining a flexible and adaptive system.

On Structure

As we contemplate the development of a comprehensive system, we find that the creation of the three components we favor is almost impelled by the realities of personal, social, and philosophical realities. We and our cohorts are the developers of any system. The system needs to accommodate all of us, and yet lead all of us to growth. We create study groups and peer-coaching groups and the blend of our personalities gives texture to our interactions. We live in faculties where norms of autonomy and privatism will pull our behavior, and yet we need to build democratic systems and collective purposes that can sustain us as a social group. Our structure pulls us apart. We have to know this and fight it as we try to build collaborative organizations.

Can we create a world where differences flourish and yet we can work together to get the job done? Yes, we can, but to do so requires perspectives that balance the nomothetic (social) and the idiographic (individual) in proper measures.

Peer-Coaching Study Teams. Perhaps no change is more needed than the development of social arrangements that enable educators to work supportively together, help one another reflect on teaching, and help one another make sensible changes. Thus, we recommend the organization of faculties *in all schools* into what we call peer-coaching study teams. The study of teaching is an intimate process. Whether one is reflecting on teaching or needs to get a change in place, one needs companionship, and we have to create structures that facilitate the type of close understanding that enables support to occur. The structure for intimate colleagueship that we see as the peer-coaching study team is the building block of an organization that provides both caring support and the reflection necessary as people think out instructional decisions and work to enhance their professional repertoire. As we will see, these microcosmic groups can also be the backbone of the changes in governance that are so needed. In the long run, the entire "teacher as inquirer" movement will depend on the creation of these small inquiring groups.

Time in the Workday.   Second, the structure of the school was not designed to engender the conditions that make it easy to stand back, reflect, study, and change course either as individuals or as faculties. Essentially, maintenance of the system is the implicit priority in the structure. Hence, we advocate making structural provision for staff development and school improvement in the creation of time within the workday. We believe that a good starting point is the establishment of a regular afternoon time period of two and a half to three hours of study. Stevenson and Stigler (1992) have put it very well in their discussions of American and Asian education, when they point out that American teachers are overworked. By that they mean that work time is scheduled to the hilt with instructional duties. When individual or collective study is proposed, the initial reaction is that the proposals create an "overload." Within the present structure, the perception of overload is accurate. So, let's change the structure.

Room for Individuals.   To put it mildly, individual personalities are extremely important and, for educators, as Myrna Cooper (1988) phrased it, "Idiosyncrasy is their culture." While autonomy will not be celebrated as much as more collaborative organizations are built, the richness of diverse personalities is the real stuff of education—thus, our advocacy of the allotment of a good-sized share of resources to a component that is very responsive to perceived needs, including provision for individual needs to affect the spectrum of opportunities. Essentially, the process of "reflective teaching" is legitimized and supported, not for small groups of volunteers or favorites, but for all. We would create a component that deliberately caters to personality differences. Does that mean that individuals will select different foci for growth and change those foci as they change? Surely it does. Does it mean that some individuals will use the individual component more often and more effectively than others? Surely it does. Does the component leave untouched the norms of autonomy and privatism and even emphasize and capitalize on them? Yes it does. We intend the creation of circumstances, within the larger system, that free the spirits of individuals *as they are*. The norms will not touch their use of that component of the system. The only condition is that they have *to do* something.

Democratic Structures.   The absence of a time structure has combined with the absence of democratic structures to create a situation where nearly everyone in the system feels helpless to bring about sensible changes. Curriculum coordinators preside over the rewriting of curriculum guides knowing that they cannot either develop shared understanding about the changes in them or the staff development necessary to implement them. Yet, the "paths" in the structure of the organization draw them repeatedly into futile and repetitive activity. Directors of "categorical" programs feel helpless in the face of legislative "mandates" to create and maintain programs while knowing that the structures to do the job well are not present. Staff development coordinators paste programs together by stealing a little time here and a little opportunity there, knowing that they will have weak implementation and will frustrate others in the organization. Principals try to lead schools where there is neither the time nor the traditions of democratic process to make integrative leadership easy. Teachers feel helpless because the lack of democratic structure means that, aside from the changes they can make in their classrooms, they have no channels through which they can get a concern aired decently in a body that can take action. Many of the teachers we work with feel the lack of a coherent curriculum—they want what they do to add up over time in the lives of the children—but they have no way of making the curriculum coherent. Nor, as it happens, does anyone else.

One of the reasons many teachers have relatively cynical views about administrators is that those administrators have not set up a good decision-making process. Teachers have a hard time realizing that the administrators are as helpless as they are, and administrators have a hard time acknowledging their helplessness. The miracle is that there is not more cross-role group-blaming activity. As it is there are many serious problems that are not solved because the mechanisms for making the change are not there. An example is the urgent need for bilingual education in our schools that serve non-English native speakers. From a technical perspective the problem is not difficult to approach, although healthy solutions require a fair magnitude of change. Few districts or schools have the social system to contemplate the solutions that are at hand.

The creation of democratic structures is the remedy at hand. Within schools, peer-coaching study teams are connected to the faculty as a whole and to the district councils as well.

The collective and systemic components we envision have many elements in common. Both require a democratic structure, both have to confine the number of initiatives taken during any one time period, and both have to reach for the proximal. The essential differences arise from the size of the units involved.

Setting up the structures for democratic decision making will not solve the problems instantly, but those structures are essential conditions to enable us to learn how to make decisions together. These structural changes will not overhaul the culture of schooling by themselves, but, where they have been developed, they start us along the way to a more satisfying and effective professional culture.

On Process

The essence of process is embedded in our beliefs, for as human beings we do not simply behave; we create understandings that make our behavior comprehensible and meaningful. We concentrate here on some of the process-related beliefs that will operate as the system is created.

Social Power and Sense of Efficacy. The autonomous world of teaching has had its virtues in that teachers and administrators have learned great self-reliance and have a sense of being able to have great influence in their own domains. The weakness is the lack of connectedness to others and the lack of a support system to help when we have trouble solving problems. For example, if you can't reach a student successfully, you have few if any places to turn in the present organization. In the process of planning one's personal staff development, one will have new opportunities—one can "buy" the service to solve problems better. In the context of study groups, one can have companionship in reflecting on teaching. Being able to help create the agenda for school and district components will increase social power and the sense of professional meaningfulness. Will everyone move at equal rates? Will everyone believe equally that actual participation will take place? Of course not. But time will increase confidence.

Confidence as a Learner. The weak support system has caused many people to underestimate their ability as learners. In our own work where we help faculties learn models of teaching that are new to their repertoires, we find that a very important, rarely surfaced cognition is that many teachers and administrators believe that adding a teaching skill to their repertoire is a lot harder than it actually is. Discovering that one can learn new skills at will changes one's view of oneself. Teachers often are criticized for being poor "risk-takers." We take quite a different view. Given adequate staff development, teachers attempt new content with aplomb. Too often in their past, they have been asked to place confidence in poorly designed training, and they have been quite right to be tentative. We envision that everyone becomes a student of staff development and learns what it takes to learn complex skills and insist on the appropriate designs and conditions. As we have seen, the peer-coaching study teams are critical in developing the sense of power that one can literally learn any educational procedure.

Trust, Differences of Opinion, and Democracy. The essence of democracy is accommodation. When you move out of the isolated classroom into a democratic process, you find that your perceptions have to be blended with others to form the conceptual matrix from which decisions emerge. You have to learn to trust the process. In your own classroom, you can trust the decision-making process to a fault. If you are wrong, you will never hear about it from other adults. Trusting collective judgment may be foreign to the school, but is a lot less risky than the alternatives. Many principals and central office personnel will have to learn a whole new range of skills (Murphy, 1992) as they join peer-coaching teams and learn to facilitate a democratic process. For everybody, the fact that individual differences in perception are valuable—that differences are to be celebrated rather than repressed and that differences are an opportunity rather than an obstacle—has to be recognized.

Professional Knowledge.   Because preservice preparation of teachers and administrators is so weak, educators have had to discover and develop their own teaching skills. Knowledge of teaching and organization comes largely from personal experience. There are many virtues to knowing one can learn to do a tough job well. And, the quality of what individuals learn should not be underestimated. An unfortunate condition is that few educators have had the benefits of connecting to the research on teaching and curriculum, and many educators are not sure that such knowledge exists. Learning to reach into the professional literature is a long-overdue process. And, yet, in the early stages of connecting to the body of literature, people are necessarily skeptical—in some cases skeptical that there *is* any body of knowledge. Also, much staff development has sometimes presented research findings as prescriptive, whereas research, as we have said repeatedly, opens up avenues for exploration and inquiry. We need to embrace the possibilities opened by research, but not assume that we should lie supine before it. Not to learn it, however, is a great loss. We need to become a knowledge-oriented community.

Public Information about Student Learning.   The individualism of the traditional structure has meant that data about student learning have been relatively private. Individuals measure student learning and then assign grades to students. Collecting information together, as, for example, on quality of writing, and watching progress is a change of considerable magnitude.

Now, information about students becomes more public. Rather than reporting grades as an unquestioned, private activity, indicators about how students are progressing—and how learning is measured—become matters of public record. The development of public indicators of progress is a significant part of the progression toward professionalism and, yet, simultaneously, is one of the most emotional of all the changes we are talking about.

We have found that the public manifestation of student growth is one of the most difficult areas involved in school improvement. Even Just Read (see chapter 9), where the only type of data has to do with the amounts of reading students do at home, upsets many professional educators because, we think, it is such a direct measure of effectiveness (can you get the kids reading at home?), but learning to collect such information and share it is essential to studying student learning and, thus, to measuring progress.

STRUCTURAL CHANGES AND BELIEFS

Thus far in this chapter we have discussed some "first step" changes in the structure of the school as an organization and a few of the many beliefs that are part of the shift from a maintenance-oriented organization to one that is oriented toward study and, as a consequence of that study, appropriate change.

Something else that is little understood is how easy it is to change and how small are the changes that make a big difference for students. Sometimes it is thought that school improvement involves changes that are nearly cataclysmic in magnitude. In fact, the important changes are of a "little bit here, little bit there" variety and are not that tough to make. Probably the tough part involves changing some beliefs about student capability and our own capacity to operate differently.

Creating Missing Elements: Changing a Culture?
Or Creating a Culture?

Proposition: That a major part of the school-related dimension of a staff development system is to help schools create the cultural conditions that will give rise to productive school improvement initiatives. Then, the task is to support those initiatives.

There have now been enough studies of site-based school improvements to make it clear that most faculties have to change how they relate and do business in order to generate school improvement programs that actually get implemented and show effects on student learning. Students of the renewal process have increasingly concentrated on the problem as one of generating a cultural change. Fullan (1982) in particular has written penetratingly about the question. His essential position is that the current culture of schools is not particularly congenial to change efforts and that substantial changes in the culture are needed if schools are to inquire into their own functioning and find ways of improving it. We agree with Fullan and believe, as he does, that the processes of making and carrying out initiatives are not inherently stressful but that trying to make changes within the current cultural configuration *is* stressful and will be alleviated only if the social side of things is attended to.

Proposition: We argue here that the cultural change process is not just one of doing business differently, but is one of creating norms and

interactive patterns in areas where they have not existed. A cultural void
has to be filled.

At the 1992 annual meeting of the Association for Supervision and Curriculum
Development, Henry Izumizaki, a specialist in organizational development and
community organization, startled the participants in a session on improving urban
schools; he remarked that the process of helping school faculties prepare to
embark on school renewal is as much one of creating a culture as it is one of
changing a culture. He pointed out that the autonomous classrooms—in a real
sense "little schools"—had not only bred the idiosyncratic norms with which
we are so familiar (Lortie, 1975) and which are pointed to by many observers
as obstacles to collective action, but have contributed something far more
injurious by causing collective norms and collegial processes *not* to develop.
Had the school format been interdependent, norms supporting collective action
would probably have emerged. As it is, those norms developed, where they
developed at all, in a truncated form. We theorize that one reason for the
truncation is that interdependent activity often collides with the norms of
autonomy, which are dominant.

What norms are essential if school improvement is to be generated at the
school level? We have culled the literature on school renewal and the following
have emerged as ones having some support:

1. *Norms that support the sharing of decisions.* What is interesting about
shared decision making is the extent to which it represents a change. The
observation has emerged from several types of inquiry. Fullan (1982) has analyzed
the literature on change, studies of innovation, the sociology of the school, and
the psychosocial dynamics of leadership. Hallinger and Murphy (1985) have made
exhaustive studies of the principalship and school renewal efforts. Huberman
(1992), and Seashore-Louis and Miles (1990) have studied schools and individuals
attempting to generate innovations. Glickman (1993) has advocated shared
decision making as part of his general strategy to professionalize faculties. Little
(1982; 1990) has studied the social dynamics of faculties. Muncey and McLellan
(1993) have studied the dynamics of leadership in schools belonging to the
Coalition of Essential Schools. Calhoun (1992) has studied the League of Professional Schools and other settings and tracked the struggle as shared leadership
norms are worked out.

All have come to a similar conclusion: that the norms supporting shared
decision making are minimal or missing in the culture of many schools and have
to be built from the ground up.

For the organization to function as a setting for collective inquiry into itself,
everyone has to be involved when it comes to the making of important decisions.

2. *Norms that accept strong and active leadership.* There is an oxymoronic
truth in the juxtaposition of this norm with the previous one. The disconnection
of role-groups has made "official" leadership a difficult passage. A good many
educators deprecate the principalship and the role of central office personnel.
Now, leaders certainly should not embrace autocracy. But the creation of the

democratic structures we envision requires aggressive leadership to build faculties into the collective problem-solving groups that can influence the shape of the education of children and also the shape of the workplace.

3. *Norms against alienation and toward self-worth.* Perhaps no change is greater than the creation of affiliation, of the caring professional relationship. The loneliness of the autonomous classroom engendered feelings of being uncared for and neglected. In personal terms the consequence of the lack of organization has been a normless situation that is prone to the development of feelings of alienation.

4. *Norms of the high purpose of education.* The belief must be created and adhered to that everybody can learn and that hard work is the key. The American educational system was created to ensure the maximum possible equity in quality of life and social participation in the society. Unfortunately, many Americans have taken a genetic deterministic view of individuals—one that accepts differences in learning ability and problem-solving ability as inevitable. From that position the educational system is relatively helpless to do more than let genetic predisposition play its way out. Schools are part of the culture and are not immune to the common social beliefs. Yet, the power of education depends on the "hard work" components of achievement, rather than the "talent driven" ones. Whoever we work with, helping them to work hard is our business; and, for whatever proportion of students may be affected by talent, helping people learn that with a little more work here and there, they, too, can make a decent contribution. And, importantly, much of what is regarded as genius is, in fact, a whole lot of work, often dull work.

SUMMARY

The words of Stevenson and Stigler (1992) summarize our thoughts:

> The belief in the importance of hard work is not alien to Americans. The mystery is why, in the later years of the twentieth century, we have modified this belief in such a destructive way. Why do we dwell on the differences among us, rather than on our similarities? Why are we unwilling to see that the whole society is advanced when all of its members, not only the privileged socioeconomic and ethnic groups, are given the opportunity to use their abilities to their fullest? How much more strongly do we need to be shocked by data that herald decline in our children's academic achievement before we devote ourselves wholeheartedly and sincerely to the improvement of the education we give our children at home and at school? (223)

chapter **11**

The States of Growth of People in the Organization

Proposition: To live is to grow. The life of the organization is embodied in its ability to enable its people to grow.

This chapter celebrates individual differences. We expect individual differences and rejoice in the mix of personalities of people in our profession. With Stevenson and Stigler (1992), we are puzzled when educators worry that people don't respond identically to the same experiences. And we worry that our common characteristics are not more celebrated and capitalized on. As we begin a chapter that is built around a long line of research into individual differences, one that reveals dramatic variety, we need to discuss some of the things that we have in common; these commonalities lead us to believe that the teachers in this world who prize individualism so highly and yet are so concerned about our variety can make common cause in the creation of a democratically operated staff development system that brings us together and yet respects our personalities.

First of all, the training research is affirmative in that it suggests that teachers are capable learners and are able to master a wide range of curricular and instructional strategies and use them effectively in the classroom. This is a strong statement about education personnel, so often maligned as "burned-out," "aging," academically impoverished (Schlecty & Vance, 1983) and as working under intolerable conditions (McLaughlin et al., 1986). Although we are in favor of recruiting the best possible talent into education and providing them with the conditions under which they will flourish, we are very pleased with the capability of present personnel, especially considering that for some the time of initial preparation is so meager and its quality is so suspect. Teachers have lots of learning ability.

Second, it appears that staff development programs can be designed to allow educators to increase their learning capability. Essentially, the more skills people develop and the more they widen their repertoire, the greater their ability to master an even greater range of skills and strategies. Learning how to solve problems increases the ability to learn how to solve problems. However, programs that increase learning capacity involve participants openly and comfortably in the shaping of the process. An unacceptable oxymoron is a "flexibility training program" designed by master teachers to teach subservient students how to think creatively.

Third, educators have the very human tendency to respond affirmatively to a positive social and organizational climate, and, given a chance, know how to create one. Faculties that are organized into study and coaching teams and that work together for the improvement of the school are more cohesive, have higher morale, and are more responsive to initiatives from one another and from administrative leadership.

It is essential that the definition of the responsibilities of teaching includes the role as a faculty member much more prominently than it has in the past. Teachers who have worked in relative isolation naturally concentrate on their roles as organizer of the classroom and as instructor. However, both school improvement and systemic initiatives require collective action. And the study of teaching, even for individuals working on their personal/professional skills and knowledge, is greatly facilitated by contact with others.

Creating a collective environment requires *time* as much as anything else. If we build in time for interaction while studying and thinking about practice, moving from the norms of autonomy that were generated by the isolating structure into norms of collaborative activity is not difficult.

INDIVIDUAL DIFFERENCES

Within our goal of a collective environment, we need a frame of reference that will enable us to think about individual differences in personnel and to take those differences into account.

There are a number of ways of thinking about individual differences that are candidates for our use at the present time. Some of these have been developed to help us think about the learning styles of children (Dunn & Dunn, 1975; Gregorc, 1982; McCarthy, 1981) and can be applied to adults as well. Some are developed to distinguish various styles of thinking (e.g., Myers, 1962) and examine how those styles affect problem solving. There is at least one current theory that attempts to describe differences between children and adults as learners (Knowles, 1978).

A number of broad conceptualizations of personality can be applied to the behavior of teachers as instructors and as learners (Harvey, Hunt, & Schroder,

1961; Maslow, 1962; Erikson, 1950). Conceptual System Theory (Hunt, 1971) has been heavily studied and has been a useful predictor of teacher-student interaction, the breadth of styles employed by teachers, sensitivity to students and responsiveness to them, and, most pertinent here, aptitude to acquire the competence to use teaching skills and strategies (for example, see Joyce, Brown, & Peck, eds., 1981).

In this chapter we will discuss a framework that was developed from the study of the professional and personal lives of teachers in the California Staff Development Study (Joyce, Bush, & McKibbin, 1982). The framework was developed to guide practice in the organization of human resource development programs and school improvement efforts (McKibbin & Joyce, 1980; Joyce, Hersh, & McKibbin, 1983). Although it was developed from a strictly practical orientation, the findings are correlated with the theories of personality growth and take conceptual development, self-concept, and psychological maturity into account.

THE CONCEPT OF STATE OF GROWTH

As we indicated earlier, the framework was developed during a large-scale longitudinal study of staff development and school improvement practices in California. The objective was to obtain a detailed picture of the opportunities for growth experienced by teachers from their school setting, the district, universities, intermediate agencies (county offices of education and professional development centers), and other institutions. Case studies were made of more than 300 educators from 21 districts in seven counties and more than 2,000 others were surveyed through questionnaires. In addition to information about participation in the formal systems of support (courses, workshops, and the services of administrators and supervisors), interaction with peers was examined as were those aspects of personal lives that might have implications for professional growth. Thus, data were collected on what came to be termed the "formal," the "peer-generated," and the "personal" domains, depending on the origins of the activities that people engaged in.

The focus was the dynamic of individual interaction with the environment. The thesis was that within any given environment (say, a school in the San Francisco Bay area), opportunities for productive interaction leading to growth would be theoretically equal. That is, formal staff development systems, colleagues, opportunities to read, attend films and events in the performing arts, engage in athletic activity, etc. would be available to all personnel in profusion. *Thus, differences in activity would be a function of the individual's disposition to interact productively with the environment.* If we discovered differences, we could proceed to try to understand their origins and develop ideas for capitalizing on them.

The Formal, Peer-Generated, and Personal Domains

The amount of interaction in all three domains varied greatly. The differences were vast in both urban and rural areas and among elementary and secondary educators. They are easily illustrated in regions like the Bay Area and the Los Angeles Basin where literally thousands of courses and workshops are available; most principals and supervisors have been trained to provide active clinical support; many professional development centers in county offices and other agencies involve teachers in the selection of staff development opportunities; and there are active organizations of teachers of writing, science, and other curriculum areas. In addition, of course, the opportunities for personal activity of all sorts abound in these great metropolitan areas which also are close to mountain ranges, waterways, and oceans. The nature of the differences in each domain is interesting.

Formal Staff Development Opportunities.   Participation ranged from persons who experienced only the activities sponsored and required by the district (possibly only one or two workshops or presentations and one or two visits by supervisors or consultants) and who were *aware* of very few options to very active, aware persons with definite plans of professional enhancement. A small number effectively exploited the opportunities in universities and the larger teacher centers.

Peer-Generated Opportunities for Growth.   The range here was from persons who had virtually no professional discussions with any other teachers to persons who had close and frequent interaction, experienced mentoring relationships (on the giving or receiving end or both), and who gathered with others to instigate the introduction of innovations or initiatives for the improvement of the school.

The Personal Domain.   In their personal lives, some educators were extremely active, with one or two well-developed areas of participation and some others made virtually no use of the rich environments in which they lived. We found some very active readers and others who barely skim the headlines of the daily paper, some Sierra Club activists and others who had never visited Yosemite, some members of performing arts groups and other who have not seen a film or a live performance in ten years or more.

STATES OF GROWTH

Somewhat to our surprise, the levels of activity were correlated across domains. That is, those who were more active professionally were also more active personally. Looking for reasons, we concluded that the differences in levels of activity were produced by the individuals' orientations toward their environments, moderated by social influence.

Orientations toward the Environment

The essence of the concept is the degree to which the environment is viewed as an opportunity for satisfying growth. Thus the more active people view the environment as a set of possibilities for satisfying interaction. They initiate contact and exploit the possibilities. Less active persons are less aware of the possibilities or more indifferent to them. The least active persons expend energy protecting themselves from what they see as a threatening or unpleasant environment, avoiding contact and fending off the initiatives of others. Also, the persons who are more active and more initiating are also more *proactive.* That is, they draw more attention from the environment, bringing more possibilities within their reach. This phenomenon multiplies the opportunities for many people. It was not unusual for us to discover that certain schools that were characterized by a cluster of active people (and generally by an active principal) were regularly approached by central office personnel, teacher centers, and universities to be the trial sites for everything from computer technology to community involvement programs. Those people and their schools receive more resources and training while some schools, characterized by a cluster of resistant persons, were approached last, and many initiatives passed them by.

Social Influence

Close friends and colleagues, and the social climate of the workplace and the neighborhood, moderate the general dispositions toward growth. Affirmative and active friends and colleagues and positive social climates induce persons to engage in greater activity than they would if left to themselves. This finding provides another dimension to the general theme of chapter 3. The synergistic environment is not only essential for collective action but to generate the kind of colleagueship that will be productive for the states of growth of individuals.

   Also, as we will emphasize later, a major goal of a human resource development system is to increase the States of Growth of the personnel in the system, potentially benefiting the individuals as well as the organization and ensuring that the children are in contact with active, seeking personalities.

LEVELS OF ACTIVITY

Although the orientations toward growth are best represented on a continuum, people gradually, over time, develop patterns that have more clearly discernible edges, and it is not unreasonable to categorize them, provided we recognize that the categories blend into one another. With that caveat, the following prototypes are presented because they can be useful in explaining behavior and in planning staff development programs and organizing faculties to exploit them vigorously.

A Gourmet Omnivore

Our prototypes here are mature high-activity people who have learned to canvass the environment and exploit it successfully. In the formal domain they keep aware of the possibilities for growth, identify high-probability events, and work hard at squeezing them for their growth potential.

They constitute the hard-core clientele for teacher centers and arrays of district and intermediate-agency offerings for volunteers. They initiate ideas for offerings and find ways of influencing the policymakers. However, they are not negative toward system initiatives. They have the complexity to balance their personal interests with the awareness that they belong to an organization.

Our prototype omnivores find kindred souls with whom to interact professionally. They learn from informal interaction with their peers. A group of omnivores may work together and generate initiatives or attend workshops or courses together. When the computer appeared on the educational scene, it was often groups of omnivores who learned to use it and developed the computer centers in their schools.

It is in their personal lives that our prototype omnivores become most clearly defined. They are characterized by a general high level of awareness, but the distinguishing feature is one or two areas in which they are enthusiastically involved. These areas vary quite a bit from person to person. One may be an omnivorous reader; another a theatergoer; a third an avid backpacker or skier; a fourth a maker of ceramics. Some run businesses. In close consort with others, they generate activities. The spouses of omnivore tennis players are likely to find themselves with rackets in their hands and the close friends of moviegoers will be importuned to share films. Because of their proactivity, our mature omnivores have learned to fend off opportunities and protect time for their chosen avocations.

What is striking is their habit of both exploiting and enriching whatever environment they find themselves in. In the workplace, they strive to learn all they can about their craft and give and take energy from their peers. In their private lives, they find opportunities for development.

They are also distinguished by their persistence. In McKibbin and Joyce's (1980) study, the gourmet omnivores both sought training that would have a high likelihood for transfer and, once back in the workplace, practiced and created the conditions of peer support that enabled them to implement a remarkably high proportion of the skills to which they were exposed. They are also more likely than others to bring the ideas they gain in their personal lives into the workplace and use them in their teaching.

A Passive Consumer

About 10 percent of the persons we studied fit the profile of our "Gourmet Omnivores," and another 10 percent were somewhat less active, although still quite engaged with aspects of their environment. By far the largest number, however, (about 70 percent) resembled the prototype we term the "Passive Consumer."

The distinguishing characteristics of our passive consumers are a more or less amiable conformity to the environment and a high degree of dependence on the immediate social context. In other words their degree of activity depends greatly on who they are with. In the company of other passive consumers, our prototype is relatively inactive. We studied one school in which all of the personnel in one "wing" of the building were passive, and their interchange with others was amiable but involved few serious discussions about teaching and learning. They visited one another's classrooms rarely. None attended staff development activities that were not required by the administration. They had no objections to being required to attend those workshops, one day in the fall and one in the spring, and they enjoyed them, but did nothing with the content.

In another wing of the school two passive consumers found themselves in the company of two omnivores and an active consumer and were drawn into many of the activities generated by their more enterprising colleagues. They found themselves helping to set up computer workstations for the students, cooperating in scheduling and the selection of software, and learning word processing and how to teach their students to use self-instructional programs. They attended workshops on the teaching of writing with the study group instigated by the omnivores and began revamping their writing programs.

In personal life, our prototype passive consumer is also dependent on a consort. If they have relatively inactive spouses and extended families, they will be relatively inactive. If they are with relatives, friends, and neighbors who initiate activity, their levels of activity will increase.

A Reticent Consumer

Whereas our passive consumer has a relatively amiable, if rather unenterprising, view of the world, about 10 percent of the persons we studied expend energy actually pushing away opportunities for growth. We speak of these persons as reticent because they have developed an orientation of reluctance to interact positively with their cultural environment. We can observe this dynamic in both professional and domestic settings.

Our prototype reticent attends only the staff development that is required and is often angry about having to be there, deprecates the content, whatever it is, and tries to avoid follow-up activities. Our reticent treats administrative initiatives and those from peers with equal suspicion and tends to believe that negative attitudes are justified because "the system" is inherently oppressive and unfeeling. Thus, even peers who make initiatives are deprecated "because they are naive" if they believe that they will gain administrative support for their "idealistic" notions. Hence our reticent tends to view our omnivores as negatively as they do the hated administration. The hard-core reticent even rejects opportunities for involvement in decision making, regarding them as coopting moves by basically malign forces.

In discussion about personal lives, the structure of attitudes was similar. Our reticents tend to emphasize what they see as defects in people, institutions, services, and opportunities in a range of fields. Film, theater, athletic activity, state and national parks, books, and newspapers all are suffering rapid decay. ("Only trash gets published these days. . . . Movies are full of sex and violence.") In the richness of an urban environment they tend to emphasize crowding as an obstacle to participation to events. ("If I could get tickets. . . . If you didn't have to wait for a court. . . . You can never get in to the good movies. . . .") In the rural environments it is lack of facilities that gets the blame.

Even so, our reticent is not unaffected by the immediate social context. In affirmative school climates, they do not "act out" their negative views as much. In the company of omnivores, they can be carried along in school improvement efforts. Affirmative spouses who tolerate their jaundiced opinions good-naturedly involve them in a surprising number of activities. In the right circumstances they learn to take advantage of the opportunities in their lives. With respect to staff development, persons who are normally quite reticent can respond positively to well-designed events and practice well in the company of their peer-coaching colleagues.

CONCEPTUAL STRUCTURE, SELF-CONCEPT, AND STATES OF GROWTH

In an attempt to seek reasons for the differences in States of Growth manifested by the teachers we were studying, we turned to a number of developmental theories. Two of them are of particular interest to us here because their descriptions of development appear to correlate with the states of growth we found (Joyce, McKibbin, & Bush, 1983). One is conceptual systems theory, (Harvey, Hunt, & Schroder, 1961; Hunt, 1971) and the other is self-concept theory (Maslow, 1962). These theories both help us understand the States of Growth and ways of thinking about education personnel, as growth-oriented programs are planned and carried out. They help us understand why people respond as they do and provide us with a basis for creating environments that are likely to be productive both in terms of the content of the programs and the people for whom they are intended.

Conceptual Development

Conceptual systems theory describes persons in terms of the structure of concepts they use to organize information about the world. In the lowest developmental stages, persons use relatively few concepts for organizing their world, tend to have dichotomous views with few "shades of grey," and much emotion is attached to their views. They tend to reject information that does not fit into their concepts or to distort it to make it fit. Thus people and events are viewed as "right" or "wrong." Existing concepts are preserved.

At higher stages of conceptual development, people develop greater ability to integrate new information, are more decentered, can tolerate alternative views better, and their conceptual structure is modified as old concepts become obsolete and new ones are developed. New experiences are tolerated and bring new information and ideas, rather than being rejected or distorted to preserve the existing state.

For an example, let us consider persons at the lower and higher developmental stages on a first visit to a foreign culture. Persons characterized by the lower conceptual levels are suspicious of the "different" and tend to find fault with it. ("You can't *believe* what they eat there.") They peer through the windows of the tour buses with increasing gratitude that they will soon be returning to America. They speak loudly to the "stupid" hotel personnel who don't speak English. They clutch their wallets to keep them away from the conniving, dishonest natives and their unclean hands.

Their higher-conceptual-level companions are fascinated by the new sights, sounds, and smells. Gingerly they order the local dishes, comparing them with the familiar, finding some new and pleasing tastes, and bargaining for a recipe. They prefer to walk, avoiding the bus unless time forbids. They ask shopkeepers to pronounce the names of things. They brush off the grime to get a better look at the interesting vase in the corner. They speak quietly and wait for the hotel personnel to indicate the local custom.

There is a substantial correlation between conceptual development and the States of Growth of the teachers and administrators we studied. The omnivores are in a continual search for more productive ways of organizing information and have more complex conceptual structures as a result. Their openness to new experience requires an affirmative view of the world and the conceptual sophistication to deal with the new ideas they encounter. Our passive consumers have more limited structures and less ability to figure out how to reach for new experience and deal with it. Our reticents are busy protecting their present concepts and act offended by the presence of the unfamiliar. They can be as negative toward children they do not understand as they are toward the facilitators who try to bring new ideas and techniques into their orbit. Conceptual development is correlated with variety and flexibility in teaching styles (Hunt & Joyce, 1967), with ease in learning new approaches to teaching (Joyce, Brown, & Peck, eds., 1981), and with ability to understand students and modulate to them.

A change to a more productive orientation involves a structural change—a more complex structure capable of analyzing people and events from multiple points of view and the ability to assimilate new information and accommodate to it.

Self-Concept

More than 35 years ago Abraham Maslow (1962) and Carl Rogers (1961) developed formulations of personal growth and functioning that have guided attempts since then to understand and deal with individual differences in response to the physical and social environment. Rather than concentrating on intellectual aptitude and development, their theories focused on individuals' views of self or self-concepts. They took the position that our competence to relate to the environment is greatly affected by the stances we take toward ourselves.

Strong self-concepts are accompanied by self-actualizing behavior, a reaching out toward the environment with confidence that the interaction will be productive. The self-actualizing person interacts richly with the milieu, finding opportunities for growth and enhancement and, inevitably, contributing to the development of others.

Some persons feel competent to deal with the environment but accept it for what it is, and are less likely to develop growth-producing relationships from their own initiatives. They work within the environment and what it brings to them, rather than generating opportunities from and with it.

Others bear a more precarious relationship with their surroundings. They are less sure of their ability to cope. Much of their energy is spent in efforts to ensure that they survive in a less than generous world.

It is not surprising that we found a relationship between the States of Growth of the people we studied and their concepts of self. Our omnivores are self-actualizing. They feel good about themselves and their surroundings. Our passive consumers feel competent but are dependent on the environment for growth-producing opportunities. Our reticents feel that they live in a precarious and threatening world. The faults that they find in their surroundings are products not of being well-developed and able to discern problems the rest of us cannot see but of an attempt to rationalize their need to protect themselves from a world of which they are afraid.

RECENT RESEARCH

Hopkins (1990) and his colleagues, measuring States of Growth and self-esteem independently, found them to be nearly congruent. In the implementation of a complex arts curriculum, scores indicating levels of use were matched with four psychological-states levels, with the following results:

Psychological State	Implementation
Group One (Highest)	71.8
Group Two	50.7
Group Three	44.7
Group Four	18.1

Hopkins also found that the organizational climate of the faculties where the teachers worked influenced implementation, but not to the extent of the psychological states.

In chapter 8, we discussed the extensive study of implementation in the Augusta project. States of Growth were measured using the interview procedure used in the California Staff Development study, and coefficients of correlation computed with two measures of implementation were .87 and .88.

In the Ames study (Joyce et al., 1994), which will be discussed in chapter 12, the responses to the Individual Growth Fund, which provided the individual teachers throughout the district with funds for their personal staff development, varied widely. About one in six teachers did not use the fund and another sixth made minor use of it, while some of the teachers generated extensive and satisfying inquiries. Although the psychological measures described above were not employed, clearly individual differences influenced both use and satisfaction to a great extent.

The Ames study confirmed again an observation about the relationship between age and experience and the response to growth opportunities. The correlation between age and response was zero and there was no curvilinear relation. In 30 years of our work in this area, we have found age to be an insignificant variable. The rhetoric about "burnout" does not stand the test of formal investigations. In studies of response to Models of Teaching (Joyce, Weil, & Showers, 1992), age correlates, if anything, with increasing power as a learner and problem solver. Sangiser (1989), studying what motivates teachers to participate in staff development activities, also found that age and experience were not factors.

STATES OF GROWTH AND PROGRAM DESIGN

As we design programs we can use information about people's States of Growth to understand why people respond as they do to initiatives of various kinds, to capitalize productively on individual differences, and to try to help in their ability to grow, not only in the technical senses that we have stressed in the previous chapters, but also in their orientations toward the world and what it offers them. During our discussion of these ways of using the study of individual differences, we will present some working hypotheses for program design, essentially principles that help us ensure that the people in the equation are treated as well as possible.

We recommend that the study of personal orientation be incorporated into the human resource development system. Whether the study utilizes the methodology for studying States of Growth, or concentrates on conceptual complexity or self-concept, or uses some other framework for studying individuals, we believe that information should be collected and employed to try to understand the human beings in the system. As a practical matter, the study will probably concentrate on a sample of people in any district, or school, or group of participants in a program. As a school principal, supervisor, staff development designer or presenter, we would want to be able to think about our clientele and try to understand why they respond to events and people as they do. Let us consider how persons in different States of Growth are likely to respond to the individual, collective, and systemic components of the system and how events and programs can be designed with individual differences in mind.

The Individual Component

The purpose of the individual component is to build an environment from which individuals and study groups can select options. We have proposed a governance system that relies greatly on surveys of individual needs and preferences, informed by information from councils and committees about options that might be productive. We can see the operation of States of Growth in this governance process. Our omnivores will participate willingly and be likely to suggest options that will stretch them. Our passive consumers will participate willingly *in an energized environment* and will tend to suggest options within their current visions of teaching. (This, we believe, is why "classroom management" programs are so often mentioned in surveys of needs.) Our reticents are likely to resist the participatory governance process itself! They may even refer to it as a "trick of management" to co-opt them into voluntary participation in a process that "will be controlled by the administration anyway." Planners need to distinguish between complaints that are based on concerns about how the process is being administered and purely reticent behavior. This is not always easy. Omnivores who offer suggestions should not be confused with reticents expressing their internal state of dissatisfaction with the world. With a differentiated view, one can ensure that the spectrum of offerings provides possibilities for persons of different visions.

Participation in programs is also likely to be related to the States of Growth of the individuals. Our omnivores are likely to participate in more programs and, once there, their active participation is likely to increase the energy and usefulness of the activities. They tend to appreciate follow-up activities. Their stronger self-concepts stand the gaff of the problems of implementation quite well and, with a little assistance from peers or supervisors, are very likely to achieve an acceptable level of transfer. On the other hand, they resent weak content and poorly developed processes and can be quite critical of events that waste their time.

Passive consumers need encouragement to participate, but are likely to be responsive. Active study teams and the company of active peers will increase their rates and amounts of participation. They are generally cooperative and are amenable to followup activities, but these have to be well-organized and enthusiastically pursued by the organizers and the study groups if they are to be effective, for the passive consumers' dependence on the environment for stimulation requires support. Left to themselves, passive consumers will achieve a very low rate of transfer. Coaching teams composed of passive consumers will need help getting started and maintaining practice.

Reticent personnel will tend to avoid participation, even in events they have theoretically helped to plan. Whether they attend voluntary programs at all will depend heavily on the level of synergy in the school and the study groups to which they belong. How they will respond to events also will depend heavily on the synergy developed in the training sessions. In positive social climates they are less likely to manifest the automatic negativism that afflicts them. When they do respond negatively, it is important to remember that their behavior is likely to be a product of poor self-images. Although they can be extremely unpleasant to deal with, they are actually not hard to "manage" in an affirmative social climate, because of their relative weakness. However, it is important to understand that they *do* have a more difficult time learning new skills and strategies (Joyce, Brown, & Peck, 1981) because their teaching strategies are more limited, their conceptual structures are more rigid and difficult to change, and their ability to understand students and respond to them is more limited. Aside from coping with their negativism, they need a great deal more help to achieve the same objective.

The Collective Component

As far as responses to governance and participation in specific program elements are concerned, the picture is similar to the one described immediately above. However, the dynamics of the collective component have some distinctive features that require sensitive planning and execution and that also provide the greatest opportunity to help people develop a more productive orientation toward themselves and their growth.

It is within the school site that the organization of coaching teams, study groups, and councils take place and all three components depend heavily on these units or similar ones. It is the task of the principal to bring this organization into existence. The affirmative orientation of the omnivores will be essential. They begin with a stake in making environments productive for themselves and others. However, woe betide the principal who involves them in pro forma activities. When our omnivores spend energy on an enterprise, they expect it to pay off. An administrator who is less than serious will have trouble from them. However, they will respond seriously to serious initiatives, and their energy will elevate the synergy in the organization. Omnivores provide affirmative leadership (although they may not have formal positions).

The passive consumers will be cooperative in general, but given their susceptibility to social influence, it is not wise to compose a study team of passive consumers and reticents only.

Active leadership and an active governance process will increase the influence of the social climate of the school and tend to "pull" faculty members toward more active States of Growth. In the most affirmative climates, reticent personnel do not "act out" their jaundice by obstructing initiatives. In fact, a productive social climate is their best opportunity for growth.

Because collective activity generally requires coordinated activity among all personnel, differences in States of Growth are critical as the faculty selects and follows directions for school improvement. The norm in many faculties (an unwritten, but powerful rule) has been to select directions and then allow those persons who do not want to participate "off the hook." The ostensible reason is that teaching styles are so different that collective action would interfere with the productive activities of some of the faculty. The real reasons are quite different. One is that collective activity has not been normative and many teachers are much more unclear about the role as faculty member than they are about the role as instructor. Collective components thus involve the establishment of some new norms. The other is that it is the seemingly easiest course of action for dealing with the most passive consumers and the reticent personnel. Faculty after faculty has started school improvement activities with the "volunteers" and the hope that the initiative would spread as it became successful, only to discover that lateral diffusion does not work and, even more important, that collective initiatives with partial participation greatly weakens the initiative.

Collective action is not dangerous to mental health, but rather the opposite. The governance process needs to emphasize the development of the affirmative climate where the energy released and the benefits to the children pull everyone into more active States of Growth in the workplace. Essentially, positive climates have therapeutic benefits for all of us.

The Systemic Component

If we can assume that systemic initiatives are focused on a few objectives during any given time period, are well-coordinated, are the product of a collaborative governance system, and have been thoroughly communicated, then the key to implementation becomes the development of a districtwide synergy that relates training and support to the schools where the implementation takes place. Individual differences in response will have parallels to those described in the discussions immediately above about the individual and collective components. However, the size and complexity of the larger organization generate some additional considerations.

First, the success of system initiatives will depend partly on whether the central administration personnel, principals, other school-site leaders, and committee and council members behave like active consumers. They have to understand that the behavior patterns characterized by the higher states of growth are infectious and lead to the affirmative stances that facilitate problem solving. Mechanical processes of implementation simply are not effective. Leaders have to model the States of Growth and affirmative stances toward the environment that they hope will be characterized by all personnel.

Second, the systemic initiatives need to be planned with increases in States of Growth as an objective. Opportunities for growth are important. The social climate of the organization is the key, however, to capitalizing on those opportunities. Leaders and staff development personnel need to study the processes of building affirmative climates and involving people in collaborative governance processes and in conducting training and the study of content positively and richly.

SUMMARY

We are what we eat, not just biologically but socially and emotionally. Rich substance, well-organized, in positive circumstances makes us richer, more outreaching, and more productive. Our task is to ensure that our organization is pervaded with the determination to enrich the lives of everyone it touches.

chapter **12**

Governance

Proposition: Democracy, democracy, democracy!!! We need to behave as democratically as we can, include everyone possible, and legitimize the governance processes. The individual, collective, and systemic components inherently differ in some aspects of governance, but all are bound by democratic behavior and the recognition that we own three kinds of citizenship: as individuals to a profession and to our society; as faculties to our school staff, its students, and its community; as system members in the communities we serve.

If we create a pervasive staff development system, what should its governance look like and what are the issues to be discussed?

Here we discuss the governance components of the system and, especially, the beliefs surrounding the governance issues. Throughout the book we have emphasized maximizing participation, essentially developing the most democratic procedures possible, and reducing the social distance between role-designations.

As a practical matter, how can we govern the system? Let us begin with the overall system, proceed to the components, and then consider some evidence about how governance affects behavior and research that is needed on how we can better work together.

THE OVERALL SYSTEM

Let's imagine that we were generating a working memorandum for a district. The contents would look something like the following:

1. All education personnel elect a council of five members who will be responsible for leading the process of developing the system. They will work with the three component councils to make a rational system that can serve the components. They are charged with creating a flexible system and working with the district legal policymakers (the superintendent and the board of education) to obtain funds and in-kind resources for the component. The teachers organizations should be heavily involved in this process, for the greater number of education personnel are teachers, and they will provide most of the service to one another. Council members who are teachers will be released appropriately from instructional duties for participation.

2. The council's first task is to generate options for structuring time for staff development and schoolwide collective decision-making activities to take place. Options are developed, presented to the entire district membership for their opinions, winnowed and presented again, and the product is then presented to the district policymakers.

3. The second task is to attend to the development of capability in the system, especially the organization and preparation of a cadre that can provide service to all components of the system. A plan for the development of the cadre should be presented to the policymakers.

4. The council's third task is to oversee the election of the component councils and, then, to coordinate the councils and work with them to present recommendations for each component to the policymakers.

5. The fourth task is to develop a formative evaluation program to provide information about the effectiveness of the components.

6. The fifth task is to facilitate the implementation of the system and arrange for its periodic revision based on results and a repeat of the governance processes described above.

The governance structures for the individual, school, and system components are parallel councils elected by their constituent groups and charged with the planning and governance functions particular to the requirements of the groups they represent.

Governance of the Individual Component

Clearly the decisions about what to do, how to do it, and how to measure the effects are in the hands of the individual professional. These are the simple questions. More complicated is how an array of opportunities is generated and how a support system can be built for individuals.

As we discussed the individual component in earlier chapters, we implied the governance processes we will recommend here. In specific terms:

1. All education personnel elect a council of five members for the governance of a district component for individuals. This council is

charged with creating a flexible and responsive staff development program and working with the district legal policymakers (the super-intendent and the board of education) to obtain funds and in-kind resources for the component. The teachers' organizations should be heavily involved in this process, for the greater number of education personnel are teachers and they will provide most of the service to one another. Council members who are teachers will be released appropriately from instructional duties for participation.

2. The council surveys needs and available options and generates a list of possibilities that are submitted to the membership of the district for their approval. The list will contain possible offerings by the district plus those by agencies in the area, such as universities, county offices, regional education agencies, and so on.

3. A final list is developed and presented again to the membership.

4. Funding and released-time options will be developed and presented to the policymakers for their approval.

5. The offerings are made and individuals choose what they believe is appropriate to their personal growth as professionals. There is no monitoring process. Individuals are trusted to select the best options they can.

Governance of the Collective Component

1. A council of five members is elected as above.

2. The council works with the cadre to ensure that it is properly connected to the schools and that either entire faculties or responsible committees at each school are connected to the cadre to study the within-school development process.

3. The council develops a formative evaluation plan that studies technical assistance needs, the development of colleagueship in the schools, and gains information about the kinds of school improvement initiatives that are generated, their progress, and reported effects on students.

4. The council reviews the component regularly and works with the cadre to improve technical assistance and program functioning within the schools.

Governance of the Systemic (District) Component

1. A council of five members is elected as above.

2. The council is responsible for working with the district curriculum office, coordinators of categorical programs, and evaluation personnel to survey all district personnel perceptions of curricular, instructional, and technological needs for the district as a whole. A list of options is developed.

3. The list is prioritized and winnowed until the most urgent options are identified that will be presented to the district faculty for a vote on perceptions of priority.
4. From the priorities identified, a series of initiatives are identified for the next three years. (Only one initiative will be selected for each year.) The council develops, with the cadre, a program to prepare the cadre to offer the training and other support necessary for the implementation of the initiatives chosen. Preparation of the cadre commences at least a year before the initiative is to be begun for the faculties as a whole. Thus, the cadre will have been able to practice using the initiative (such as an integrated language arts approach) in their schools for a year before they begin to offer service to the district faculty.
5. The council develops a formative study of implementation and effects and revises the initiatives as appropriate.
6. The process continues. Initiatives are not abandoned, nor are others begun, until the previous one is well established.

Essence

Essentially, all components are governed through a basically democratic process until the basic offerings are developed. Then, however, individuals select their options, schools theirs, and everyone works together to implement the initiatives that, *one by one,* are selected for the entire community. Let us now visit a district that has done a fine job of developing each of the components and has studied not only implementation and the effects on students, but teacher perceptions of each component as well.

Toward a Comprehensive System: A Case Study

Here follows the description of a district whose staff development program is reaching in the direction of a comprehensive system that is conducted as a districtwide inquiry as well—actually a district action research study (Joyce et al., 1994). The program enables us to understand the process of developing a staff development system that reaches individuals and schools and serves the district initiatives. The embedded formative evaluation system permits the community of professionals to follow the implementation of the program, estimate effects and satisfaction, and discover whether student learning is being affected. In chapter 4, we discussed the same program from a school-improvement perspective. Here we explore the governance that legitimized and lead the program.

Knowledge production in staff development comes slowly and many important issues are debated, sometimes hotly, in an environment where hard evidence is scarce. To a degree, the slow pace of knowledge production is due to the inherent complexity of the area. Essentially, the only available research laboratory is the field where staff development programs are implemented. "Intermediate" and interacting variables abound, and programs are modified continually in the course of implementation. Yet, we must continue to weigh the research that we have and, as we create programs, try to test their assumptions as we proceed by embedding research in the program as this district has done.

Thanks to the energy of the professional staff of the Ames (Iowa) Community Schools and the policy support of its exceptionally fine board of education, we have had the opportunity to study a multidimensional program through implementation and including some aspects of student achievement (see Joyce et al., 1994).

We will concentrate on the productivity of this extensive staff development/ school improvement program in this school district of 11 schools, 350 teachers, and 5,000 students, and interpret the findings in terms of several of the "theses" that are argued as programs are planned. The Ames staff development program provided the opportunity to observe the effects of three governance options in staff development, in terms of both the types of objectives generated, the activities pursued, the implementation of innovations, and the effects on students. The 1992–93 academic year, when all three governance options were operating in the nine elementary schools, is the time frame of the study. The formative evaluation system permitted the collection of information relevant to several of the common theses that are currently argued in the staff development field.

THE FOCUS OF THE STUDY:
THREE TYPES OF GOVERNANCE
AND THEIR UNDERLYING RATIONALES

The district has created strong and balanced support for staff development generated by teachers as individuals, by school faculties in the action-research mode, and by the district as a unit. District policy has acknowledged the measures of "truth" underlying often-competing theses. The current theses in staff development provide rationale for all three governance modes. The district policy supports the energy of individuals and generating options where the locus of control is with the person who will pursue a course of action, making the actions congruent with the individual's perceptual world. Individually generated staff development acknowledges the division of the workplace into units (class-rooms) where individual teachers need to use their perceptions and strengths to create innovations to which they can be committed. Whole-faculty generated action research is supported because the curricular and social climate dimensions of the school can be addressed in a way not possible through individual action alone. Further, schoolwide action research directly addresses the goal of developing shared-governance modes and increasing the capacity of the faculty to inquire into and solve problems requiring concerted, democratic action. The districtwide initiatives emphasize the importance of curricular coherence and the development of faculties who embrace professional citizenship in the larger sense of belonging to a community whose children deserve equity in educational opportunity and a common core of knowledge and skills.

By supporting individually oriented, site-based, and district-generated initiatives simultaneously, the district has created a condition where information relative to the success of all three can be obtained.

On Colleagueship: A Cadre to Support All Spheres

Another component is the organization of a cadre who will study curriculum, teaching, and school improvement. All principals are members, as are teachers who represent a range of specialties. The group has been studying several models of teaching and has been working with the Just Read and Write initiative.

For the long term, the cadre needs to have the capability to provide service to building leadership teams and faculties. Its functions include:

1. providing training on generic teaching skills and a wide variety of models of teaching;
2. providing training on the implementation of curriculum areas as content and processes are changed;
3. building the capacity of leadership teams to organize the faculties into productive problem-solving teams, including the organization of study groups for the implementation of training in curriculum and instruction;
4. developing training materials and procedures, including creating training for innovations that emerge as priorities;
5. applying understanding of the change process to curricular and instructional innovation and helping all personnel understand change; and
6. studying implementation and modifying procedures accordingly, and facilitating the study by teachers of the effects on students.

On Study Groups and Colleagueship

All faculties have organized themselves into study groups. The study group structure is intended to increase collegial interaction in the study of teaching and curriculum and, especially, to implement teaching strategies and curriculum changes. Each faculty has organized a group of action-research facilitators. These facilitators will work with our action-research consultants to study the action-research process and how to lead it.

DESIGN OF THE FORMATIVE EVALUATION SYSTEM

In a real sense, the entire program was conducted as districtwide action research, with school wide action research and the inquiry of individuals and small groups nested therein.

The evaluation component was designed to obtain multiple sources of information about reactions to, implementation of, and effects of each of the component initiatives of the program.

1. *The Interview Study: Perspectives of Teachers.* The perspectives of the teachers about the effects of the initiatives on themselves, the implementation of each, and effects on students and the organizational climate of the schools were obtained through interviews (The Teacher Satisfaction and Productivity Interview) with a sample of teachers in each of the elementary schools.
2. *The Ethnographic Study: On-Site Participant-Observation.* Perspectives of principals, leadership teams, and central office personnel were also obtained through interviews and the observation of meetings. Interviews with participants, observations of teaching, and formal and informal discussions with teams, study groups, and individuals provided other information. Quantitative data were obtained through records of implementation of program components and included logs of use, records of student reading, action-research plans, observations of teaching, and a school-climate questionnaire survey administered to all teachers.
3. *The Formal Study of Writing.* An intensive study was made of quality of writing in grades 4, 6, and 8 by collecting samples of expository, persuasive, and narrative writing from all students at the beginning and end of the 1992–93 school year and submitting them to a content analysis for quality. Writing scores were compared with a baseline obtained the prior year and compared to the results of the National Assessment of Writing Progress.

We will begin with the perceptions of the teachers, proceed to the ethnographic study, then discuss the measures of student learning in writing, finally returning to the relevance of the study to the current theses relating to policy in staff development.

RESULTS: THE TEACHER SATISFACTION/ PRODUCTIVITY INTERVIEWS

The interviews were designed to explore the teachers' perceptions of the content of the three initiatives (IGE, Action Research, and Models of Teaching/Language Arts) and the satisfaction and productivity that emerged from each of them. Thirty-five questions were asked of each teacher, and their general opinions were solicited through open-ended questions.

The interviews, completed between May 17 and June 7, 1993, lasted from about 15 minutes to two hours, were conducted by four persons: two consultants from outside the district, one teacher who is past-president of the

Ames teachers' association, and one representative of the central office. The results did not differ by interviewer. Sixty-four teachers, a random sample drawn from the faculties of each of the nine schools, were interviewed. Altogether there were 163 full-time teachers assigned to classrooms and support roles in the nine elementary schools. Thus, 39 percent of the classroom teachers were interviewed.

Years of Teaching Experience

There was one first-year teacher and one veteran of 36 years, with the rest distributed between as shown in Table 12.1.

The distribution approximates that of the entire staff of the elementary schools. The broad distribution of experience and, thus, age allowed us to examine the current theses in the field about the influence of age on receptivity to initiatives.

Teacher Perceptions of Impact: Cross-Initiative Comparisons

The interview schedule asked the 64 teachers to discuss their perceptions of each program component initiative in detail. For cross-initiative comparisons, the critical items were four questions tapping teachers' estimates of the worth of the components, items that were parallel for each initiative: whether the initiative should be continued in Ames, whether they would recommend it to another school district, whether there were positive effects for students, and what were their general feelings about the component. To interpret the results, it is important to know that 12.5 percent of the sample did not make use of the Individual Growth Fund (IGF) initiative at all and 18.5 percent used the IGF money to develop instructional plans or materials and, thus, did not use the resources for staff development. Another 18.5 percent had not yet used the initiative when the interviews were conducted but planned to (and did) use it

TABLE 12.1 Years of teaching experience

Years	Number
1–5	5
6–10	9
11–15	17
16–20	15
21–25	7
26–30	5
31–36	5
NA	1

in the summer. Many of those who either did not use the initiative or who used it to purchase materials declined to comment about the worth of the initiative. Table 12.2 provides the results for the three governance systems with respect to the question, "Should the initiative be continued?"

TABLE 12.2 Comparison of initiatives: Should the initiative be continued? (For IGF, "Would you do it again?")

Initiative	Yes N (%)	No N (%)	Don't Know or No Comment	Total N
IGF	38 (59.4%)	4 (6.3%)	22 (34.4%)	64
ACTION RES.	49 (78.4%)	3 (4.7%)	12 (18.7%)	64
MODELS/LA	61 (95.1%)	1 (1.6%)	2 (3.1%)	64

Clearly, the majority favored the continuance of all three initiatives, but the largest percentage favored continuing the Models of Teaching/Language Arts initiative (although a half-dozen felt it should be modified), with the next largest favoring the continuance of the Action Research initiative. Table 12.3 presents the results of responses to the question, "Would you recommend the initiative to another district?"

TABLE 12.3 Cross-initiative comparison: Would you recommend the initiative to another district? (Or person, in the case of the IGF)

Initiative	Yes N (%)	No N (%)	Unsure, Missing or No Comment N (%)
IGF	36 (56.3%)	0	28 (43.7%)
ACTION RES.	50 (76.6%)	3 (4.7%)	9 (14.1%)
MODELS/LA	56 (87.5%)	3 (4.7%)	5 (7.8%)

Again, the majority would recommend each of them. The differences favoring the Models of Teaching/Language Arts and Action Research initiatives were similar to the responses to the question asking whether the initiatives should be continued. Table 12.4 presents the responses to the question of perceptions of impact on students for each of the three initiatives.

TABLE 12.4   Cross-initiative comparison: Did the initiative have an effect on students?

Initiative	Yes N (%)	No N (%)	Unsure N (%)	Missing or NC N (%)
IGF	35 (54.7%)	1 (1.6%)	2 (3.1%)	26 (40.6%)
ACTION RES.	48 (75%)	8 (12.5%)	2 (3.2%)	6 (9.4%)
MODELS/LA	54 (84.4%)	3 (4.7%)	2 (3.1%)	4 (6.3%)

The results closely approximated those of the other two questions designed to obtain an assessment of the teachers' general perceptions of the three initiatives. The findings are pertinent to the current theses of staff development regarding individual motivation, "buy-in," and the role of the district offices in generating initiatives. In the case of Ames, the perceptions of the teachers certainly do not suggest that the districtwide initiative was regarded as unworthy by very many of the teachers. Also, the schoolwide action research, which is necessarily more complicated to carry out than the individual teacher-oriented initiative, is apparently held in high esteem by more of the teachers than is the IGF program. Table 12.5 presents teacher feelings of satisfaction with each of the three initiatives.

TABLE 12.5   Cross-initiative comparison: How do you feel about . . . ?

Initiative	Good/O.K. N (%)	Indifferent N (%)	Worse N (%)	Missing N (%)
GF	41 (61.4%)	1 (1.6%)	0	22 (33.4%)
ACTION RES.	51 (79.3%)	8 (12.5%)	1 (1.6%)	4 (6.3%)
MODELS/LA	61 (95.3%)	0	1 (1.6%)	2 (3.1%)

The results are in line with those of the other three questions. Again, the two collective components were apparently viewed very positively and the IGF initiative was viewed as positive in terms of general feeling by three out of five persons. Cross-tabulations were made to determine the consistency of responses within and across initiatives and there was great consistency.

Although these overall results of the comparison of responses to the three initiatives are somewhat different from what many might expect—the high approval of the central-office initiative and the considerable support for the schoolwide action research—the real puzzle is the large number of persons who did not express direct and positive support for the IGF.

Estimated Changes in Classrooms

The open-ended questions enabled the teachers to speak in their individual terms and from their perspectives. Generally, they described changes in instruction, in students, and in instructional strategies and materials, and in the effect on themselves, including their morale. Overall, specific, and positive changes were mentioned for the Individual Growth Fund initiative by 26 teachers; for the Action Research initiative by 39 teachers; and for the Language Arts initiative by 49 teachers.

Estimated Effects on Students

For the various initiatives, teachers' perceptions of positive effects on their students were:

Individual Growth Fund	35 (54.7%)
Action Research	48 (75.0%)
Models of Teaching/LA	54 (84.4%)

Experience in Teaching and Responses

Cross-tabulations were computed between years of teaching experience and the four variables with respect to each initiative. Thus, 12 comparisons were made. In all 12 cases, the distributions fitted almost exactly. In other words, experience does not appear to be a factor influencing response to any of the three components of the program.

The Perceptual World: Summary

From a vote-count perspective, all the components are doing nicely from the teachers' perspective with the collective initiatives apparently being in somewhat better shape than the IGF. However, *it* is not doing badly. All can use some design attention to ensure congruent cognitions about purposes and to extend comfortable and purposeful implementation.

THE STUDY OF QUALITY IN WRITING

The study was created to support what can be termed districtwide action research and concentrated on comparing students of writing for grades 4, 6, and 8 from the early fall of 1992 and the late spring of 1993. The study was directed particularly at the goals of the Models of Teaching/Language Arts initiative. Some of the results were presented in tables in chapter 4 and will not be repeated here. Overall, very large gains were reported in the expository mode of writing, which was strongly emphasized in the initiative, for grades 4 to 6—gains *several times* the average annual gain of previous years or compared to the national assessment educational progress. Grade 4 gained substantially in the narrative and persuasive types of writing, but the results still indicated that almost none of the students in any of the grades had reached the point where they could focus and structure persuasive discourse. The lack of transfer from one genre to the other suggests that each genre of importance may have to be targeted specifically.

GOVERNANCE REVISITED

The interesting aspect of the Ames study is that all three components were operating with their particular governance system, and the district conducted an open, action-research study to find out how each mode was doing. The finding that will startle many is that all three modes were well accepted and the district initiative fared very well, in the opinion of the teachers, probably because its governance base was so broad and its design was so carefully constructed. By conducting such a thoroughgoing formative evaluation, Ames, like Augusta, is in a position to make each mode better. The district committee for the Individual Growth Fund initiative needs to involve the teachers and administrators to consider ways of making the initiative more satisfying for all. The collective component continues to need support and a group of teachers and administrators has undertaken to study the action-research process so that they will become a support cadre for that component. The planners for the districtwide component are organizing to generate an initiative in mathematics, ensuring that it will build on the models of teaching utilized in the Language Arts initiative and will extend the uses of writing-to-learn into the mathematics curriculum area.

SUMMARY

Democracy! Democracy! Democracy! Together with a formal inquiry into the system, the democratic process will shape and reshape the components. The inquiry will continue until we have established an inclusive democratic process, which will generate its own questions. Bureaucratic administration will be replaced by a collective problem-solving mode.

The issues of governance that so frequently create conflict in the design of staff development systems may indeed be red herrings. As was evident in the Ames case study, programs governed by individuals, schools, and the district were all perceived as valuable by substantial portions of the relevant populations. We believe that democratic processes involving all roles and levels of the organization in decisions regarding staff development will make moot the issue of who controls such decisions.

part V

Beliefs and Philosophies

We are what we believe, and belief propels our decisions, sometimes despite the evidence. In this last chapter, we examine our traditions and return to the theses presented in the opening chapter. We end with a call for continued inquiry and the innovative action that makes us revisit our ideas, especially our ideas about what is possible.

chapter 13

Theses about Staff Development: Impact on Policy

Proposition: Interpretation of reality generates and is driven by beliefs. Our inquiry needs to include the ideas that we use when making decisions.

Staff development is rarely discussed in philosophical terms—the language is generally pragmatic and problem-oriented. Yet, in fact, strong beliefs underly many of the decisions to pursue certain paths rather than others. Many of these beliefs reflect the philosophical traditions of the Western world, and some of the controversies reflect differences that are centuries old.

TRADITIONS OF THOUGHT AND CONTEMPORARY BELIEFS

Let us take a few pages to reflect on some of the traditions before we return to the theses we presented in chapter 1.

Governance and Democracy

We can find Thomas Jefferson everywhere: in Glickman (1993), who directly recommends that schools develop a "charter," in the discussions about democratic collegiality and collective action advocated by Goodlad (1984) and Sizer (1985), and in the involvement of parents and students in the decision-making process advocated by Joyce, Hersh, and McKibbin (1983). The Jeffersonian tradition is part of the much larger movement toward democracy that can be found in the writings of writers from such different backgrounds as Rousseau (1983) and Comenius (1896), whose view from his seventeenth-century monastery attempted to move education toward a thoughtful and collaborative community that would have educated far beyond the doctrine generally attributed to monasticism. For persons reflective of this tradition, the belief in the creation of democratic governance of schools is quite different from the pragmatic view that people should be involved so they will "buy in." They believe (we are among the "they") that democracy is an essential element of our search for quality in human life and that the schools, to imbue students with the philosophy on which our governmental traditions are based, have to reflect those traditions. John Dewey (1916) appears in the basic approach we take to the development of the system—the idea that everybody participates in decision making and that the scientific process be used to discipline the group process.

Not only is the Jeffersonian tradition antithetical to the pragmatic, manipulative traditions that see involvement as a practical necessity but not necessarily as a philosophical good; but it also conflicts with the Royalist traditions that have dominated the structures of American business and commerce. The feudal governmental structures, based on power and control, were inherited by many of our economically based institutions and many of the structures for the bureaucratic control of schools that were developed in the nineteenth century.

As education tries to borrow reform programs from the "private sector," we need to reflect on whether they will work at all or in a manipulative fashion or whether they can be adapted to increase the social quality of education. When we are asked, "Suppose teachers and administrators *don't want* democracy as you propose it?" we have to engage philosophically, and counter, "What kind of social order do you propose the school system reflect to its students?"

Myrna Cooper (1988) has wisely pointed out the riddle we are in at the present time. Essentially, can one "impose" democracy? We hope the proposition that the schools and school districts move toward a democratic organization can be seen rather as a movement within our tradition that is long overdue, than as an issue of workers' rights. The fact that the question is raised indicates just how much of a cultural change democracy will bring to the schools. However, educators were brought up in the Jeffersonian tradition and have the cognitive and social tools to operate democratically. Those tools have just not been exercised much in the workplace.

Equity

We can find Locke (1927), Hobbes (1651), Bentham (1789), and Rawls (1971) in arguments about the nature of equity and whether schools should seek opportunities for all or allow socioeconomic differences to affect the outcomes of the educational process (Stevenson & Stigler, 1992). The issues over multicultural and bilingual education are very much involved in the seeking for equity, as are, of course, the arguments about tracking, students with "special" needs, and the conduct of education for the economically poor. In the case of staff development, the question nests in issues about ensuring that all children are educated by educators who have the best possible tools for their work.

Inquiry and Knowledge

We can find Aristotle in arguments about accumulated knowledge and inquiry and their places in the inquiry of both teachers and students (Schwab & Brandwein, 1962). The current arguments about whether education has a knowledge base (*Review of Educational Research,* 1993) turns less on the quality of the knowledge base than the issues over whether it is possible to have general knowledge. The action-research tradition is certainly Aristotelian in the approach, but democratic in that it would make everyone producers of knowledge, while drawing on the knowledge of the field (Calhoun, 1994).

Personalism

Existentialism and situationism (Sartre, 1956; De Bouvoir, 1957; Camus, 1946) reappear in the arguments by Stenhouse (1975), Elliott (1991), and Hollingsworth and Sockett (1994) that knowledge is very individual and that the very legitimization of the "organization" and the "research establishment" are at question. The situationism characteristic of the 1960s (see Reich, 1970) is apparent in their writing. They are suspicious of the possibility of general, common knowledge and of the power relationships that they believe are inherent in the development of a community of "professional researchers" who hand down knowledge to others.

Constructivism

The current discussions of constructivism (Brooks & Brooks, 1993) are very much reflected in the arguments over which theses should be dominant as programs are constructed. There are three varieties of constructivism. They differ in their emphases on:

Personal, idiosyncratic knowledge out of the existentialist, situationist tradition.

Collective, consensual knowledge out of the democratic, pragmatic tradition.

Construction as a part of the societal accrual of knowledge—the dialectic between science and personal experience.

THE INQUIRY INTO STAFF DEVELOPMENT: STUDYING OUR BELIEFS

We believe that the continual study of our beliefs and a testing of those beliefs against the developing knowledge base are an essential part of our inquiry. Coming as we do from the Jeffersonian and Aristotelian traditions (although with a dollop of Rousseau, as witnessed not just by the individual component but also the shape of the other components), we feel comfortable playing ideas against the knowledge base, and will do so, as best we can, in the next few pages.

In the first chapter, we identified a number of theses that are subscribed to by varying numbers of people as policies are made for designing events and approaching the larger task of developing a staff development system. We believe strongly that the evolution of the field should be conducted as a nationwide inquiry into the development of a system and that this inquiry needs to be conducted by a surfacing of our beliefs and the collection of information about them. The purpose should not be a search for doctrine, rather it should be a genuine inquiry that acknowledges that our knowledge will emerge gradually and that our needs will propel us into areas where we are uncertain. We need to reach forward in a fashion that permits us to advance ideas, test them through research and practice, modify them, and proceed forward in the most scholarly fashion we can muster.

THESES REVISITED

In these pages we will revisit the theses, discuss them from the point of view of the evidence we have been able to find about them, and discuss their implications for action and further inquiry.

On Personal Motivation, Selection of Options, and Probable Effects

Thesis One: If individual teachers select their own staff development options, "buy-in" will ensure satisfaction and implementation.

Thesis Two: Personal motivational factors and knowledgeability vary considerably, and individually designed staff development programs will have equally variable effects and satisfaction.

The studies of States of Growth (chapters 8 and 11) and the Ames study (discussed in chapters 4 and 12) lead us to celebrate differences while acknowledging that people will respond differently both to particular events and to the process of decision making. The idea that personal control will solve all problems doesn't stand up. Creating components that flexibly respond to differences is a good bet.

On Collegial Locus of Control

Thesis Three: Staff development should be based at the school site, with the faculty making the decisions about directions and how to get there.

Normative beliefs: A currently popular belief that guides many decisions.

Thesis Four: Many schools are "stuck" and site-based restructuring efforts create frustration and disappointment unless the faculties transform themselves into problem-solving groups.

Normative belief: Not as popular as Thesis Three, but many people agree with this one.

The literature: The studies of site-based school improvement (chapters 2, 3, 4) provide strong support for Thesis Four.

Needed research: How to guide facilitation of faculties. Although we believe that the development of a pervasive staff development system will make a big difference, many schools are being asked to change and the technology of how to support them with the current level of support personnel is not developed. This area needs serious attention from researchers.

On Credibility and "Buy-In"

Thesis Five: Start with a group of enthusiasts, and, when the others see what they are doing, they will buy-in.

Normative belief: Another popular thesis.

The literature: This thesis is not systematically studied at present. Evidence from the California Staff Development Study (Joyce, McKibbin, & Bush, 1983) would not support the thesis.

Needed research: Much more needs to be done in this area and can be embedded in school-renewal programs that operate on the thesis. The question about whether starting with enthusiasts "infects" others with enthusiasm should not be difficult to study.

Corollary Thesis Six: Action research is best conducted by individuals and small groups.

Normative belief: Advocated by some theorists, but a relative unknown to much of the population.

The literature: Virtually all the studies reporting success are of schoolwide action research, and some studies have reported outstanding success. Schoolwide action research is a clear option for school improvement. Individual and small-group action research is certainly feasible as an option under the individual component, but should not be confused with a general school improvement program, which requires participation by the entire faculty.

Needed research: Questions about needed facilitation for all types of action research need to be pursued.

Thesis Seven: Schoolwide action research knits the faculty and gets results for children.

Normative belief: Has intuitive appeal and is strongly advocated by some theorists.

The literature: Generally positive (chapter 3).

Needed research: There is a considerable need for research on how to conduct action research so that a self-renewing school (the major objective) will result. The odds are good that it will pay off.

On Central Planning

Thesis Eight: Carefully articulated initiatives in curriculum and instruction generate colleagueship and bring about changes in curriculum and instruction that are satisfying to teachers and effective for students.

Normative belief: This is not a popular item at this time, although it is the thesis on which most curriculum initiatives are based.

The literature: Strong and positive support (chapter 4), if the operational aspect is well designed. Many successful school improvement efforts have operated from this position.

Needed research: Failure to study implementation carefully has impeded development in this area. A good deal of work is needed, especially in the areas of governance. Poorly designed initiatives will fail, but the belief that centrally designed initiatives cannot work does not hold up.

Thesis Nine: Centralized initiatives are doomed to failure because of resistance and lack of "buy-in."

Normative belief: Has high popularity at this time, but nearly all central offices generate initiatives on the belief that it is at least partly untrue.

The literature: Rejecting of the thesis, for the most part (chapters 4 and 12). Some initiatives that have had great effect have been centralized. Again, weakly designed initiatives will have little effect, regardless of who designs them. The Ames study shows how acceptable districtwide initiatives can be, as do the Just Read initiative and the Augusta Project.

Needed research: How to build broad-based governance and "vertical collegiality" so that the development of districtwide initiatives has legitimacy.

On the Culture of the School

Thesis Ten: Begin with the development of collegiality, then initiatives will emerge.

Normative belief: A very popular item.

The literature: A mixed bag (see chapters 3 and 4). Most site-based initiatives have labored. The "Essential Schools" version has run into serious difficulty. The "Effective Schools" version has fared better. The generic "OD" movement has its problems.

Needed research: How to develop collegiality so that initiatives for school improvement develop. May need research on the combined effects of several approaches to school renewal.

Thesis Eleven: Begin with initiatives and generate collegiality through action.

Normative belief: Less popular that the preceding one, but has support from a number of people.

The literature: Has worked out quite a number of times (chapters 7 and 8). Clearly a viable option. However, has not proven that it can change the culture of the school.

Needed research: Needs a lot more detail work, especially to ensure that things don't stop with the first initiatives, but true school-renewal effects occur.

On Time and the Culture of the School

Thesis Twelve: The implementation of an initiative in curriculum, instruction, or technology takes three years or more.

Normative belief: Uncertain. Most people are not sure.

The literature: (chapter 4) Supports a short time frame, not more than one or two years. Design of the initiative is a critical variable.

Needed research: More work on design, including governance. We believe the time frame can be shortened.

Thesis Thirteen: Well-designed initiatives can be implemented during the first year.

As with Thesis Twelve.

Thesis Fourteen: Well-designed initiatives can change the culture of the school immediately in certain ways and, by steady increments, create self-renewing schools and school districts.

Normative belief: Difficult to ascertain. Most people are pessimistic however.

The literature: Certain structural features can be changed rapidly (chapter 4). Probably "deep" changes will take some time.

Needed research: We badly need longitudinal studies of deep cultural change.

Thesis Fifteen: Changing the culture of the school takes from five to ten years.

Normative belief: Again, there appears to be no conclusion about this one. Many take a "who knows" view.

The literature: In the absence of long-term studies, the literature is no better than anybody's opinion.

On Age and Experience

Thesis Sixteen: Age decreases motivation and the stresses of teaching lead to "burnout."

Normative belief: Has mixed support. Most reject.

The literature: Strongly rejecting (chapter 11).

Needed research: The strengths of the older learner need exploration, counterbalancing the concern with possible deficits.

Thesis Seventeen: Maturity increases strength as learners and problem solvers.

As with Thesis Sixteen.

On Technical Assistance and Research

Thesis Eighteen: To get "moving" most schools need technical support, especially to bring the research base to bear on problem solving.

Normative belief: Most people are unsure about this one, but lean toward the need for support.

The literature: The literature on site-based school improvement strongly supports the thesis (chapters 2 and 4). Nearly all schools appear to need facilitation to become "schools as centers of inquiry."

Thesis Nineteen: Knowledge is personal and situation-specific. External sources provide little of value to local problem solving.

Normative belief: There is wide variance on this question. Few reject external knowledge out-of-hand. On the other hand, many educators are suspicious of research and other forms of knowledge generated at a distance from "their" school.

The literature: Many school improvement projects that have successfully affected student learning have used knowledge generated elsewhere (chapters 4 and 5).

MORE INQUIRY

We believe we are at a beginning. In these theses there is plenty of meat for research personnel and plenty of food for thought for all of us. Knowledge about staff development does not permit the development of a static, "this will do it" series of ideas. We hope it never does.

On the other hand there *is* knowledge, and we need to build on it as well as we can.

Epilogue: Reflections
from a Practitioner

James M. Wolf
Director, Dept. of Defense Dependents Schools, Panama/Islands Area

What follows are *reflections from a practitioner* after reading the last page of *Student Achievement through Staff Development* and thinking about how to use its rich content and store of fresh ideas. The 1988 edition was widely accepted as a state-of-the-art book on the subject and, like others, my practice was directly affected by it. We used peer coaching to bring teachers into the process of following up on training. We concentrated on fewer initiatives, studied implementation more carefully, and looked at effects on students more formatively. The challenge to the authors now is to meet the greater expectations generated by those who found the first edition so valuable. For me they have succeeded and I have much to reflect on about how we practioners can use the book.

First we can use the book with many audiences. We can share it with those who operate in the policy-making arena, such as school board members and legislatures, because its blend of research and ideas can be integrated into the design of reform proposals and used to justify and defend such proposals.

The style of writing makes information available to persons of quite different levels of sophistication. The "advance guard" will find assistance as they fine-tune their programs. They will use the information on successful initiatives and find guidance in their constant search for content that produces positive effects on student learning. They will use the section on governance to increase involvement at all levels of the organization. They will improve their evaluation components, embedding the study of implementation more fully and studying student learning formatively.

Those who recognize that we have evolved to the point that the need for a comprehensive staff development program can no longer be ignored will find guideposts to get them started. They will find that the time is ripe to create a comprehensive program and that they have the material to provide direction and rationale to the teachers and administrators who have to be involved in its design.

Those who are new to the role of design will find a handy guide to projects and programs that work and ideas to use with school faculties as they move in the direction of building a community of learners. As teachers are asked to become creators of staff development at school sites, they will need a primer on the subject so that their involvement avoids the mistakes of the past and results in effects on students and satisfaction for the faculties. This book will be a useful guide for this purpose and for all practioners as they make plans to meet the requirements of the new Goals 2000: Educate America Act that establishes a new goal for professional development.

Perhaps most important is that the authors, rather than telling us what to do, invite us to become action researchers, treating what we do as an inquiry in our own settings and in the field of staff development. For example, at the end of the first chapter they present, via a questionnaire, a series of "theses" which many people embrace or reject as they develop programs. The readers are invited to take a position on the theses and test them as research is presented and as they inquire into their own practice.

I intend to make good use of these theses as I work with school faculties and administrative personnel as they initiate or redefine staff development and school improvement plans. After administering the questionnaire, the ten propositions formulated by the authors can be presented to the faculty or utilized in study groups for the purpose of discussion. Worksheets can be easily developed for each study group to complete after each chapter and list the research that supports the propositions and the findings that support or negate the 19 beliefs. A process such as this offers a powerful procedure for developing consensus on beliefs and goals for staff development. Hopefully, we can begin to overcome the "paradigm paralysis" that has kept so many efforts weak because they are based on strongly held but dysfunctional beliefs.

Several of the theses and propositions will attract immediate attention:

- The key to student growth is educator growth and everyone must participate in growth.
- "Top down" innovations can be successful if governance is broad and they are well designed.
- Well-designed initiatives can be implemented and have effects on student learning.
- Any significant changes in curriculum, instruction, and technology need to be supported by intensive staff development.
- To get "moving," most schools need technical support.
- School initiatives and district initiatives that involve the total faculty(ies) are more likely to get and stay implemented.

My faculties and administrators will find these provocative, to say the least, and if I can bring increasing numbers into a mode where they can examine them seriously, my attempt to build a learning community throughout my district will be enhanced.

A unique feature of the book is found in chapter 13 where the authors relate the theses or beliefs to our philosophical traditions. The introduction to the conclusions formulated about the 19 theses is just a few pages but is a real gem and may help us reflect seriously on our beliefs. We practioners are a very pragmatic group and spend our days interacting with others, planning, facilitating, and problem solving—there is little time to reflect on our philosophical traditions. We need to be reminded of this heritage—the influence of Aristotle, Rousseau, Comenius, Locke, Jefferson, Hobbes, Dewey, and others on our present goal of developing the school setting into a community of learners where inquiry and collaboration of both students and educators are valued.

Although we are so pragmatic, we are not always effectively practical. Another idea I intend to use with my community is the *proximal principle*, which gives us a new perspective for evaluating potential initiatives. We need to select initiatives that focus on "the student as learner. . . . The closer an innovation is to the interactive process that helps the learner manage learning better, the greater the effect will be. . . . Reciprocally, the farther (more distal) the innovation is from the environment where teacher and learners interact, the slower and lesser will be the effects, if there are any." Like other communities, mine often selects the distal in the hope that the proximal will follow. Not so, say these authors, and we need to take them seriously.

Finally, we practioners are inundated with the day-to-day, and we need help thinking ahead so that changes surprise us less and create fewer crises that could have been avoided with foresight. Joel Barker, the futurist, describes three keys to the future success of any organization. They are (1) anticipation, (2) innovation, and (3) excellence. *Excellence* is a requirement and goal for all schools as they enter the twenty-first century. *Innovation* is an essential ingredient of school improvement. But excellence and innovation are not enough. *Anticipation* provides us with information that allows us to make better decisions about innovations and to implement them at the right time. I hope to use the content of this book to further our future thinking—to help my community think more reflectively not only about the tasks requiring our immediate attention, but about the evolving world and how we can accept its challenges more strongly.

I accepted with degrees of both eagerness and trepidation the invitation to read the manuscript and write my reflections as a practitioner. The time I spent was minimal when compared to what I have learned and the reflecting I have been induced to do.

References

Abrams, P. (1984). Educational seduction. *Review of Educational Research, 52* (3), 446-464.

Allen, J., J., Combs, M., Hendricks, P., Nash, & S. Wilson. (1988). Studying change: Teachers who became researchers. *Language Arts, 65* (4), 379-387.

Almy, M. (1970). *Logical thinking in second grade.* New York: Teachers College Press.

Anderson, H., & Brewer, H. (1939). Domination and social integration in the behavior of kindergarten children and teachers. *Genetic Psychology Monograph, 21,* 287-385.

Anderson, L., Evertson, C., & Brophy, J. (1979). An experimental study of effective teaching in first grade reading groups. *Elementary School Journal, 79,* 193-223.

Anderson, L. W., & Pellicer, L. O. (1990). Synthesis of research on compensatory and remedial education. *Educational Leadership, 48* (1), 10-16.

Apple, M. (1979). *Idiology and curriculum.* London: Routledge and Kegan Paul.

Applebee, A., Langer, J., Jenkins, L., Mullis, I., & Foertsch, M. (1990). *Learning to write in our nation's schools.* Washington, D.C.: U.S. Department of Education.

Aspy, D. N., & Roebuck, F. (1973). An investigation on the relationship between student levels of cognitive functioning and the teacher's classroom behavior. *Journal of Educational Research, 65,* 365-368.

Aspy, D. N., Roebuck, F., Willson, M., & Adams, O. (1974). *Interpersonal skills training for teachers.* (Interim report #2 for NIMH Grant #5PO 1MH 19871.) Monroe, LA: Northeast Louisiana University.

Atkinson, R. (1975). Nemotechnics in second language learning. *American Psychologist, 30,* 821-828.

Ausubel, David (1963). *The psychology of meaningful verbal learning.* New York: Grune and Stratton, Inc.

Baker, R. G., & Showers, B. (1984). *The effects of a coaching strategy on teachers' transfer of training to classroom practice: A six-month followup study.* Paper presented at the annual meeting of the American Educational Research Association, New Orleans, LA.

Baldridge, V., & Deal, T. (1975). *Managing change in educational organizations.* Berkeley, CA: McCutchan.

Ball, S., & Bogatz, G. A. (1970). *The first year of sesame street.* Princeton, NJ: Educational Testing Service.

Bangert-Drowns, R. L. (1993). The word processor as an instructional tool: A meta-analysis of word processing in writing instruction. *Review of Educational Research, 63* (1), 69-93.

Barnes, B., & Clawson, E. (1973). The effects of organizers on the learning of structured anthropology materials in the elementary grades. *Journal of Experimental Education, 42,* 11-15.

Barnes, B., & Clawson, E. (1975). Do advance organizers facilitate learning? Recommendations for further research based on an analysis of 32 studies. *Review of Educational Research, 45* (4), 637-659.

Barth, R. (1990). *Improving schools from within.* San Francisco: Jossey-Bass Publishers.

Baveja, B. (1988). An exploratory study of the use of information-processing models of teaching in secondary school biology science classes. Delhi, India: Delhi University, Ph.D. thesis.

Becker, W. C. (1978). Teaching reading and language to the disadvantaged—What we have learned from field research. *Harvard Educational Review, 47,* 518-543.

Becker, W., & Carnine, D. (1980). Direct instruction: An effective approach for educational intervention with the disadvantaged and low performers. In B. Lahey and A. Kazdin (Eds.), *Advances in child clinical psychology,* pp. 429-473. New York: Plenum.

Becker, W., & Gersten, R. (1982). A followup of Follow Through: The later effects of the direct instruction model on children in the fifth and sixth grades. *American Educational Research Journal, 19* (1), 75-92.

Bennett, B. (1987). *The effectiveness of staff development training practices: A meta-analysis.* Ph.D. thesis, University of Oregon.

Bentham, J. (1789). *An introduction to the principles of morals and legislation.* New York: Penguin, 1982.

Bentzen, M. (1974). *Changing schools: The magic feather principle.* New York: McGraw-Hill.

Bereiter, C. (1984). How to keep thinking skills from going the way of all frills. *Educational Leadership, 42* (1), 75-77.

Berman, P., & Gjelten, T. (1983). *Improving school improvement.* Berkeley, California: Berman, Weiler Associates.

Berman, P., & McLaughlin, M. (1975). *Federal programs supporting educational change, Vol. IV: The findings in review.* Santa Monica, CA: The Rand Corporation.

Beyer, B. (1988). *Developing a thinking skills program.* Boston: Allyn Bacon.

Block, J. (1971). *Mastery learning: Theory and practice.* New York: Holt, Rinehart, & Winston.

Block, J. W., & Anderson, L. W. (1975). *Mastery learning in classrooms.* New York: Macmillan.

Bloom, B. S. (1971). Mastery learning. In J. Block (Ed.), *Mastery learning: Theory and practice.* New York: Holt, Rinehart, & Winston.

Bloom, B. S. (1981). *The new direction in educational research and measurement: Alterable variables.* Paper presented at the annual meeting of the American Educational Research Association, Los Angeles, CA.

Bloom, B. S. (1984). The 2 sigma problem: The search for group instruction as effective as one-to-one tutoring. *Educational Researcher, 13,* 4-16.

Bondi, J. C., Jr. (1970). Feedback from interaction analysis: Some implications for the improvement of teaching. *Journal of Teacher Education, 21,* 23-30.

Bonsangue, M. V. (1993). Long term effects of the Calculus Workshop Model. *Cooperative Learning, 13* (3), 19-20.

Boocock, S., & Schild, E. O. (1968). *Simulation games in learning.* Beverly Hills, CA: Sage Publications, Inc.

Borg, W. R., & others (1969). Videotape feedback and microteaching in a teacher training model. *Journal of Experimental Education, 37,* 9-16.

Bredderman, T. (1983). Effects of activity-based elementary science on student outcomes: A quantitative synthesis. *Review of Educational Research, 53* (4), 499-518.

Brookover, W., Schwitzer, J. H., Schneider, J. M., Beady, C. H., Flood, P. K., & Wisenbaker, J. M. (1978). Elementary school social climate and school achievement. *American Educational Research Journal, 15* (2), 301-318.

Brooks, J. G., & Brooks, M. G. (1993). *The case for constructivist classrooms.* Alexandria, VA: Association for Supervision and Curriculum Development.

Brophy, J. (1992). Probing the subtleties of subject-matter teaching. *Educational Leadership, 49* (7), 4-8.

Brophy, J., & Evertson, C. (1974). *The Texas teacher effectiveness project: Presentation of non-linear relationships and summary discussion.* Austin, TX: Research and Development Center for Teacher Education, University of Texas.

Brophy, J., & Good, T. (1986). Teacher behavior and student achievement. In Merlin Wittrock (Ed.), *Handbook of Research on Teaching, 3rd Edition,* pp. 328-375. New York: Macmillan Publishing Co.

Bruner, J. (1961). *The process of education.* Cambridge, MA: Harvard University Press.

Byers, J. (1984). The predictions of commitment to the teaching profession. Paper presented at the annual meeting of the American Educational Research Association, New Orleans.

Calderon, M. (1994). *Bilingual Teacher Development within School Learning Communities: A Synthesis of the Staff Development Model.* El Paso: University of Texas at El Paso.

Calderon, M., Hertz-Lazarowitz, R., & Tinajero, J. (1991). Adapting CIRC to multiethnic and bilingual classrooms. *Cooperative Learning, 12,* 17-20.

Calhoun, E. F. (1991). A wide-angle lens: How to increase the variety, collection, and use of data for school improvement. Paper presented at the annual meeting of the American Educational Research Association, Chicago.

Calhoun, E. F. (1992). A status report on action research in the League of Professional Schools. Paper presented at the annual meeting of the American Educational Research Association, San Francisco.

Calhoun, E. F. (1994). *How to use action research in the self-renewing school.* Alexandria, VA: Association for Supervision and Curriculum Development.

Camus, A. (1946). *The stranger.* New York: Vintage Books.

Chamberlin, C., & Chamberlin, Enid (1943). *Did they succeed in college?* New York: Harper and Row.

Cochran-Smith, M., & Lytle, S. L. (1992). *Inside-outside: Teacher research and knowledge.* New York: Teachers College Press.

Cogan, M. L. (1973). *Clinical supervision.* Boston: Houghton-Mifflin.

Cohen, D. K., & Farrar, E. (1977). Power to the parents? The story of education vouchers. ERIC document number EJ165190.

Coleman, J. S., Campbell, E. Q., Hobson, C. J., McPortland, J., Mood, A. M., Weinfield, E. D., & York, R. L. (1966). *Equality of educational opportunity.* Washington, D.C.: Government Printing Office.

Collins, K. (1969). The importance of strong confrontation in an inquiry model of teaching. *School Science and Mathematics, 69* (7), 615–617.

Comenius, J. A. (1628–32). *The great didactic.* (English trans. 1896.)

Cooper, M. (1988). Whose culture is it, anyway? In A. Lieberman (Ed.), *Building a professional culture in schools.* New York: Teachers College Press.

Corey, S. M. (1953). *Action research to improve school practices.* New York: Teachers College Press.

Costa, Arthur (1985). *Developing minds: A resource book for teaching thinking.* Alexandria, VA: Association for Supervision and Curriculum Development.

Costa, A. L., & Garmston, R. (1985). Supervision for intelligent teaching. *Educational Leadership, 42* (5), 70–80.

Crandall, David, et al. (1982). *People, policies, and practices: Examining the chain of school improvement.* Vols. I–X. Andover, MA: The NETWORK, Inc.

Crawford, J., Gage, N., Corno, L., Stayrook, N., Mittman, A., Schunk, D., Stallings, J., Baskin, E., Harvey, P., Austin, D., Cronin, D., & Newman, R. (1978). An experiment on teacher effectiveness and parent-assisted instruction in the third grade. (3 vols.) Stanford, CA: Center for Educational Research at Stanford, Stanford University.

CRESST (1994). Measurement-driven reform: The more things change, the more they stay the same. CRESST Technical Report 373. Los Angeles: Center for the Study of Education, U.C.L.A.

Cuban, L. (1990). Reforming again, again, and again. *Educational Researcher, 19* (1), 3–13.

David, J. L. (1989). *Restructuring in progress: Lessons from pioneering districts.* Washington, D.C.: National Governors' Association.

David, J. L. (1990). Restructuring: Increased autonomy and changing roles. Invited address presented at the annual meeting of the American Educational Research Association, Boston.

David, J. L., & Peterson, S. M. (1984). Can schools improve themselves? A study of school-based improvement programs. Palo Alto, CA: Bay Area Research Group.

De Bouvoir, S. (1957). *The second sex.* New York: Alfred A. Knopf.

Devaney, K., & Thorn, L. (1975). *Exploring teacher centers.* San Francisco: Far West Laboratory for Educational Research and Development.

Dewey, John (1916). *Democracy in education.* New York: Macmillan, Inc.

Downey, L. (1969). *The secondary phase of education.* Waltham, MA: Blaisdell.

Drucker, P. (1988). Knowledge, work, and the structure of the schools. *Educational Leadership, 45* (5), 44–46.

Dunn, R., & Dunn, K. (1975). *Educator's self-teaching guide to individualizing instructional programs.* West Nyack, NY: Parker.

Edmonds, R. (1979). Some schools work and more can. *Social Policy, 9* (5), 28–32.

Elefant, E. (1980). Deaf children in an inquiry training program. *The Volta Review, 82,* 271–279.

Elliott, J. (1991). *Action research for educational change.* Buckingham: Open University Press.

Elmore, R. F. (1990). On changing the structure of public schools. In R. F. Elmore (Ed.), *Restructuring schools.* San Francisco: Jossey-Bass.

El Nemr, M. (1979). *Meta-analysis of the outcomes of teaching biology as inquiry.* Ph.D. thesis, University of Colorado.

Erikson, E. (1950). *Childhood and society.* New York: Norton.

Evans, M., & Hopkins, D. (1988). School climate and the psychological state of the individual teacher as factors affecting the use of educational ideas following an inservice course. *British Educational Research Journal, 14* (3), 211-230.

Evertson, C. (1982). Differences in instructional activities in higher and lower-achieving English and math classes. *The Elementary School Journal, 82* (4), 329-350.

Evertson, C., Anderson, C., Anderson, L., & Brophy, J. (1980). Relationships between classroom behaviors and student outcomes in junior high mathematics and English classes. *American Educational Research Journal, 17* (1), 43-60.

Feeley, Theodore (1972). *The concept of inquiry in the social studies.* Ph.D thesis, Stanford University.

Fisher, C. W., Berliner, D. C., Filby, N. N., Marliave, R., Ghen, L. S., & Dishaw, M. M. (1980). Teaching behaviors, academic learning time, and student achievement: An overview. In C. Denham and A. Lieberman (Eds.), *Time to learn.* Washington, D.C.: National Institute of Education.

Flanagan, A. (1994). The Vermont writing portfolio is revised. *The Council Chronicle, 3* (4), 1-2. Washington, D.C.: The National Council of Teachers of English.

Flanders, N. (1970). *Analyzing teacher behavior.* Reading, MA: Addison-Wesley.

Fullan, M. G. (1990). Staff development, innovation, and institutional development. In B. Joyce (Ed.), *Changing school culture through staff development: 1990 ASCD yearbook.* Alexandria, VA: Association for Supervision and Curriculum Development.

Fullan, M. (1982). *The meaning of educational change.* New York: Teachers College Press.

Fullan, M. G., & Miles, M. B. (1992). Getting reform right: What works and what doesn't. *Phi Delta Kappan, 73* (10), 744-52.

Fullan, M., Miles, M., & Taylor, G. (1980). Organization development in schools: The state of the art. *Review of Educational Research, 50* (1), 121-84.

Fullan, M., & Park, P. (1981). *Curriculum implementation: A resource booklet.* Toronto: Ontario Ministry of Education.

Fullan, M. & Pomfret, A. (1977). Research on curriculum and instruction implementation. *Review of Educational Research, 47* (2), 335-397.

Fullan, M. G., & Stiegelbauer, S. (1991). *The new meaning of educational change.* New York: Teachers College Press.

Gage, N. L. (1978). *The scientific basis for the art of teaching.* New York: Teachers College Press.

Gamoran, A., & Berends, M. (1987). The effects of stratification in secondary schools: Synthesis of survey and ethnographic research. *Review of Educational Research, 57* (4), 415-435.

Gardner, J. W. (1963). *Self renewal: The individual and the innovative society.* New York: Harper and Row.

Garmston, R. J. (1987). How administrators support peer coaching. *Educational Leadership, 44* (5), 18-26.

Garmston, R. J., & Eblen, D. R. (1988). Visions, decisions, and results: Changing social culture through staff development. *The Journal of Staff Development, 9* (2), 22-29.

Garmston, R., Linder, C., & Whitaker, J. (1993). Reflections on cognitive coaching. *Educational Leadership, 51* (2), 57-61.

Glass, G. V. (1982). Meta-analysis: An approach to the synthesis of research results. *Journal of Research in Science Teaching, 19* (2) 93-112.

Glickman, C. D. (1990). *Supervision of instruction: A developmental approach.* Boston: Allyn and Bacon.

Glickman, C. D. (1993). *Renewing America's schools: A guide for school-based action.* San Francisco: Jossey-Bass.

Goldhammer, R. (1969). *Clinical supervision: Special methods for the supervision of teachers.* New York: Holt, Rinehard, and Winston.

Good, T., Grouws, D., & Ebmeier, H. (1983). *Active mathematics teaching.* New York: Longman, Inc.

Goodlad, J. (1984). *A place called school.* New York: McGraw-Hill.

Goodlad, J., & Klein, F. (1970). *Looking behind the classroom door.* Worthington, OH: Charles A. Jones.

Gordon, W. J.J., & Poze, T. (1971). *The metaphorical way of learning and knowing.* Cambridge: Porpoise Books.

Graves, N., & Graves, T. (1990). *Cooperative learning: A resource guide.* Santa Cruz: The International Association for the Study of Cooperation in Education.

Gregorc, A. F. (1982). *An adult's guide to style.* Maynard, MA: Gabriel Systems.

Habib, F., Cook, T., Marcantonio, R., Anson, A., & Clifford, E. (1993). The Comer middle school development program after two years. Paper presented at the annual meeting of the American Educational Researcher Association, Atlanta.

Hall, G. (1986). *Skills derived from studies of the implementation of innovations in education.* A paper presented at the annual meetings of the American Educational Research Association, San Francisco.

Hall, G. E., & Hord, S. M. (1987). *Change in schools: Facilitating the process.* New York: State University of New York.

Hall, G., & Loucks, S. (1977). A developmental model for determining whether the treatment is actually implemented. *American Educational Research Journal, 14* (3), 263–276.

Hallinger, P., & Murphy, J. (1985). Assessing the instructional management behavior of principals. *Elementary School Journal, 86* (2), 217–247.

Harter, S. (1982). The perceived competence scale for children. *Child Development, 53,* 87–97.

Harvey, O. J., Hunt, D. E., & Schroder, H. M. (1961). *Conceptual systems and personality organization.* New York: John Wiley & Sons, Inc.

Hawley, W. D., Rosenholtz, S., Goodstein, H. J., & Hasselbring, T. (1984). Good schools: What research says about improving student achievement. *Peabody Journal of Education, 61* (4), 1–178.

Hertz-Lazarowitz, R. (1993). Using group investigation to enhance Arab-Jewish relationships. *Cooperative Learning, 13* (3), 26–28.

Hertz-Lazarowitz, R., & Shachar, H. (1990). Changes in teachers' verbal behavior in cooperative classrooms. *Cooperative Learning, 11* (2), 13–14.

Hillocks, G. (1987). Synthesis of research on teaching writing. *Educational Leadership, 44* (8), 71–82.

Hobbes, T. (1651). *Leviathan.*

Hoetker, J., & Ahlbrand, W. (1969). The persistence of the recitation. *American Educational Research Journal, 6,* 145–167.

Hollingsworth, S., & Sockett, H. (1994). *Teacher research and educational reform.* Chicago: University of Chicago Press.

Holloway, S. D. (1988). Concepts of ability and effort in Japan and the U.S. *Review of Educational Research, 58* (3), 327–346.

Hopkins, D. (1990). Integrating staff development and school improvement: A study of teacher personality and school climate. In B. Joyce (Ed.), *Changing school culture through staff development* (pp. 41–70). Alexandria, VA: Association for Supervision and Curriculum Development.

Huberman, A. M. (1992). Critical introduction. In M. Fullan, *Successful school improvement*. Philadelphia: The Open University Press.

Huberman, A. M., & Miles, M. B. (1984). Rethinking the quest for school improvement: Some findings from the DESSI study. In A. Lieberman (Ed.), *Rethinking school improvement: Research, craft, and concept*. New York: Teachers College Press.

Hunt, D. (1971). *Matching models in education*. Toronto: Ontario Institute for Studies in Education.

Hunt, D. (1981). *Teachers' personal theorizing*. Toronto: Ontario Institute for Studies in Education.

Hunt, D. E., Butler, L. F., Noy, J. E., & Rosser, M. E. (1978). *Assessing conceptual level by the paragraph completion method*. Toronto: Ontario Institute for Studies in Education.

Hunt, D. E., & Gow, J. (1984). How to be your own best theorist II. *Theory Into Practice, 23* (1), 64–71.

Hunt, D., & Joyce, B. (1967). Teacher trainee personality and initial teaching style. *American Educational Research Journal, 4*, 253–259.

Hunter, M. (1980). Six types of supervisory conferences. *Educational Leadership, 37*, 408–412.

Hunter, M., & Russell, D. (1981). Planning for effective instruction: Lesson design. In *Increasing your teaching effectiveness*. Palo Alto, CA: Learning Institute.

Ivany, George (1969). The assessment of verbal inquiry in elementary school science. *Science Education, 53* (4), 287–293.

Jencks, C., et al. (1970). *Education vouchers: A report on financing elementary education by grants to parents*. Cambridge, MA: Center for the Study of Public Policy.

Johnson, D. W., & Johnson, R. T. (1975). *Circles of learning*. Englewood Cliffs: Prentice-Hall.

Johnson, D., & Johnson, R. (1979). Conflict in the classroom: Controversy in learning. *Review of Educational Research, 49* (1), 51–70.

Johnson, D., & Johnson, R. (1981). Effects of cooperative and individualistic learning experiences on inter-ethnic interaction. *Journal of Educational Psychology, 73* (3), 444–449.

Johnson, D. W., & Johnson, R. T. (1990). *Cooperation and competition: Theory and research*. Edina, MI: Interaction Book Company.

Johnson, D. W., Johnson, R. T., & Skon, L. (1979). Student achievement on different types of tasks under cooperative, competitive, and individualistic conditions. *Contemporary Educational Psychology, 4*, 99–106.

Johnson, D., Maruyama, G., Johnson, R., Nelson, D., & Skon, L. (1981). Effects of cooperative, competitive, and individualistic goal structures on achievement: A meta-analysis. *Psychological Bulletin, 89* (1), 47–62.

Joyce, B. (Ed.), (1990). *Changing school culture through staff development*. The 1990 ASCD Yearbook. Alexandria, VA: The Association for Supervision and Curriculum Development.

Joyce, B. R. (1991). Doors to school improvement. *Educational Leadership, 48* (8), 59–62.

Joyce, B. R. (1992). Cooperative learning and staff development: Teaching the method with the method. *Cooperative Learning, 12* (2), 10–13.

Joyce, B., Bush, R., & McKibbin, M. (1982). *The California staff development study. The January, 1982 report.* Palo Alto, CA: Booksend Laboratories.

Joyce, B., Brown, C., & Peck, L. (Eds.) (1981). *Flexibility in Teaching.* New York: Longman, Inc.

Joyce, B., Calhoun, E., Halliburton, C., Simser, J., Rust, D., & Carran, N. (1994). The Ames Community Schools staff development program. Paper presented at the annual meeting of the Association for Supervision and Curriculum Development, Chicago.

Joyce, B., Hersh, R., & McKibbin, M. (1983). *The structure of school improvement.* New York: Longman.

Joyce, B. R., McKibbin, M., & Bush, R. (1983). The seasons of professional life: The growth states of teachers. Paper presented at the annual meeting of the American Education Research Association, Montreal, Canada.

Joyce, B., Murphy, C., Showers, B., & Murphy, J. (1989). School renewal as cultural change. *Educational Leadership, 47* (3), 70–78.

Joyce, B., & Showers, B. (1980). Improving inservice training: The messages of research. *Educational Leadership, 37* (5), 379–385.

Joyce, B. R., & Showers, B. (1982). The coaching of teaching. *Educational Leadership, 40* (1), 4–16.

Joyce, B., & Showers, B. (1983). *Power in staff development through research on training.* Washington, D.C.: Association for Supervision and Curriculum Development.

Joyce, B., & Showers, B. (1988). *Student achievement through staff development.* New York: Longman, Inc.

Joyce, B., Showers, B., Dalton, M., & Beaton, C. (1985). The search for validated skills of teaching: Four lines of inquiry. A paper presented to the annual meeting of the American Educational Research Association, Chicago.

Joyce, B., Showers, B., & Rolheiser-Bennett, C. (1987). Staff development and student learning: A synthesis of research on models of teaching. *Educational Leadership, 45* (2), 11–23.

Joyce, B., Weil, M., & Showers, B. (1992). *Models of teaching* (4th ed.). Boston: Allyn & Bacon.

Joyce, B., & Wolf, J. (1992). Operation just read and write: Toward a literate society. Paper presented at the annual meeting of the Association for Supervision and Curriculum Development, New Orleans.

Joyce, B., Wolf, J., & Calhoun, E. (1993). *The self-renewing school.* Alexandria, VA: Association for Supervision and Curriculum Development.

Kent, K. M. (1985). A successful program of teachers assisting teachers. *Educational Leadership, 43* (3), 30–33.

Kerman, Sam (1979). Teacher expectations and student achievement. *Phi Delta Kappan, 60* (10), 716–718.

Knowles, M. (1978). *The adult learner: A neglected species* (2nd ed.). Houston: Gulf Publishing Co.

Kulik, C. C., Kulik, J. A., & Bangert-Drowns, R. L. (1990). Effectiveness of mastery learning programs: A meta-analysis. *Review of Educational Research, 60,* 265–299.

Lara, A. V., & Medley, D. M. (1987). Effective teacher behavior as a function of learner ability. *Professional School Psychology, 2* (1), 15–23.

Lawton, J. T., & Wanska, S. (1977). Advance organizers as a teaching strategy: A reply to Barnes and Clawson. *Review of Educational Research, 47* (1), 233–244.

Lawton, J. T., & Wanska, S. K. (1979). The effects of different types of advance organizers on classification learning. *American Educational Research Journal, 16* (3), 223–39.

Leithwood, K. (1990). The principal's role in teacher development. In B. Joyce (Ed.), *Changing school culture through staff development.* Washington, D.C.: Association for Supervision and Curriculum Development.

Leithwood, K. (1992). The move toward transformational leadership. *Educational Leadership, 49* (5), 8-12.

Leithwood, K., & Montgomery, D. (1982). The role of the elementary school principal in program improvement. *Review of Educational Research, 52,* 309 339.

Levin, J., Shriberg, L., & Berry, J. (1983). A concrete strategy for remembering abstract prose. *American Educational Research Journal, 20* (2), 277-290.

Levin, M. E., & Levin, J. R. (1990). Scientific mnemonics: Methods for maximizing more than memory. *American Educational Research Journal, 27,* 301-321.

Levine, D. U. (1991). Creating effective schools: Findings and implications from research and practice. *Phi Delta Kappan, 72* (5), 389-393.

Levine, D., & Lezotte, L. (1990). *Creating unusually effective schools: A review and analysis of research and practice.* Madison, WI: National Center for Effective Schools.

Lieberman, A. (Ed.) (1988). *Building a professional culture in schools.* New York: Teachers College Press.

Little, J. W. (1982). Norms of collegiality and experimentation: Workplace conditions of school success. *American Educational Research Journal, 19* (3), 325-340.

Little, J. W. (1990). The persistence of privacy: Autonomy and initiative in teachers' professional relations. *Teachers College Record, 91,* (4), 509-536. San Francisco.

Locke, J. (1927). In R. H. Quick (Ed.), *Some thoughts concerning education.* Cambridge: Cambridge University Press.

Lortie, Dan (1975). *Schoolteacher.* Chicago: The University of Chicago Press.

Luiten, J., Ames, W., & Ackerson, G. (1980). A meta-analysis of the effects of advance organizers on learning and retention. *American Educational Research Journal, 17* (2), 211-218.

McCarthy, B. (1981). *The 4Mat system: Teaching to learning styles with right/left mode techniques.* Barrington, IL: Excel, Incorporated.

McDonald, F., & Elias, P. (1976). *Executive summary report: Beginning teacher evaluation study, phase two.* Princeton, NJ: Educational Testing Service.

McKibbin, M., & Joyce, B. (1980). Psychological states and staff development. *Theory into Practice, 19* (4), 248-255.

McLaughlin, M. W. (1990). Rand change agent study revisited. *Educational Researcher, 19* (9), 11-15.

McLaughlin, M., Pfeifer, R. S., Swanson-Owens, D., & Yee, S. (1986). Why teachers won't teach. *Phi Delta Kappan, 67* (6), 420-426.

Mandeville, G. H., & Rivers, J. L. (1991). The South Carolina PET study. *Elementary School Journal, 91* (4), 377-407.

March, H. W., & O'Neill, R. (1984). Self-description Questionnaire III: The construct validity of multidimensional self-concept ratings by late adolescents. *Journal of Educational Measurement, 21,* 153-174.

Maslow, A. (1962). *Toward a psychology of being.* New York: Van Nostrand.

Medley, D. (1977). *Teacher competence and teacher effectiveness.* Washington, D.C.: American Association of Colleges of Teacher Education.

Medley, D. M., Coker, H., Coker, J. G., Lorentz, J. L., Soar, R. S., & Spaulding, R. L. (1981). Assessing teacher performance from observed competency indicators defined by classroom teachers. *Journal of Educational Research, 74,* 197-216.

Medley, D., & Mitzel, H. (1958). A technique for measuring classroom behavior. *Journal of Educational Psychology, 49,* 86–92.

Medley, D., & Mitzel, H. (1963). Measuring classroom behavior by systematic observation. In N. L. Gage (Ed.), *Handbook of Research on Teaching,* pp. 247–328. Chicago: Rand McNally and Co.

Medley, D., Soar, R., & Coker, H. (1984). *Measurement-based evaluation of teacher performance.* New York: Longman.

Meyer, L. (1984). Long-term academic effects of the Direct Instruction Project Follow Through. *Elementary School Journal, 84,* 380–394.

Miles, M., & Huberman, A. M. (1984a). *Innovation up close.* New York: Praeger.

Miles, M., & Huberman, A. M. (1984b). Qualitative data analysis: A source-book of new methods. Beverly Hills, CA: Sage.

Moore, D. R., & Davenport, S. (1989). *The new improved sorting machine: Concerning school choice.* Chicago: Designs for Change.

Muncey, D. (1994). Individual and schoolwide change in eight coalition schools: Findings from a longitudinal ethnographic study. Paper presented at the annual meeting of the American Educational Research Association, New Orleans.

Muncey, D., & McQuillan, P. (1993). Preliminary findings from a five-year study of the Coalition of Essential Schools. *Phi Delta Kappan, 74* (6), 486–489.

Murphy, J. (1992). *The landscape of leadership preparation.* Newbury Park, CA: Corwin Press.

Murphy, J., & Hallinger, P., (Eds.) (1987). *Approaches to administrative training.* Albany: SUNY Press.

Murphy, J., & Louis, K. S., (Eds.) (1994). *Reshaping the principalship: Insights from transformational change efforts.* Newbury Park, CA: Corwin.

Myers, I. B. (1962). *The Myers-Briggs type indicator.* Palo Alto, CA: Consulting Psychologists Press.

Myers, M. (1985). *The teacher-researcher: How to study writing in the classroom.* Urbana: The National Council of Teachers of English.

National Assessment of Educational Progress (NAEP) (1992). *The reading report card for the nation and the states.* Washington, D.C.: National Center for Educational Statistics. U.S. Department of Education.

National Council of Teachers of Mathematics (1989). *Curriculum and evaluation standards for school mathematics.* Reston, VA: NCTM.

National Council of Teachers of Mathematics (1991). *Professional standards for teaching mathematics.* Reston, VA: NCTM.

Nelson, J. (1971). *Collegial supervision in multi-unit schools.* Ph.D. thesis, University of Oregon.

Neubert, G. A., & Bratton, E. C. (1987). Team coaching: Staff development side by side. *Educational Leadership, 44* (5), 29–33.

Oakes, J. (1985). *Keeping track: How schools structure inequality.* New Haven: Yale University Press.

Oja, S. N. (1989). *Collaborative action research: A developmental perspective.* London: Falmer Press.

Orlich, D., Remaley, A., Facemyer, K., Logan, J., & Cao, Q. (1993). Seeking the link between student achievement and staff development. *Journal of Staff Development, 14* (3), 2–8.

Orme, M. (1966). *The effects of modeling and feedback variables on the acquisition of a complex teaching strategy.* Ph.D. thesis, Stanford University.

Perkins, D. N. (1984). Creativity by design. *Educational Leadership, 42* (1), 18–25.

Pinnell, G. S. (1989). Reading recovery: Helping at-risk children learn to read. *Elementary School Journal, 90* (2), 161–83.

Potter, D. C., & Wall, M. E. (1992). Higher standards for grade promotion and graduation: Unintended effects of reform. Paper presented at the annual meeting of the American Educational Research Association, San Francisco.

Pressley, M. (1977). Children's use of the keyword method to learn simple Spanish vocabulary words. *Journal of Educational Psychology, 69* (5), 465–472.

Pressley, M., & Dennis-Rounds, J. (1980). Transfer of a mnemonic keyword strategy at two age levels. *Journal of Educational Psychology, 72* (4), 575–582.

Pressley, M., Levin, J., & Delaney, H. (1982). The mnemonic keyword method. *Review of Educational Research, 52* (1), 61–91.

Pressley, M., Levin, J., & Ghatala, E. (1984). Memory-strategy monitoring in adults and children. *Journal of Verbal Learning and Verbal Behavior, 23* (2), 270–288.

Pressley, M., Levin, J., & McCormick, C. (1980). Young children's learning of foreign language vocabulary: A sentence-variation of the keyword method. *Contemporary Educational Psychology, 5* (1), 22–29.

Pressley, M., Levin, J., & Miller, G. (1981a). How does the keyword method affect vocabulary, comprehension, and usage? *Reading Research Quarterly, 16,* 213–226.

Pressley, M., Levin, J., & Miller, G. (1981b). The keyword method and children's learning of foreign vocabulary with abstract meanings. *Canadian Psychology, 35* (3), 283–287.

Pressley, M., Samuel, J., Hershey, M., Bishop, S., & Dickinson, D. (1981). Use of a mnemonic technique to teach young children foreign-language vocabulary. *Contemporary Educational Psychology, 6,* 110–116.

Purkey, S., & Smith, M. (1983). Effective schools: A review. *Elementary School Journal, 83* (4), 427–452.

Quellmalz, E., & Burry, J. (1983). *Analytic scales for assessing students' expository and narrative writing skills.* Los Angeles: Center for the Study of Evaluation, UCLA Graduate School of Education.

Ralph, J., & Fennessey, J. (1983). Science or reform: Some questions about the effective schools model. *Phi Delta Kappan, 64* (10), 689–694.

Rand Corporation. (1981). *A study of alternatives in American education, Vol. VII: Conclusions and policy implications.* Santa Monica, CA: Rand.

Rawls, J. (1971). *A theory of justice.* Cambridge: Harvard University Press.

Raywid, M. A. (1993). Finding time for collaboration. *Educational Leadership, 51* (1), 30–35.

Reich, C. A. (1970). *The greening of America.* New York: Random House, Inc.

Review of Educational Research, (1993), *63,* (3).

Rhine, W. (Ed.) (1981). *Making schools more effective: New questions from follow-through.* New York: Academic Press.

Ripple, R., & Drinkwater, D. (1981). Transfer of learning. In H. E. Mitzel (Ed.), *Encyclopedia of educational research, Vol. 4,* pp. 1947–1953. New York: The Free Press, Macmillan Publishing Company.

Roebuck, F., Buhler, J., & Aspy, D. (1976). *A comparison of high and low levels of human teaching/learning: Conditions on the subsequent achievement of students identified as having learning difficulties.* Final report: Order # PLD6816-76. The National Institute of Mental Health. Denton, TX: Texas Women's University Press.

Rogers, C. (1961). *On becoming a person.* Boston: Houghton-Mifflin.

Rogers, C. (1982). *Freedom to learn in the eighties.* Columbus: Charles E. Merrill.

Rogers, S. (1987). If I can see myself, I can change. *Educational Leadership, 45* (2), 64–67.

Rolheiser-Bennett, C. (1986). *Four models of teaching: A meta-analysis of student outcomes.* Ph.D. thesis, University of Oregon.

Ronnestad, M. H. (1977). The effects of modeling, feedback and experimental methods on counselor empathy. *Counselor Education and Supervision, 16,* 194–201.

Roper, S., Deal, T., & Dornbusch, S. (1976). Collegial evaluation of classroom teaching: Does it work? *Educational Research Quarterly,* Spring, 56–66.

Rosenholtz, S. J. (1989). *Teachers' workplace: The social organization of schools.* White Plains, NY: Longman.

Rosenshine, B. (1971). *Teaching behaviors and student achievement.* London: National Foundation for Educational Research.

Rousseau, J. J. (1783). *Emile.* New York: E. P. Dutton, 1983.

Rowe, M. B. (1969). Science, soul and sanctions. *Science and Children, 6* (6), 11–13.

Rowe, M. B. (1974). Wait-time and rewards as instructional variables, their influence on language, logic, and fate control. *Journal of Research in Science Teaching, 11,* 81–94.

Rowen, B., Bossert, S. T., & Dwyer, D. C. (1983). Research on effective schools: A cautionary note. *Educational Researcher, 12* (4), 24–31.

Rutter, M., Maughan, R., Mortimer, P., Oustin, J., & Smith, A. (1979). *Fifteen thousand hours: Secondary schools and their effects on children.* Cambridge, MA: Harvard University Press.

Sagor, R. (1992). *How to conduct collaborative action research.* Alexandria, VA: Association for Supervision and Curriculum Development.

Sangiser, R. L. (1989). Teacher participation in discretionary professional development activities. Doctoral Thesis. College Park: Pennsylvania State University.

Sarason, S. (1982). *The culture of the school and the problem of change* (2nd ed.). Boston: Allyn and Bacon.

Sarason, S. (1990). *The predictable failure of school reform: Can we change the course before it's too late?* San Francisco: Jossey-Bass.

Sartre, J.-P. (1956). *Being and nothingness.* New York: Philosophical Library.

Schaefer, R. J. (1967). *The school as a center of inquiry.* New York: Harper and Row.

Schiffer, J. (1980). *School renewal through staff development.* New York: Teachers College Press.

Schlechty, P. C., & Vance, V. S. (1983). Institutional responses to the quality/quantity issue in teacher training. *Phi Delta Kappan, 65* (2), 94–101.

Schmuck, R. A., & Runkel, P. J. (1985). *The handbook of organizational development in schools* (3rd ed.). Palo Alto, CA: Mayfield Press.

Schmuck, R., Runkel, P., Arends, J., & Arends, R. (1977). *The second handbook of organizational development in schools.* Palo Alto, CA: Mayfield Press.

Schon, D. (1982). *The reflective practitioner.* New York: Basic Books.

Schrenker, G. (1976). *The effects of an inquiry-development program on elementary school children's science learning.* Ph.D. thesis, New York University.

Schwab, J. (1982). *Science, curriculum, and liberal education: Selected essays.* Chicago: University of Chicago Press.

Schwab, J., & Brandwein, P. (1962). *The teaching of science.* Cambridge: Harvard University Press.

Seashore-Louis, K., & Miles, M. B. (1990). *Improving the urban high school.* New York: Teachers College Press.

Senge, P. M. (1990). *The fifth discipline: The art and practice of the learning organization.* New York: Doubleday.

Sergiovanni, T. J. (1985). Landscapes, mindscapes, and reflective practice in supervision. *Journal of Curriculum and Supervision, 1* (1), 5-17.

Sharan, S. (1980). Cooperative learning in small groups: Recent methods and effects on achievement, attitudes, and ethnic relations. *Review of Educational Research, 50* (2), 241-271.

Sharan, S. (Ed.) (1990). *Cooperative learning: Theory and research.* New York: Praeger.

Sharan, S. (Ed.) (1992). *Research on cooperative learning.* New York: Praeger.

Sharan, S., & Hertz-Lazarowitz, R. (1980). A group investigation method of cooperative learning in the classroom. In Shlomo Sharan, P. Hare, C. Webb, R. Hertz-Lawarowitz (Eds.), *Cooperation in Education,* pp. 14-46. Provo, UT: Brigham Young University Press.

Sharan, S., & Hertz-Lazarowitz, R. (1982). Effects on an instructional change program on teachers' behaviors, attitudes, and perceptions. *The Journal of Applied Behavioral Science, 18* (2), 185-201.

Sharan, S., & Shachar, H. (1988). *Language and learning in the cooperative classroom.* New York: Springer-Verlag.

Shavelson, R., & Dempsey-Atwood, M. (1976). Generalizability of measures of teacher behavior. *Review of Educational Research, 46* (4), 553-661.

Shirley, J. R., & Anderson, L. (1994). A study of South Carolina's Project Relearning. Paper presented at the annual meeting of the American Educational Research Association, New Orleans.

Showers, B. (1982). *Transfer of training: The contribution of coaching.* Eugene, OR: Center for Educational Policy and Management.

Showers, B. (1984). *Peer coaching: A strategy for facilitating transfer of training.* Eugene, OR: Center for Educational Policy and Management.

Showers, B. (1985). Teachers coaching teachers. *Educational Leadership, 42* (7), 43-49.

Showers, B. (1989). School improvement through staff development: Levels of implementation and impact on student achievement. Paper presented at the International Conference on "School-based Innovations: Looking Forward to the 1990's," Hong Kong.

Showers, B., Joyce, B., & Bennett, B. (1987). Synthesis of research on staff development: A framework for future study and a state-of-the-art analysis. *Educational Leadership, 45* (3), 77-87.

Sirotnik, K. (1983). What you see is what you get: Consistency, persistence, and mediocrity in classrooms. *Harvard Educational Review, 53* (1), 16-31.

Sizer, T. R. (1985). *Horace's compromise.* Boston: Houghton-Mifflin.

Sizer, T. R. (1991). No pain, no gain. *Educational Leadership, 48* (8), 32-34.

Slavin, R. (1983). *Cooperative learning.* New York: Longman, Inc.

Slavin, R. (1986). The Napa evaluation of Madeline Hunter's ITIP: Lessons learned. *The Elementary School Journal, 87* (2), 165-171.

Slavin, R. E. (1987). Ability grouping and student achievement in elementary schools: A best-evidence systhesis. *Review of Educational Research, 57,* 293-336.

Slavin, R. (1990). Achievement effects of ability grouping in secondary schools. *Review of Educational Research, 60* (3), 471-500.

Slavin, R., et al. (1991). Preventing early school failure: What works. Center for research on effective schooling for disadvantaged students. Baltimore, MD: Johns Hopkins University.

Slavin, R., & Madden, N. (1994). Lee Conmigo: Effects of Success for All in bilingual first grades. A paper presented at the annual meeting of The American Educational Research Association, New Orleans.

Slavin, R. E., Madden, N. A., Karweit, N., Livermon, B. J., & Dolan, L. (1990). Success for all: First-year outcomes of a comprehensive plan for reforming urban education. *American Educational Research Journal, 27,* 255-278.

Smith, K., & Smith, M. (1966). *Cybernetic principles of learning and educational design.* New York: Holt, Rinehart, and Winston.

Smith, M. L. (1980). *Effects of aesthetics education on basic skills learning.* Boulder, CO: Laboratory of Educational Research, University of Colorado.

Soar, R. (1973). *Follow Through classroom process measurement and pupil growth.* (1970-71 final report.) Gainesville, FL: Institute for the Development of Human Resources, University of Florida.

Snow, R. (1982). *Intelligence, motivation, and academic work.* Paper presented for a symposium on "The student's role in learning," conducted by the National Commission for Excellence in Education, U.S. Department of Education, San Diego, California.

Sparks, D. (1993). Organization development in schools. *The Developer,* October, p. 1.

Sparks, D., and Loucks-Horsley, S. (1992). *Five models of staff development for teachers.* Oxford, Ohio: The National Staff Development Council.

Spaulding, R. (1970). *Educational Improvement Program.* Durham, NC: Duke University Press.

SRI International (1981). Evaluation of the implementation of Public Law 94-142. Menlo Park, CA: SRI International.

Stallings, J. (1979). *How to change the process of teaching reading in secondary schools.* Menlo Park, CA: SRI International.

Stallings, J., & Kaskowitz, D. (1972-73). *Follow Through classroom observation evaluation.* Menlo Park, CA: SRI International.

Stallings, J., Needels, P., & Stayrook, N. (1979). *The teaching of basic reading skills in secondary schools, Phase Two and Phase Three.* Menlo Park, CA: SRI International.

Stenhouse, L. (1975). *An introduction to curriculum research and development.* London: Heinemann.

Sternberg, R. (1986). *Intelligence applied: Understanding and increasing your intellectual skills.* San Diego: Harcourt Brace Jovanovich.

Sternberg, R., & Bahna, K. (1986). Synthesis of research on the effectiveness of intellectual skills programs: Snake-oil remedies or miracle cures? *Educational Leadership, 44* (2), 60-67.

Stevenson, H., & Stigler, J. (1992). *The learning gap.* New York: Summit Books.

Stone, C. (1983). A meta-analysis of advance organizer studies. *Journal of Experimental Education, 51* (4), 194-199.

Suchman, R. (1964). Studies in inquiry training. In R. Ripple and V. Bookcastle (Eds.) *Piaget reconsidered.* Ithaca, NY: Cornell University Press.

Taba, H. (1966). *Teaching strategies and cognitive functioning in elementary school children.* (Cooperative Research Project 2404.) San Francisco: San Francisco State College.

Thelen, H. (1960). *Education and the human quest.* New York: Harper and Row.

Thelen, H. (1967). *Classroom grouping for teachability.* New York: John Wiley and Sons, Inc.

Timar, T. (1989). The politics of school restructuring. *Phi Delta Kappan, 71,* (4), 265-276.

Tobin, K. (1986). Effects of teacher wait time on discourse characteristics in mathematics and language arts classes. *American Educational Research Journal, 23* (2), 191-200.

Voss, B. (1982). *Summary of research in science education.* Columbus, OH: ERIC Clearinghouse for Science, Mathematics, and Environmental Education.

Walberg, H. (1985). *Why Japanese educational productivity excels.* Paper presented at the annual meetings of the American Educational Research Association, Chicago.

Walberg, H. (1986). What works in a nation still at risk. *Educational Leadership, 44* (1), 7-11.

Walberg, H. J. (1990). Productive teaching and instruction: Assessing the knowledge base. *Phi Delta Kappan, 71* (6), 70-78.

Walberg, H. J. (1992). *The knowledge base for educational productivity.* Lancaster, PA: Technomic Publishing Company.

Wallace, R. C., LeMahieu, P. G., & Bickel, W. E. (1990). The Pittsburgh experience: Achieving commitment to comprehensive staff development. In B. Joyce, (Ed.) *Changing school culture through staff development.* Alexandria, VA: Association for Supervision and Curriculum Development.

Wallace, R. C., Young, J. R., Johnston, J., Bickel, W. E., & LeMahieu, P. G. (1984). Secondary educational renewal in Pittsburgh. *Educational Leadership, 41* (6), 73-77.

Wang, M., Haertel, G., & Walberg, H. (1993). Toward a knowledge base for school learning. *Review of Educational Research, 63* (3), 249-294.

Weil, M., Marshalek, B., Mittman, A., Murphy, J., Hallinger, P., & Pruyn, J. (1984). Effective and typical schools: How different are they? Paper presented at the annual meeting of The American Educational Research Association, New Orleans.

White, W. A. T. (1986). The effects of direct instruction in special education: A meta-analysis. Ph.D. thesis, University of Oregon.

Wolf, J. (1994) *BLT: A resource handbook for building leadership teams.* Minneapolis: The North Central Association of Schools and Colleges.

Wolpe, J., & Lazarus, A. (1966). *Behavior therapy techniques: A guide to the treatment of neuroses.* Oxford: Pergamon Press, Inc.

Worthen, B. R. (1968). A study of discovery and expository presentation: Implications for teaching. *Journal of Teacher Education, 19,* 223-242.

Index

Taba, H., 76
Teaching practices
   research on, 79
TESA, 79
Thelen, H., 71
Theses about
   age and experience, 22, 211
   centralized planning, 20, 210
   collegial locus of control, 19, 209
   credibility and "buy-in," 19-20, 209
   culture of school, 20-21, 210
   personal motivation, 18, 208
   technical assistance and research,
      22-23, 64, 212
   time and the culture of the school,
      21-22, 211
Thorn, L., 117
Timar, T., 64
Tinajero, J., 72
Tobin, K., 79
Training design, 108-113

Transfer of training, 132
   levels of, 133-136

Vance, V., 173
Voss, B., 76
Voucher plans, 64-65

"Wait" time, 79
Walberg, II., 15, 68
Wall, M., 65,
Wallace, R., 43, 57-58
Wang, M., 15, 68
Wanska, S., 73
Weil, M., 15, 31, 68, 69, 70, 85, 86
White, W., 78
Whole-faculty participation
   in school renewal, 13-15, 55-56
Wolf, J., 59, 155, 213-215
Wolpe, J., 78
Worthen, B., 76